Waterloo BASIC

**Primer and
Reference Manual**

A Structured Programming Approach

J W Graham
J W Welch
K I McPhee

*Computer Systems Group
University of Waterloo*

Published by
WATFAC Publications Ltd.
P.O. Box 803
Waterloo, Ontario
N2J 4C2

Canadian Cataloguing in Publication Data

Graham, J. W. (James Wesley), 1932–
  Waterloo BASIC

Includes index.
ISBN 0-919884-22-9

1. Basic (Computer program language)
  I. Welch, J. W. (James William), 1947–
II. McPhee, K. I. (Kenneth Ian), 1950–
III. Title.

QA76.73.B3G73   001.64'24   C81-094038-8

WATFAC
Series in Computer Science and Computer Applications

An Introduction to COBOL with WATBOL
by Cowan, Dirksen and Graham

An Introduction to WATIAC and WATMAP
*by Cooper, Cowan, Dirksen, Graham,
Penton and Treadwell*

Waterloo BASIC for the Commodore PET
by Graham, Wilkinson and Cowan

Pascal Reference Manual and
Waterloo Pascal User's Guide
by Boswell and Welch

The BASIC language was originally developed and implemented at Dartmouth College in New Hampshire as a cost-effective way of teaching introductory computing to undergraduate students. Over the years it has evolved to the point where it is widely used not only in educational applications, but in industry as well.

In recent years many new programming techniques have evolved which have received broad acceptance; the most well-known is structured programming. The BASIC language as originally developed required enhancements to permit the effective use of these new techniques. Early in 1978 it was decided by the Computer Systems Group at the University of Waterloo to incorporate a few new powerful language and systems extensions into BASIC to meet these needs. An important objective was to retain the inherent simplicity and consistency of BASIC in order to preserve the proven and accepted advantages of the original system developed at Dartmouth.

In June 1978, the Computer Systems Group at the University of Waterloo began programming the Waterloo BASIC system for the IBM Series/1. The primary members of the team were:

> Dave Boswell
> Fred Crigger
> Carl Durance
> Trevor Grove
> Ian McPhee
> Doug Mulholland
> Jim Welch

Although this group had direct responsibility for the development, all members of the Computer Systems Group contributed substantially to the development process. In December 1978 the initial coding was completed. During the months of January to March 1979, the Waterloo BASIC system was extensively tested, in order that the system would be highly reliable when it was placed into productive use. At the same time, an agreement was made with the IBM Corporation permitting IBM to distribute the system as an IBM Installed User Program (IUP). The first such systems were distributed in August 1979.

One of the design goals of Waterloo BASIC was to implement the system in a manner which would facilitate its implementation on other systems. In the first half of 1979, the system was implemented under the VM/CMS operating system for IBM 370, 3030, and 4300 computer series. This was accomplished by Romney White and Bruce Hay, working part-time during this period.

In September 1979, a new development phase was entered which involved all members of the Computer Systems Group in varying capacities. This project was completed in March 1980 resulting in the Waterloo BASIC system for the IBM Series/1 with the CPS operating system. The new system included substantial functional enhancements, particularly with respect to facilities for programming commercial applications, as well as significant improvements in areas of performance and 'ease of use'.

During the summer of 1980, the new system was re-implemented under the VM/CMS operating system for the IBM 370 class of computers. As part of this project, new tools for the implementation were developed which have resulted in performance improvements of approximately 300% compared to the previous VM/CMS version.

This edition of the book incorporates the enhanced features of the new Waterloo BASIC systems. Consequently, the book is not totally applicable to the older version of IBM Series/1 Waterloo BASIC with the RPS operating system being distributed by IBM at the time of printing.

The authors would like to thank the many people who have contributed their time to criticize and review the first draft of this manuscript. In particular, Don Cowan and Paul Dirksen deserve special thanks for their suggestions. The authors would also like to thank Cathy Dunlop, Sharon Malleck and Charlotte Ross for the many hours they have spent in preparing the manuscript for publication. Heather Lennox made a significant contribution by running all the example programs on the system.

This book is organized into two parts. The first part is a primer which is intended to introduce the BASIC language supported by Waterloo BASIC. The primer does not attempt to cover all aspects in complete detail. Further information on particular features can be obtained by consulting the second part, a reference manual for Waterloo BASIC.

University of Waterloo   J.W. Graham
Waterloo, Ontario, Canada, N2L 3G1   J.W. Welch
October 1980   K.I. McPhee

TABLE OF CONTENTS -- PRIMER

Table of Contents -- Reference Manual

CHAPTER 1

AN INTRODUCTION TO WATERLOO BASIC

This chapter will serve as an introduction to programming using the Waterloo BASIC system. Simple examples are used to illustrate the basic principles, without going into details. The programming novice will be presented with an overview of the terminology; the experienced programmer will see examples of how familiar concepts are implemented in BASIC. The various features discussed are more completely explained in subsequent chapters, and in the Reference Manual.

1.1 BASIC PRINCIPLES

BASIC is a computer programming language developed initially at Dartmouth College in New Hampshire. It has been widely used, and many dialects of the language have appeared over the years. Waterloo BASIC is the particular version of the language developed at the University of Waterloo. It has been implemented on various computers used on that campus.

Example 1.1 illustrates how you could write a BASIC program to calculate the Fahrenheit equivalent of 100 degrees Centigrade. This is too trivial a problem to be considered for solution using a computer, but nevertheless it serves to illustrate a number of important points.

```
1        !EXAMPLE 1.1
2        ! A SIMPLE CALCULATION
3        C = 100
4        F = (C*9)/5 + 32
5        PRINT C,F
6        STOP
```

This example consists of six _statements_, each preceded by a line _number_ or _statement_ _number_. The first two statements are _comments_ which describe the problem. These comment statements are recognizable by the ! which appears immediately following the statement number. Comments are used to identify and describe the program, and are used only for documentation purposes; they are not executed by the computer.

The last four statements are _executable_ statements, and will be processed by the computer in the order in which they appear. Statement 3 causes the value 100 to be assigned to the variable C. Then statement 4 causes the <u>expression</u>

$$(C*9)/5 + 32$$

to be computed, with its value being assigned to F. Note that this expression is similar to expressions used in algebra, with the * to denote multiplication and the / to denote division.

Since this is the formula used to convert Centigrade to Fahrenheit, F would at this point have the value 212, which is the boiling point of water. The fifth statement will cause the current values of C and F to be printed on the computer terminal, and statement six causes the computer to terminate execution of the program. These statements are therefore executed <u>sequentially</u> by the computer, and the entire collection of statements is referred to as a <u>program</u>.

1.2 LINE NUMBERS

It is not necessary to number the statements from 1 to 6, as shown in Example 1.1. In fact, it is more desirable to number the statements leaving <u>gaps</u> between the statement numbers in case it should be required to insert a new statement between two existing statements. Thus a more common form of the same program appears as Example 1.2.

```
10      !EXAMPLE 1.2
20      ! A SIMPLE CALCULATION
30      C = 100
40      F = (C*9)/5 + 32
50      PRINT C,F
60      STOP
```

1.3 LOOPING

It would be more useful and interesting to calculate F for C having a number of values, for example 100, 110, 120, ... etc. This is accomplished in Example 1.3 by using a <u>loop</u>.

```
10      ! EXAMPLE 1.3
15
20      C = 100
22
25      LOOP
30         F = (C*9)/5 + 32
40         PRINT C,F
45         C = C + 10
47      ENDLOOP
48
50      STOP
```

Two new statements have been used, namely LOOP and ENDLOOP, to determine the beginning and ending of a group of statements which are to be executed repeatedly by the computer. Thus when Example 1.3 is executed, the statements

```
30      F = (C*9)/5 + 32
40      PRINT C,F
45      C = C + 10
```

are repeated indefinitely. Consequently the computer never stops, and the program is said to be in an _infinite loop_, a most undesirable state of affairs. A method for overcoming this short-coming is illustrated in the next example.

NOTES: 1. Each time through the loop, the value of C is _incremented_ by 10 in the statement

```
        C = C + 10
```

2. The = in BASIC means "is assigned the value". Thus this statement is not an algebraic equation, but means "calculate the expression C+10 and assign its value to C". By incrementing C each time through the loop, a table of values of F for C starting from 100 and increasing in steps of 10 degrees, is produced.

3. The reader may have noticed that all statements in the _range_ of the loop have been indented. This is to make the program more readable, and has no effect on its operation within the computer.

4. Line numbers 15, 22 and 48 contain only spaces. These lines are inserted for readability of the program and no action takes place when the computer executes them. They are referred to as _null_ statements.

1.4 TERMINATING THE LOOP

```
10      !EXAMPLE 1.4
18
20      C = 100
22
25      LOOP
30         F = (C*9)/5 + 32
40         PRINT C,F
45         C = C + 10
46         IF C > 200 THEN QUIT
47      ENDLOOP
48
50      STOP
```

Example 1.4 shows how simple it is to cause the computer to terminate the loop at a desired value of C. A single statement

    IF C > 200 THEN QUIT

has been inserted in the loop, and when C is incremented to the value 210 the computer will exit from the loop, and continue to the statement immediately following the ENDLOOP statement. In this case that statement is STOP, so the process is terminated.

The quantity C > 200 is known as a <u>relational</u> <u>expression</u>, and when computed has the value "true" or "false". The operator > is known as a relational operator, and there are six such operators available, namely

    =   equals
    >   greater than
    <   less than
    >=   greater than or equal
    <=   less than or equal
    <>   not equal to

1.5 KEYWORDS

In this chapter, several BASIC <u>keywords</u> have been introduced. These include PRINT, STOP, LOOP, ENDLOOP, IF, THEN and QUIT. These are reserved words which cannot be used as variable names. There are dozens of such keywords in BASIC; a complete list is given in the Reference Manual.

1.6 SPACING WITHIN A STATEMENT

In the various examples blank characters have been used extensively to improve readability. For example, line 20 in Example 1.3 could be written in various ways as follows:

    20 C = 100
    20 C=100
    20   C = 100
    20C=100

All of these are equivalent, and the blank characters are used at the programmer's discretion, and are ignored by the computer.

It would seem that blank characters are never significant in BASIC. However there are important instances in which a blank is necessary. One example is contained in line 40 of the same program.

    40 PRINT C,F

The blank following the keyword PRINT must be used. Otherwise the computer would interpret the string of characters PRINTC to be a variable name. The general rule is that keywords must be separated from other keywords or variable names by at least one blank, or by some other <u>delimiter</u> such as a comma. Examples where these other delimiters are used are introduced as needed in subsequent chapters.

1.7 SUMMARY

This chapter has introduced many programming terms, and illustrated their application in the BASIC language. No attempt has been made to rigorously define the terms. It is suggested that the reader should proceed immediately to Chapter 2 to learn how to submit these examples to the computer, and run them to observe their operation. The definitions of terms used are covered more rigorously in the Reference Manual, and in subsequent chapters.

1.8 EXERCISES

1.1 Make the required changes to Example 1.4 to produce a table of Fahrenheit values for Centigrade values ranging from 0 to 100 degrees in increments of one degree.

1.2 Further change the program to produce only those Fahrenheit values for Centigrade values ranging from -5 to 20 degrees in increments of 2 degrees.

1.3 Further change each of the programs to produce the tables in reverse order. That is, the largest temperatures should be computed and printed first, with the smallest at the end of the table.

1.4 Write a program to produce a table showing Fahrenheit to Centigrade conversion values. (The subtraction operator in BASIC is the symbol '-' as in algebra).

1.5 With the switch to metric it is important to be able to compare English units and metric units.

a) Write a program which converts 100 miles to kilometers. Use the conversion factor one kilometer equals 5/8 of a mile.

b) It is necessary to produce a speedometer with both miles per hour and kilometers per hour showing on its face in increments of 10 miles per hour and 10 kilometers per hour. Write a program which produces two lists, the first one showing miles per hour from 0 to 100 in 10 miles per hour increments, and the corresponding kilometers per hour values, and the second one showing kilometers per hour from 0 to 160 in 10 kilometers per hour increments and the corresponding miles per hour values.

CHAPTER 2

RUNNING A BASIC PROGRAM

The basic principles of writing a simple BASIC program were described in Chapter 1. The next step is to enter the program into the computer, and then put it into operation. This is accomplished using the BASIC editor and run-time systems. In this chapter many of the features of these two systems are discussed.

2.1 SIGNING ON TO WATERLOO BASIC

When you first approach the BASIC terminal it will be displaying the following message:

USERID?

This is inviting the user to type his or her user identification, which has been assigned by the computer system management when permission was granted to use the terminal. You should respond at the key-board with the appropriate USERID, depress the ENTER key, and the following message will be displayed:

PASSWORD?

At this point type your password, also assigned by the system manager, and depress the ENTER key. The terminal will respond with the message

READY

which means it is prepared for you to enter and run BASIC programs. If you should be unlucky enough to enter the incorrect USERID or PASSWORD you will have to repeat the procedure until you obtain the READY message. At this time the system is said to be in the READY status.

NOTES: 1. The above sign-on procedure is typical of that used with the IBM Series/1 with CPS. This procedure will vary, depending on the environment. The reader should consult the computer system management to determine appropriate sign-on procedures.

2. The ENTER key may have another name, depending upon the terminal being used.

2.2 TYPING IN A BASIC PROGRAM

When you first sign on to BASIC you are provided with a workspace which is empty. You can then enter each line of the program by typing it, together with its statement number, and then depressing the ENTER key. If you make a mistake simply type the line again and the computer system will replace the old line with the new line, provided they have the same statement number.

If you wish to check your typing, enter the editor command LIST and the contents of the entire workspace will appear on the terminal.

As you enter your program you usually make errors. Either you type incorrectly, or you misunderstand the rules of the BASIC language. When this happens you receive an error message immediately after typing the line. These messages are usually self-explanatory, and you can correct the statement immediately by re-typing it at the terminal.

2.3 RUNNING A BASIC PROGRAM

Assuming you have entered the program correctly, you are now ready to place it into execution. This is done by typing RUN and then depressing the ENTER key. After a brief pause, the message

EXECUTION BEGINS...

appears, and the computer starts executing BASIC statements in your workspace, beginning with the first executable statement (the statement with the lowest statement number). Execution continues from statement to statement until the STOP statement is encountered, at which time the message

...EXECUTION ENDS

appears, and the terminal once again returns to READY status.

All too often an error occurs during execution (usually referred to as "at execution time"). For example, if you try to compute the square root of a negative number, the computer must terminate execution because it is unable to perform this function. When this happens an error message occurs. Hopefully the message is self-explanatory, but you may have to refer to the Reference Manual for further explanation. When the reason for the execution-time error has been determined, simply enter the correction into your workspace, thus _modifying_ your original program, and RUN it again.

Occasionally the computer will remain in execution endlessly. It is then said to be in an "infinite loop". When this occurs you must use the BREAK key to _interrupt_ operation of the program. This returns the computer to the READY status.

2.4 OUTPUT FROM A BASIC PROGRAM

When Example 1.4 is run on the computer, the output at the terminal appears as follows:

```
100               212
110               230
120               248
130               266
140               284
150               302
160               320
170               338
180               356
190               374
200               392
```

On each line the numbers are arranged in 18-position _zones_ or _windows_. This means the first number on any line appears in columns 1 to 18 inclusive, the second number in columns 19 to 36 inclusive, etc. Each number appears _left-justified_ in a window, with the sign in the left-most position. When the sign is positive, this position is left blank.

2.5 STORING A BASIC PROGRAM

When you have completed your program you may wish to STORE a copy into your private library of programs. First you think of a name for it such as PROGONE, type

    STORE 'PROGONE'

and then depress the ENTER key. The program is then copied from your workspace onto a secondary storage area such as disk, and will be permanently saved until you subsequently erase it. The method for erasing or "scratching" programs is discussed in a later section.

The name you choose for your program should contain no more than 8 letters or digits and should begin with a letter. Actually, your program is stored as a <u>file</u>, and the name you choose is referred to as the <u>file</u> <u>name</u>.

When you have STOREd a copy of your program, it remains in your workspace as well. If you wish to erase it from your workspace you should enter the command

    CLEAR

and the workspace is in its original status, just as if you had signed on.

2.6 <u>RETRIEVING</u> <u>A</u> <u>BASIC</u> <u>PROGRAM</u> <u>FROM</u> <u>THE</u> <u>LIBRARY</u>

At some point in time you will probably want to copy a selected program from your library into your workspace. When the system is in READY status, simply type

    LOAD 'PROGONE'

followed by ENTER and the workspace is automatically cleared; your program is then copied from the library into the workspace. The program is not erased from the library and can be recalled as frequently as you like.

2.7 <u>SIGN</u> <u>OFF</u> <u>PROCEDURE</u>

When you have completed your session at the terminal you sign off by entering the command BYE. This will clear your workspace and display the message USERID?, thus inviting another user to "sign on".

2.8 <u>MANAGING</u> <u>THE</u> <u>LIBRARY</u>

When you have a number of programs stored in the library, it is difficult to remember their names. Enter the command DIR, and a listing of the names of all of your programs (or files) will appear on the terminal.

Should you wish to erase a program such as PROGONE enter the command

    SCRATCH 'PROGONE'

and it will be removed from the library.

If you wish to change a library entry, LOAD it into your workspace, alter it as required and STORE it back using the same name. This destroys the original entry, and copies the modified program from your workspace into the library under the same name.

2.9 CHANGING A PROGRAM

It has been explained that any line in your workspace can be changed by re-entering it with the same statement number. However, it is possible to change any group of characters in a line using the CHANGE command as follows:

CH 10/X/Y/

This causes the first occurrence of an X in line 10 to be changed to a Y. The slanted strokes are called "delimiters" and in fact can be any character you choose to use.

Other program editing features are illustrated in the following examples:

a) If you wish to delete a line, say line 10, simply type

DEL 10

b) If you wish to delete all lines between 10 and 100 inclusive type

DEL 10 - 100

c) If you wish to delete all lines up to line 100 inclusive type

DEL -100

d) If you wish to delete all lines from line 100 then type

DEL 100-

e) There is also a universal CHANGE command which permits the user to change the first occurrence of a given string of characters in any line to another string of characters. For example

CH 10-100/CAT/HORSE/

would change the first occurrence of the string CAT to HORSE in all lines from 10 to 100 inclusive.

f) The LIST command also can be used with a range of line numbers. For example LIST 10-100 will list only lines 10 to 100 inclusive, and LIST 100- causes all lines beyond 100 inclusive to be printed at the terminal.

2.10 SUMMARY

A number of commands such as LOAD, STORE, RUN, CLEAR, LIST, DIRECTORY, DELETE, CHANGE and BYE have been introduced in this chapter. These commands are not part of the BASIC language, and are _editor_ _commands_ or _system_ _commands_ because they are associated with the editing, managing and operation of the program. There are other commands of this type, including OLD, SAVE and RUNLIB. These are described in the Reference Manual.

2.11 EXERCISES

2.1 Enter each of the examples from Chapter 1 into the computer and run them to ensure that the output is as expected. Store these programs into the library for later reference.

2.2 Enter solutions for the Exercises at the end of Chapter 1 and run the programs to be sure they work.

2.3 Try every editor or system command introduced in this chapter to verify that they work as described.

2.4 In example 1.4 we would like to change the letter C to the word Centigrade. The CHANGE commands described in this chapter will allow you to make these modifications. You should be careful of the line C = C+10; you will have to apply the change command to this line a second time.

CHAPTER 3

THE FLAVOUR OF WATERLOO BASIC

In Chapter 1 simple programs were discussed, and presumably the reader has entered these examples into the computer, run them, and modified them in various ways. In this chapter further examples are used to introduce the reader to additional features of the BASIC language. The purpose of the chapter is to give the reader a feeling for the "flavour" of the system, and to allow more interesting problems to be attempted before examining all of the details. Subsequent chapters repeat most of the material covered, and provide more formal definitions and descriptions.

3.1 MAKING HEADINGS IN BASIC

```
10      ! EXAMPLE 3.1
13
15      PRINT 'CENTIGRADE','FAHRENHEIT'
18
20      C = 100
22
25      LOOP
30         F = (C*9)/5 + 32
40         PRINT C, F
45         C = C + 10
46         IF C > 200 THEN QUIT
47      ENDLOOP
48
50      STOP
```

Example 3.1 is identical to Example 1.4, except that one additional statement has been added, namely

PRINT 'CENTIGRADE','FAHRENHEIT'

When the computer runs the program this statement is encountered before the loop begins, and the words CENTIGRADE and FAHRENHEIT are printed in the first two windows of the first line. These quantities are referred to as <u>string</u> <u>constants</u> and can be recognized because they are enclosed between quotation marks. Such string constants can be printed and used as headings or special text in any window of any line.

The reader should type the program into the system, run it and confirm that the output appears as follows:

CENTIGRADE	FAHRENHEIT
100	212
110	230
120	248
130	266
140	284
150	302
160	320
170	338
180	356
190	374
200	392

Notice that the words CENTIGRADE and FAHRENHEIT are printed left-justified in the windows. Actually the numbers are also left justified but the + sign is not printed.

Example 3.2 shows another interesting use for string constants.

```
10      ! EXAMPLE 3.2
15
20      C = 100
22
25      LOOP
30        F = (C*9)/5 + 32
40        PRINT 'CENTIGRADE =',C,'FAHRENHEIT =',F
45        C = C + 10
46        IF C > 200 THEN QUIT
47      ENDLOOP
48
50      STOP
```

Here the PRINT statement contains quantities to be printed in four windows on every line. The first and third quantities are string constants, while the second and fourth are variables. When the program is placed into execution the output appears as follows:

CENTIGRADE =	100	FAHRENHEIT =	212
CENTIGRADE =	110	FAHRENHEIT =	230
CENTIGRADE =	120	FAHRENHEIT =	248
CENTIGRADE =	130	FAHRENHEIT =	266
CENTIGRADE =	140	FAHRENHEIT =	284
CENTIGRADE =	150	FAHRENHEIT =	302
CENTIGRADE =	160	FAHRENHEIT =	320
CENTIGRADE =	170	FAHRENHEIT =	338
CENTIGRADE =	180	FAHRENHEIT =	356
CENTIGRADE =	190	FAHRENHEIT =	374
CENTIGRADE =	200	FAHRENHEIT =	392

NOTE: The output of Example 3.2 contains a considerable number of blank spaces in each line because each of the windows is not completely used. This problem can be overcome by using the following alternative for line 40.

    40 PRINT 'CENTIGRADE =';C;'FAHRENHEIT =';F

The only change is that the commas have been replaced by semi-colons. This has the effect of setting the size of the window to the size of data being printed, thus eliminating the unwanted blank spaces. The reader should make this change to Example 3.2 and observe the output.

3.2 MORE EXAMPLES OF ALGEBRAIC EXPRESSIONS

a)   In Example 1.4 an expression was calculated, namely

    (C*9)/5 + 32

It was noted that this expression is similar to expressions used in algebra. The corresponding expression for conversion of Fahrenheit to Centigrade would be as follows:

    ((F - 32)*5)/9

Here the subtraction operator - has been introduced, as well as two sets of parentheses which are nested. First the computer will calculate the innermost expression, namely F-32. This quantity will be multiplied by 5, and finally this result will be divided by 9. Thus parentheses determine the order in which expressions are computed, and is similar to the method used in algebra.

    The reader should write a program similar to Example 1.4 which converts Fahrenheit to Centigrade. Run it on the computer to verify that it works as expected.

b)   Suppose it is required to calculate the 6th power of X, and assign this value to Y. A BASIC statement could be written as follows:

    Y = X*X*X*X*X*X

However, there is a shorter way of accomplishing the same result by using the exponentiation operator as follows:

    Y = X ** 6

The two asterisks immediately following one another are a signal to the computer to perform a computation which is equivalent to multiplying the current value of X by itself 6 times.

c) <u>Built-In</u> <u>functions</u> can be used to perform common computations such as the square root. The statement

    Y = SQR(2)

will cause the computer to use a previously programmed routine or built-in function which is designed to calculate the square root, this routine being invoked with the use of the letters SQR. The value of the expression contained in the parentheses following SQR is called the <u>argument</u> and is the quantity which is submitted to the built-in function called SQR. In this example the argument is 2; thus Y will be assigned a value which is the square root of 2. Note that this built-in function will only calculate the square root if the argument is non-negative.

    Examples of other built-in functions are SIN and COS, for calculation of sine and cosine respectively. There are many more which will be introduced during the course of this text, with a complete list being available in the Reference Manual.

```
10      ! EXAMPLE 3.3
15
20      X = 1
25
30      LOOP
40         Y = X**3
50         Z = SQR(X)
60         PRINT X, Y, Z
70         X = X + 1
80         IF X > 10 THEN QUIT
90      ENDLOOP
95
100     STOP
```

    Example 3.3 is a program which calculates the third powers and the square roots of all integers from 1 to 10 inclusive. Enter this program into the computer, run it, and observe the following output:

1	1	1
2	8	1.414214
3	27	1.732051
4	64	2
5	125	2.236068
6	216	2.44949
7	343	2.645751
8	512	2.828427
9	729	3
10	1000	3.162278

Note that the third powers are all printed accurately, but in most cases the square roots are terminated after 6 decimal places. In a later chapter format control will be introduced which will allow the programmer to obtain more than 6 digits of decimal places in the output. However, owing to hardware limitations, the computer saves only 16 digits internally, and this will be the maximum accuracy normally obtained, even with format control.

3.3 INPUT DURING EXECUTION

It is often desirable to enter data from the terminal under program control during execution. Example 3.4 is another version of the Centigrade-to-Fahrenheit conversion program which incorporates this new feature. The reader should type this program into the computer and run it to observe its operating characteristics.

```
10      ! EXAMPLE 3.4
15
20      LOOP
30         INPUT C
40         F = (C*9)/5 + 32
50         PRINT C, F
60      ENDLOOP
65
70      STOP
```

When the computer encounters the statement

INPUT C

a ? appears at the terminal. This is referred to as a prompt and is a signal to the user to enter data. The program then pauses until the user types a number such as 110 and depresses the ENTER key. The variable C is assigned the value which has been typed, and the computer goes on to the next statement following the INPUT statement.

This program is designed to permit the user to enter Centigrade data endlessly and have it converted to Fahrenheit. To stop the program's operation you can type an alphabetic string constant such as QUIT and it will terminate with an error. This occurs because the computer is expecting a number to be assigned to C, and when it receives the letters there is a conversion error which causes the program to cease operation. This is not a "professional" way to stop a program, but in our case it works, and introduces an example of an error which can occur during execution of the program.

Another version of the program which incorporates a prompt message is illustrated in Example 3.5.

```
10      ! EXAMPLE 3.5
12
15      OPTION NOPROMPT
18
20      LOOP
25        PRINT 'ENTER DEGREES CENTIGRADE'
30        INPUT C
40        F = (C*9)/5 + 32
50        PRINT C, F
60      ENDLOOP
65
70      STOP
```

Type this example into the computer and note how much more pleasant it is to use the terminal; you have the feeling of carrying on a "conversation" with the computer. The terms interactive computing or conversational computing are often used to refer to this type of programming system.

The statement at line 15 is called an OPTION statement. This particular OPTION is followed by the keyword NOPROMPT which is a message to the computer to eliminate the question mark (?) which normally occurs as in Example 3.4.

3.4   SELECTION USING IF-ELSE-ENDIF

Example 3.6 is a program which converts either Centigrade to Fahrenheit or vice versa.

```
10      ! EXAMPLE 3.6
12
15        OPTION NOPROMPT
18
20      LOOP
30        PRINT 'ENTER 1 FOR CENTIGRADE TO FAHRENHEIT'
40        PRINT '   OR 2 FOR FAHRENHEIT TO CENTIGRADE'
50        INPUT TYPE
60        IF TYPE = 1
70          PRINT 'ENTER DEGREES CENTIGRADE'
80          INPUT C
90          F = (C*9)/5 + 32
100         PRINT C,F
110       ELSE
120         PRINT 'ENTER DEGREES FAHRENHEIT'
130         INPUT F
140         C = ((F-32)*5)/9
150         PRINT F,C
160       ENDIF
170     ENDLOOP
175
180     STOP
```

The computer first asks the user to enter a 1 or a 2 depending on which type of conversion is to be done. This constant is assigned to the variable TYPE. In the loop, two separate calculations are made, depending on the current status of TYPE. The value of TYPE is tested using an IF statement with a relational expression as follows:

IF TYPE = 1

If the relational expression has the value "true" the statements immediately following the IF are executed, stopping when the ELSE is encountered. If the relational expression has the value "false" the statements immediately following the ELSE are executed, up to the ENDIF. Thus the IF statement allows the programmer to logically select one of two sets of statements, depending on the value of a relational expression. When the IF-ELSE-ENDIF combination has been executed, the computer continues with the statement following the ENDIF.

IMPORTANT NOTE: Two distinctly separate kinds of IF statements have been introduced. The IF-THEN-QUIT is used only to terminate processing in loops and is a single statement. The IF-ELSE-ENDIF combination is a collection of several statements used to select two separate blocks of statements, depending upon whether the relational expression is true or false.

Enter the program into the computer and run it. Once again you can terminate its operation by typing QUIT.

3.5 SUMMARY

The reader should now have a sufficient introduction to the fundamentals of programming in BASIC to experiment with a number of interesting problems. The following exercises which reinforce these fundamental concepts should be completed before proceeding to subsequent chapters.

3.6 EXERCISES

3.1 Make the following modifications to the program in Example 3.1, enter the resulting programs into the system and run them.

a) The initial value of C is assigned in line 20. Incorporate appropriate statements so that this initial value is entered from the terminal at execution time. A prompting message should ask the operator to enter the starting value.

b) The program as modified in a) will produce one table of output. Incorporate further statements so that the program does not stop after producing a table, but "loops", each time requesting a new starting value for C. Thus several tables can be produced. The program can be terminated by typing QUIT as the value for the variable for C when the terminal prompts for the value.

3.2 In Example 3.1 the conversion table is printed in increments of 10 degrees Centigrade. Modify the program so that this increment changes to 2 degrees when C has reached a value of 170 degrees.

3.3 Further modify the solution for problem 2 so that the increment of 2 degrees is reset to an increment of 10 degrees when C has reached 180 degrees.

3.4 Write a program which permits the user to type several numbers into the computer, and receive their average as output. Note that in order to terminate the input a special number will have to be used and recognized by the program.

3.5 In exercise 3.4 a special number was used to terminate input. However, another method is to ask the question

IS THERE MORE INPUT? (Y OR N)

When the user types Y, the terminal then prompts for the next numeric quantity; if the user types N, the program computes the average and displays it at the terminal.

Modify the solution of exercise 3.4 to include this feature; it will be necessary to learn about string variables in a subsequent chapter before attempting this problem.

3.6 Suppose $100 is placed in a bank account at the beginning of each year. Interest of 8 percent is added to the account at the end of the last day of each year. There are no withdrawals. Write a program which shows the current balance in the account at the end of the first day of each year, for the first 10 years.

3.7 Modify the program for exercise 3.6 so the terminal prompts the user for the interest rate, annual deposit amount, and number of years, thus making a more general-purpose program.

3.8 Marks for a particular course are assigned integer values ranging from 0 to 100 inclusive.

A mark below 50 is a failure
A mark from 50 to 59 inclusive is a D grade
A mark from 60 to 69 inclusive is a C grade
A mark from 70 to 79 inclusive is a B grade
A mark from 80 to 100 inclusive is an A grade.

Write a program which permits the teacher to enter a mark for each student in the class, and receive as output a statistical report which indicates the number of students in each of the five categories. Use appropriate prompts for the input and headings in the output.

3.9 Modify Example 3.6 so that it terminates if a third value other than 1 or 2 is given.

3.10 Write a program which converts miles to kilometers or kilometers to miles. It should ask the user to specify what conversion should be done by specifying either a 1 or 2, and then give the value to be converted. The reader should refer to Example 3.6 for guidance. The answer should be displayed on the terminal.

3.11 Modify the program in problem 3.10 so that it terminates if a third value other than 1 or 2 is given.

DEBUGGING PROGRAMS

Writing BASIC programs would be fairly straight-forward if they always ran properly. Unfortunately this is seldom the case. The process of finding errors in a program is known as debugging, that is, eliminating the "bugs". This process includes many different techniques for testing programs and locating errors. Some of these techniques are discussed in this chapter.

4.1 IMMEDIATE MODE

Whenever you enter a BASIC statement without a line number it is executed immediately. For example, if you type

    PRINT 'HELLO'

the word HELLO will be echoed back at the terminal as soon as the statement is entered. This immediate mode of operation seems at first glance to be of limited use, since it appears that you can only execute one BASIC statement. However it turns out to be quite powerful in the preparation and debugging of programs.

4.2 AN EXAMPLE

```
10        ! EXAMPLE 4.1
15
20        I = 1
30        TOTAL = 0
35
40        LOOP
50          TOTAL = TOTAL + 1
60          I = I + 2
70          IF I = 100 THEN QUIT
80        ENDLOOP
85
90        PRINT TOTAL
95
100       STOP
```

Suppose you have written the program in Example 4.1. You intend it to calculate the sum of all the odd integers up to 100, namely 1+3+5+7+...+99. When you place the program into execution, the message

    EXECUTION BEGINS...

appears, but nothing else ever appears at your terminal, regardless of how long you wait. You are in an infinite loop. You can recover by depressing the BREAK key one or more times, and finally you return to READY status. One method of finding the bug is to stare at the program until it occurs to you what went wrong. A better way is to examine the current contents of the key variables to see if this gives you a clue. For example, you could type

    PRINT I

Immediate-mode execution takes place and the value of I is printed. You are shocked to find it to be 493! How could this be, since you carefully arranged to stop the loop when I reached 100? Hopefully at this point it occurs to you that I never does reach 100, as it skips from 99 to 101. However, should you fail to make this observation you should insert a new line in the program, namely

    55 PRINT I

and place the program into execution again. This will cause the values of I to be printed each time through the loop. Surely now you will observe that it skips from 99 to 101, and you will then change the program by re-entering line 70 as follows

    70   IF I>100 THEN QUIT

This technique of interrupting the program and examining the values assumed by various variables is of inestimable value when debugging larger and more complex programs.

4.3 MONITORING THE OPERATION OF A PROGRAM

Some programs are expected to operate for several hours before they produce the required output. For example, you may want the computer to sort the names of all the people in Canada into alphabetical order, and then produce a list. While the program is operating, you are worried because nothing has appeared for 30 minutes or more. You can interrupt the program with the BREAK key. Then a message appears indicating the statement number which was just about to be executed, let us say number 260 to be specific. You can now "browse" around looking at partial results to see if things seem to be going well, all the time using immediate mode BASIC operations. If you are satisfied, you can resume execution at precisely the proper statement by typing

CONTINUE

which is an immediate command to transfer control back to statement 260 and the program resumes normal operation.

4.4 TESTING THE PROGRAM IN SMALL PARTS

Many programs are quite large and you may wish to test only small parts of them to be sure those parts seem to work well. Suppose in Example 4.1 you wish to test the instructions contained within the loop. You could insert a statement as follows

65 PAUSE

Then you could set any value you like for TOTAL and I, using immediate mode assignment statements. You could then type

GO TO 50

This would cause statements 50, 60 and 65 to be executed, and the computer would pause. Then you can examine the current value for TOTAL and I to be sure they have increased as you expected them to.

4.5 SUMMARY

This chapter has only scratched the surface of methodology relative to debugging and the use of immediate-mode computing. Hopefully it contains enough guidance to enable the user to begin to develop a debugging style which will produce effective results in the shortest possible time.

4.6 EXERCISES

4.1 The following program prints a conversion table relating Centigrade and Fahrenheit temperatures. It is supposed to print the conversion table from -20 to 100 degrees Centigrade in increments of 10 Centigrade degrees except for the comfort range from 10 to 35 degrees where it should print the temperatures for every 2 degrees Centigrade. After 35 degrees the table is again printed in 10 degree increments. Run this program and examine the output. Does it work? Attempt to repair the program so it will work. If you have difficulties use the debugging techniques described in this chapter to help you.

```
10    C = -20
20    DEGREES = 10
30    PRINT 'CENTIGRADE', 'FAHRENHEIT'
40    LOOP
50      IF C=100 THEN QUIT
60      F = (C*9)/5 + 32
70      PRINT C,F
80      IF C = 10
90        DEGREES = 2
100     ELSE
110       IF C = 35
120          DEGREES = 10
130       ENDIF
140     ENDIF
150     C = C + DEGREES
160   ENDLOOP
170   STOP
```

4.2 The following program prints a conversion table relating
     Centigrade and Fahrenheit temperatures. It is supposed to
     print the conversion table from -20 to 100 degrees
     Centigrade in increments of 10 Centigrade degrees except
     for the range from 0 to 5 degrees where it should print the
     temperatures for every .2 Centigrade degrees. After 5
     degrees the table is again printed in 10 degree increments.
     Run the program and examine the output. Does it work?
     Find the bugs and fix them. If you have difficulties use
     the debugging techniques described in this chapter.

```
10    C = -20
20    DEGREES = 10
30    PRINT 'CENTIGRADE', 'FAHRENHEIT'
40
50    LOOP
60      IF C = 100 THEN QUIT
70      F = (C*9)/5 + 32
80      PRINT C,F
90      IF C = 0
100        DEGREES = .2
110     ELSE
120       IF C = 5
130          DEGREES = 10
140       ENDIF
150     ENDIF
160     C = C + DEGREES
170   ENDLOOP
```

ARITHMETIC IN BASIC

In earlier chapters there have been several examples of arithmetic operations within BASIC programs. The purpose of this chapter is to approach the subject more formally, in order to tidy up many of the ideas which have been introduced.

5.1 NUMERIC CONSTANTS

BASIC programs and the data they process usually contain many numeric constants, several examples of which follow:

(a) (i)   126
     (ii)   -126
     (iii)   0
     (iv)   1112223334445556
     (v)   -1112223334445556

(b) (i)   .126
     (ii)   -.126
     (iii)   .0
     (iv)   111222.3334445556
     (v)   -111222.3334445556

(c) (i)   12.6 E3
     (ii)   12.6 E-3
     (iii)   -12.6 E3
     (iv)   -12.6 E-3
     (v)   999.9999999999999 E13
     (vi)   1.0E75
     (vii)   1.0E-78

Group a) contains a number of examples of integers. Integers contain no decimal point, as it is assumed to be to the immediate right of the least significant digit. They can be positive or negative, and can contain at most 16 digits as shown in examples a) (iv) and a) (v).

Group b) contains several examples of real constants. Each contains a decimal point, can be positive or negative, and has at most 16 digits of precision.

Group c) contains several examples of real constants expressed using exponent or scientific notation, usually referred to as E-notation. In all cases the signed integer following the E indicates the power of ten which is used to multiply the number which precedes it. For example 12.6E3 means 12.6 multiplied by 10 to the third power and is therefore equivalent to 12600. On the other hand 12.6E-3 is equivalent to .0126 because the -3 indicates that 12.6 should be multiplied by 10 to the -3rd power, which is equivalent to dividing by 10 to the 3rd power.

E-notation is used to allow the programmer to use very large or very small constants in the program or data. Example c) (vi) is a number which is so large it could almost be considered infinite. On the other hand example c) (vii) shows a number which is so small it could almost be considered to be zero. All E-notation constants can contain up to 16 digits of precision. The largest magnitude is approximately 10 to the 75th power, and the smallest magnitude, other than zero, is approximately 10 to the -78th power.

The following are examples of errors which can be made when using numeric constants in BASIC.

111222333444555666	Too many digits of precision
142.6.7	Two decimal points
1,462,271.439	Cannot use commas
$126.42	Cannot use $
14.E16.2	Cannot use decimal in exponent part
14.6E93	Too large.

5.2 NUMERIC VARIABLES

Numeric variables are used in BASIC programs, and are for the purpose of being assigned numeric values. Consider the following examples.

a) In the statement

$$X = 7.6$$

the symbol X is a numeric variable, and is assigned the value 7.6 when the statement is executed.

b) In the statement

INPUT Y

the symbol Y is a numeric variable, and is assigned a value when any numeric constant is entered at the keyboard during execution.

c)   In the statement

        PRINT K

the numeric variable K has previously been assigned a
numeric value, and this value is displayed on the terminal.

A numeric variable always begins with a letter, and can
contain as many letters or digits as can conveniently be used on
the line being entered into the computer (in other words, a
numeric variable cannot by typed partly on one line, and partly
on the next). Examples of numeric variables are as follows:

    (i)   CAT
    (ii)   G72
    (iii)   THIS_IS_A_LONG_VARIABLE_NAME

NOTES: 1. In example (iii) we use the <u>underscore</u> character to
       make the variable name more readable. This is the only
       special character allowed in numeric variable names.

       2. Some computer terminals permit lowercase letters to
       be entered. When used in variable names, lowercase
       letters are treated as being different from uppercase
       letters: CAT and CaT are different variables.

Examples of erroneous numeric variable names are as
follows:

    7K   Must begin with a letter
    C$K   Must not contain the special character $

5.3 <u>NUMERIC</u> <u>EXPRESSIONS</u>

Any expression which, when evaluated, produces a numeric
result is said to be a <u>numeric</u> <u>expression</u>. Some examples are;

    (i)   (X + 6.92)/8.6
    (ii)   (A + T)*(J - 2)
    (iii)   7.493
    (iv)   K
    (v)   -K
    (vi)   A+B**5
    (vii)   A+B**.5
    (viii)   A/B*C
    (ix)   -7.9**2

The conventions used in evaluating numeric expressions are
similar to those used in algebra. For example in (i) the
expression X + 6.92 would be evaluated first because it is
contained in parentheses. The result would then be divided by
8.6 (recall that the slanted stroke / is used to denote the
division operation).

Example (ii) introduces * as the multiplication operator. Here the two expressions A + T and J - 2 are evaluated, and the two results are multiplied together. Note that in BASIC the multiplication operator * must always be used when multiplication is to be done, whereas in algebra we are allowed an implied multiplication, with the expression written as (A+T)(J-2).

Examples (iii) and (iv) are included to show that the simple numeric constant and numeric variable are each simple cases of numeric expressions.

Example (v) introduces the <u>unary minus</u>. This operator is the same symbol as the subtraction operator, but serves to multiply the value of K by negative or minus one, thus changing its sign.

Example (vi) introduces the exponentiation operator **. First B**5 is evaluated to produce B multiplied by itself five times. Then the result is added to A. This is because of the <u>priority</u> of operators. The operators in order of decreasing priority are

    **
    * and /
    + and -

Example (vii) indicates the use of a fractional exponent, namely .5. Here B is raised to the power .5 to produce the square root of B; the result is added to A. Note that B must be positive or an error message would be produced by the computer.

Example (viii) seems to provide two possible results. Will A/B be evaluated, with the result multiplied by C? Or will B*C be evaluated with the result divided into A. The rule is that when equal priority operators are encountered the expression is evaluated from left to right, so the A/B is evaluated then multiplied by C. It is usually best to use parentheses and then no possible misunderstanding can take place. Thus the expression could be written as (A/B)*C.

Example (ix) produces the negative of 7.9 squared. The expression (-7.9)**2 would produce the same result with a positive sign.

5.4 <u>NUMERIC ASSIGNMENT STATEMENTS</u>

The general form of a <u>numeric assignment statement</u> is

numeric variable = numeric expression.

First, the value of the numeric expression is computed; this value is then assigned to the numeric variable.

Examples are:

(i)   SALARY = HOURS * 6.25 -DEDUCTIONS
(ii)   TIME = 7

An alternative form of the assignment statement is to use the BASIC keyword LET as follows:

(i)   LET SALARY = HOURS * 6.25 - DEDUCTIONS
(ii)   LET TIME = 7

An error frequently caused by beginning programmers is to try to use an assignment statement such as the following:

X + Y = 7 * Z

The item to the left of the equals sign is not a variable. You cannot have an expression to the left of the equals sign when you are using an assignment statement.

5.5 SOME EXAMPLES

a)   Suppose a loan of $10,000 is to be repaid at the rate of $750.00 per month, payable at the end of each month. This payment is to include interest of 1 percent per month on the outstanding portion of the loan (principal). Example 5.1 is a BASIC program which calculates the number of months required to repay the loan. It also prints out the schedule of monthly payments to show the declining principal amount.

```
5       ! EXAMPLE 5.1
10
15      OPTION PRTZO 14
20
30      PRINCIPAL = 10000
40      MONTH = 1
50      PRINT 'MONTH','PRINCIPAL','INTEREST','PAYMENT'
55
60      LOOP
70        INTEREST = PRINCIPAL * .01
80        PAYMENT = 750 - INTEREST
90        IF PAYMENT >= PRINCIPAL THEN QUIT
100       PRINT MONTH, PRINCIPAL, INTEREST, PAYMENT
110       PRINCIPAL = PRINCIPAL - PAYMENT
120       MONTH = MONTH + 1
130     ENDLOOP
140
160     PRINT MONTH,PRINCIPAL,INTEREST,PRINCIPAL
170     PRINT
180     PRINT 'THE NUMBER OF MONTHS TO REPAY IS';MONTH
190
200     STOP
```

The first few lines in the program which appear before the main loop are used for _initialization_. The numeric variables PRINCIPAL and MONTH are assigned their initial values of 10000 and 1 respectively. Then a heading is printed for the report which is to be calculated.

Each time the LOOP is executed the payment schedule for one month is computed and printed. Then the new principal amount is recalculated and the month is incremented by one. The loop is terminated by testing to determine whether the calculated payment equals or exceeds the outstanding principal amount. If so, the exit from the loop is taken and a line for the final month is printed with a payment equal to the outstanding principal amount. Finally a message is printed which indicates the total number of months in which payments must be made to repay the loan completely. The output produced by the computer appears as follows:

MONTH	PRINCIPAL	INTEREST	PAYMENT
1	10000	100	650
2	9350	93.5	656.5
3	8693.5	86.935	663.065
4	8030.435	80.30435	669.69565
5	7360.73935	73.607393	676.392606
6	6684.346743	66.843467	683.156533
7	6001.190211	60.011902	689.988098
8	5311.202113	53.112021	696.887979
9	4614.314134	46.143141	703.856859
10	3910.457276	39.104573	710.895427
11	3199.561848	31.995618	718.004382
12	2481.557467	24.815575	725.184425
13	1756.373041	17.56373	732.43627
14	1023.936772	10.239368	739.760632
15	284.17614	2.841761	284.17614

THE NUMBER OF MONTHS TO REPAY IS 15

NOTES: 1. All quantities are recorded to six decimal places, even though they represent dollars and cents. In a subsequent chapter it is shown how to truncate and round these numbers using the _format_ facility in BASIC.

2. The statement OPTION PRTZO 14 is used to change the size of the print window or zone from 18 to 14.

3. The reader should note that the decimal points do not line up vertically. This is because all numeric output is left-justified in the print window. In a subsequent chapter, format control will be introduced to help overcome this difficulty.

4. In line 170 the PRINT keyword has no associated list of variables or constants. When the computer executes this statement a line of blank spaces is printed.

5. The reader should observe that the values in the column labelled PAYMENT vary, but that INTEREST plus PAYMENT equals $750 (the monthly payment) for every month except the last one.

b)   Example 5.2 is identical to the previous example, except that the program contains an important change of _style_. Most of the numeric constants have been replaced by numeric variables which are initialized _once_ in the initialization portion of the program. For example, each time .01 appears it is replaced by RATE. This makes the program much easier to modify when these important parameters change. For example, if the interest rate becomes 2 percent, it is only necessary to change one line in the initialization, namely

RATE = .02

The program will now function correctly and produce a corresponding result for the new rate.

This point of programming style cannot be emphasized too much. Often programs are used repeatedly for years by different people. These people or users wish to introduce different data (such as interest rates), so the initial assignments of variables will have to be changed. The effort involved to make this change becomes relatively trivial if all such changes are isolated in the initialization portion of the program.

```
5       ! EXAMPLE 5.2
10
15      OPTION PRTZO 14
20
25      INSTALLMENT = 750
30      PRINCIPAL = 10000
35      RATE = .01
40      MONTH = 1
50      PRINT 'MONTH','PRINCIPAL','INTEREST','PAYMENT'
55
60      LOOP
70        INTEREST = PRINCIPAL * RATE
80        PAYMENT = INSTALLMENT - INTEREST
90        IF PAYMENT >= PRINCIPAL THEN QUIT
100       PRINT MONTH,PRINCIPAL,INTEREST,PAYMENT
110       PRINCIPAL = PRINCIPAL - PAYMENT
120       MONTH = MONTH + 1
130     ENDLOOP
140
160     PRINT MONTH,PRINCIPAL,INTEREST,PRINCIPAL
170     PRINT
180     PRINT 'THE NUMBER OF MONTHS TO REPAY IS';MONTH
190
200     STOP
```

5.6 NUMERIC BUILT-IN FUNCTIONS

In Chapter 3 the built-in function SQR was introduced, and others such as SIN and COS were mentioned. A complete list of available functions and their characteristics can be found in the Reference Manual. However, a number of observations are useful.

Every function such as SQR can be considered to be a numeric variable which is assigned its value when the function is encountered. Thus it is not possible to use the numeric variable name SQR for any other purpose, as it is "reserved" for use as the built-in function. The variable name SQR can only be used in conjunction with parentheses which contain the proper argument. Thus SQR(2) will calculate the square root of 2. Note that a few of the functions can contain more than one argument. For example MIN(X,Y,Z) calculates a result which is the minimum value of X, Y and Z.

The arguments used in functions can be expressions. For example SQR(X + Y * Z) is evaluated by first computing the expression X + Y * Z, followed by the evaluation of the square root. Note that the value of the expression must be non-negative in order for the SQR function to produce a result.

The arguments can also be expressions which contain another function. For example SQR(SQR(2)) will produce the 4th root of 2.

5.7 INTEGER COMPUTATIONS IN WATERLOO BASIC

Sometimes it is important to do arithmetic which ignores the fractional component of a numeric quantity. Consider the following example. Suppose you wish to calculate the maximum number of quarters (25-cent pieces) contained in the quantity $3.15. Obviously the answer is 12 with $.15 left over. To compute this the following BASIC statements could be incorporated into a program.

```
NUMBER_OF_QUARTERS = 315/25
PRINT NUMBER_OF_QUARTERS
```

Unfortunately the answer would appear on the terminal as 12.6 because it is indeed true that $3.15 contains 12.6 quarters! However, since .6 of a quarter is not legal currency, 12 is the required answer. To obtain an integer answer for the number of quarters the following statements are used:

```
NUMBER_OF_QUARTERS = IP(315/25)
PRINT NUMBER_OF_QUARTERS
```

Note that the built-in function IP (which stands for "Integer Part") has been used. First the expression 315/25 is computed to produce 12.6, and then the integer part, namely 12 is selected and is finally assigned to the variable NUMBER_OF_QUARTERS. There is another function FP which returns the fractional part of a numeric quantity.)

Suppose it is further required to know that there is a "remainder" of 15 cents after the number of quarters has been calculated. Another built-in function called REM is used, which automatically returns the correct remainder as illustrated in the following BASIC statements.

```
NUMBER_OF_QUARTERS = IP(315/25)
REMAINDER = REM(315,25)
PRINT NUMBER_OF_QUARTERS, REMAINDER
```

Note that REM is another function which uses more than one argument.

Many people have a habit of collecting one-cent coins in an old cigar box, usually located in the bedroom. This habit drives the government to distraction, but prevents many holes from developing in pants pockets. Example 5.3 is a program which permits the user to indicate the number of cents in the collection. The program proceeds to compute the minimum number of coins required to make up this sum, using 5 denominations, namely 50-cent pieces (halves), 25-cent pieces (quarters), 10-cent pieces (dimes), 5-cent pieces (nickels) and 1-cent pieces (pennies). The reader should study the program to observe the use of the IP and REM built-in functions.

```
10   ! EXAMPLE 5.3
90
100 PRINT 'HOW MANY CENTS DO YOU HAVE?'
110 INPUT AMOUNT
115
120 NUMBER_OF_HALVES = IP (AMOUNT / 50)
130 REMAINDER = REM (AMOUNT, 50)
140 NUMBER_OF_QUARTERS = IP (REMAINDER / 25)
150 REMAINDER = REM (REMAINDER, 25)
160 NUMBER_OF_DIMES = IP (REMAINDER / 10)
170 REMAINDER = REM (REMAINDER, 10)
180 NUMBER_OF_NICKELS = IP (REMAINDER / 5)
190 NUMBER_OF_PENNIES = REM (REMAINDER, 5)
200
201 PRINT
202 PRINT AMOUNT; 'CENTS MAY BE REPRESENTED BY:'
210 PRINT NUMBER_OF_HALVES, 'HALVES'
220 PRINT NUMBER_OF_QUARTERS,'QUARTERS'
230 PRINT NUMBER_OF_DIMES,'DIMES'
240 PRINT NUMBER_OF_NICKELS,'NICKELS'
250 PRINT NUMBER_OF_PENNIES,'PENNIES'
260
300 STOP
```

When the program is run the following output is produced when the number of cents in the collection is 280.

HOW MANY CENTS DO YOU HAVE?

```
280 CENTS MAY BE REPRESENTED BY:
5              HALVES
1              QUARTERS
0              DIMES
1              NICKELS
0              PENNIES
```

5.8 SUMMARY

Arithmetic operations appear in arithmetic expressions which include operands, operators, built-in functions and parentheses. The operands are either numeric constants or numeric variables. The operators are +, -, *, /, and **. All calculations proceed retaining 16 digits of precision.

Results of arithmetic operations can be assigned to a numeric variable. However they can be printed directly without assignment by including them in the list of items specified in a PRINT statement. For example, the following statements would produce the result of the expression X+2.

PRINT X+2

In order to conserve space within the machine, it is possible to store all numeric quantities to only 6 digits of precision. This is done by including the statement

OPTION SPREC

at the beginning of the program.

5.9 EXERCISES

5.1 A retired school teacher has $60,128.42 in his bank account. Interest of one-half of one percent is credited at the end of each month. Assume the teacher must withdraw $1,020.00 for living expenses at the beginning of each month. Write a BASIC program which calculates the number of months until the bank account has reached a balance which is less than $1,020.00.

5.2 Write a program which converts a time in seconds to a time in hours, minutes and seconds. The program should continue in a loop; each time the user is requested to type a time in seconds, and the converted time is printed at the terminal.

5.3 Write a program which computes and prints all the integers up to 1000 which are perfect squares. (625 is a perfect square because its square root is 25, which is an integer.)

5.4 Write a program which converts a distance in inches to a distance in miles, yards, feet and inches. The program should continue in a loop; each time the user is requested to type a distance in inches, and the converted distance is printed at the terminal.

CHAPTER 6

HARDWARE-DEPENDENT LIMITATIONS

When using a computer, sometimes surprising and unexpected results can occur. These are usually related to the limitations of the hardware, and it is helpful to be forewarned. This chapter outlines some of these problems, and gives partial explanations. It is possible to skip this chapter on an initial reading of the text, as future chapters do not depend on the material.

6.1 AN EXAMPLE

```
10      ! EXAMPLE 6.1
15
20      X = 1.0
25
30      LOOP
40        Y = SQR(X)
50        PRINT X, Y
60        X = X + .1
70        IF X = 2.0 THEN QUIT
80      ENDLOOP
85
90      STOP
```

Consider Example 6.1 which tabulates the square roots of the set of numbers 1.0, 1.1, 1.2, 1.3, ... 2.0. It would be reasonable to expect this program to terminate but in fact it does not.

The problem is that the computer represents numbers using binary notation and it is not possible to represent .1 accurately using binary notation. The computer must use an <u>approximation</u> for .1 which is slightly too small. This means that X never actually becomes equal to 2.0 and the program does not terminate. The program is easily corrected by changing line 70 as follows:

```
70   IF X > 2.0 THEN QUIT
```

It is therefore common to avoid equality tests when terminating loops. However, if the numbers involved are all integers this problem does not arise (unless the integers are very large). This is because most useful integer values are represented accurately in binary.

To further help the reader understand the problem, perhaps an analogy using decimal arithmetic would be of assistance. Suppose it is required to write the fraction one third as a decimal. It is written as .3333333, a number which never terminates; thus no computer could ever have enough capacity to accurately represent this fraction, if the computer recorded its numbers in common decimal notation. If we accept .3333333 as the approximation it is slightly too small, but the error is less than 1 part in ten million.

6.2 ANOTHER EXAMPLE

```
10      ! EXAMPLE 6.2
15
20      X = 3.1
30      Y = 3.1E20
40      Z = Y - Y + X
50      T = Y + X - Y
55
60      PRINT Z, T
65
70      STOP
```

In Example 6.2 you would expect Z and T to be assigned identical values. In actual fact, Z becomes 3.1 and T becomes zero! This happens because computation of expressions proceeds from left to right, and numeric constants contain only 16 digits of precision. When computing Z, the quantity Y-Y is evaluated first, yielding zero; then X is added to produce the result 3.1. When computing T, the quantity Y+X is evaluated first. Since the computer retains only 16 significant digits, the result is 3.1E20 because X is insignificant relative to Y. Then Y is subtracted producing the zero result for T. This points out that operations which are associative in ordinary algebra are not necessarily associative in BASIC.

6.3 SUMMARY

The reader who is not familiar with computers may be disturbed by the points made in the two examples. However, experienced computer users have learned over the years to cope with these difficulties, and they seldom present problems in straight-forward real-life situations. The most serious difficulties arise in complex scientific or engineering calculations where millions of computations are taking place. Since the numbers used are approximations, the errors can have a tendency to compound upon one another. In extreme cases the error becomes larger than the numbers themselves, so the results are meaningless! A separate discipline called numerical analysis has concerned itself with the propagation of errors. These studies have yielded good algorithms for solving common scientific problems keeping the error in the results to a minimum.

CHAPTER 7

STRING MANIPULATION IN BASIC

Many problems involve the processing of alphabetic data. Examples include names, addresses, and product descriptions, to name just a few. Waterloo BASIC permits the programmer to manipulate alphabetic data with reasonable ease. The purpose of this chapter is to introduce the subject of string processing, and to formalize a number of the pertinent rules of BASIC.

7.1 STRING CONSTANTS

In previous chapters there have been examples in which headings were produced by printing strings of characters contained between quotation marks. Examples of these string constants are as follows:

(i)	'CAT'
(ii)	"CAT"
(iii)	' '
(iv)	''
(v)	"IT'S A BOY!"

Examples (i) and (ii) show that a string can be delimited by either the single quote or the double quote. However, for any given string constant, it must begin and end with the same type of quote. Both strings are said to have a length of 3.

Example (iii) shows a string of blank characters, while example (iv) illustrates the null string. This null string is of length zero and contains no characters.

Example (v) illustrates what to do if a string is to contain quotation marks as in the word IT'S. Double quotes are used to delimit the string, and the single quote is used within it.

7.2 STRING VARIABLES

A string variable is a variable which can assume a string of characters as its value. String variables are similar to numeric variables except that they always end with a $ character. Thus the following are typical string variables:

    A$
    NAME$
    NAME2$

As with numeric variables, they must begin with a letter, and
contain no special characters except the underscore and of
course the final $ character.

7.3 STRING EXPRESSIONS

    There is only one string operation, namely concatenation,
which is denoted by a + or &. For example

        'CAT' + 'DOG'
    or 'CAT' & 'DOG'

is a string expression which, when executed, causes the two
strings to be joined together (concatenated) to form a single
string, namely 'CATDOG'. In a similar fashion, three strings
can be concatenated as follows

        'CAT' + ' ' + 'DOG'

to form the string 'CAT DOG'. As many strings   can   be
concatenated together as required in a particular problem.

    String variables and string constants can also appear in
the same string expression. For example

        'CAT' + X$

will concatenate the string 'CAT' to the current value assigned
to the string variable X$, thus forming a new string.

    The following are examples of invalid string expressions.

    'CAT' + 6   Cannot concatenate a string
                     with a numeric constant

    'CAT' + DOG   Here, DOG is not contained
                     within quotes so is not a
                     string constant

    'CAT' * 'DOG'   The * operator is not allowed
                     in string expressions.

    Later in this chapter built-in string functions   are
introduced; they can also be used in string expressions.

7.4 STRING ASSIGNMENT STATEMENTS

The general form of a string assignment statement is

string variable = string expression

Examples are:

```
(i)      X$ = 'CAT' + 'DOG'
(ii)     NAME$ = 'JOHN HENRY'
(iii)    T$ = X$ & NAME$
(iv)     T$ = T$ + T$
```

In each example the string variable on the left of the equals sign is assigned the value of the string expression on the right. Note in example (iv) the variable T$ is concatenated to itself to form a string of twice the original length.

7.5 AN EXAMPLE

```
10  ! EXAMPLE 7.1
13
15  OPTION NOPROMPT
18
20  PRINT 'WHAT IS YOUR SURNAME?'
30  INPUT SURNAME$
40  PRINT 'WHAT IS YOUR FIRST NAME?'
50  INPUT FIRST_NAME$
60  PRINT 'WHAT IS YOUR MIDDLE INITIAL?'
70  INPUT INITIAL$
75
80  FULL_NAME$=FIRST_NAME$+' '+INITIAL$+'. '+SURNAME$
90  PRINT FULL_NAME$
95
100 STOP
```

Example 7.1 is a program which prompts the user for surname, first name and middle initial. The three items are entered at the keyboard, and are assigned to three separate string variables. The full name is formed by concatenating the three strings together in the proper order. Note that a period is placed after the initial, and blank characters are inserted between the components of the full name.

When the program is run, the user is prompted to enter three string constants. To make things easier, it is not necessary to use the beginning and ending quotes around the input string. Thus when the surname is requested you can type either 'SMITH' or SMITH as a response. (When you choose to omit the quotation marks, the string constant must not contain a comma (,) as this becomes a delimiter. This unusual situation is discussed further in Chapter 8.)

The computer _never_ prints strings on the terminal (or on any file device) with the quotes included. Thus when the full name is printed it looks as we would want it to, for example

JOHN H. SMITH

It should be noted that in Chapter 2 we discussed the concept of print "windows" which are 18 characters wide. If a string longer than 18 characters is printed, it uses two or more of these windows. In fact, if a string is longer than a line, the output is automatically continued on the next line, and is said to "wrap around".

7.6 BUILT-IN FUNCTIONS FOR STRINGS

While built-in functions play a minor role in most numeric calculations, it is rare that a string manipulation operation can be done effectively without the use of built-in functions. Hence these functions play an important role, and appear in many string expressions. The following examples illustrate the application of some of the more common functions. Many others can be found in the Reference Manual.

a) It is often necessary to select a string of characters from within an existing string, thus forming a new string, often referred to as a _substring_. This is accomplished using the STR$ function with three arguments as follows:

```
Y$ = 'ABCDEFGH'
X$ = STR$(Y$,3,4)
```

The string Y$ is selected, and the new string is formed beginning at the 3rd character, namely the C, and continuing for 4 characters. Thus the string X$ will be assigned the value 'CDEF' and will have a length of 4.

```
10 ! EXAMPLE 7.2
13
15 OPTION NOPROMPT
18
20 PRINT 'PLEASE ENTER A 3-LETTER WORD'
30 INPUT X$
35
40 LETTER1$ = STR$(X$,1,1)
50 LETTER2$ = STR$(X$,2,1)
60 LETTER3$ = STR$(X$,3,1)
70 NEW_STRING$ = LETTER1$+' '+LETTER2$+' '+LETTER3$
75
80 PRINT NEW_STRING$
85
90 STOP
```

Example 7.2 illustrates a simple application of this function. It requests the terminal operator to enter a three-letter word such as CAT. The program then composes a new string, placing a blank between each letter, and the terminal output becomes C A T.

b) The previous example is somewhat restrictive in application because it processes only 3-letter words. In order to be able to input a word of any length, it would be convenient to have a facility which determines the length of any given string. The built-in function LEN is used for this purpose. For example

```
INPUT X$
N =LEN(X$)
Y$=STR$(X$,N,1)
PRINT Y$
```

will permit the user to enter a string constant of any reasonable length; it will be assigned to X$, and then the length is determined and is assigned to N. Finally the _last_ character in the string is selected using the STR$ function, and it is printed on the terminal.

```
10        ! EXAMPLE 7.3
13
15        OPTION NOPROMPT
18
20        PRINT 'PLEASE ENTER A WORD'
30        INPUT X$
35
40        N = LEN(X$)
50        Y$ = STR$(X$,1,1)
60        I = 2
65
70        LOOP
80           IF I > N THEN QUIT
90           Y$ = Y$ + ' ' + STR$(X$,I,1)
100          I = I + 1
110       ENDLOOP
115
120       PRINT Y$
125
130       STOP
```

Example 7.3 uses the LEN function to generalize Example 7.2 so that a string of any reasonable length can be entered. The output is the same string, with a single blank inserted between each character. Study this example carefully to be sure the algorithm is thoroughly understood, because the technique illustrated is commonly used in string processing.

Initially Y$ is a string of length 1 which contains the
first character in X$. Each time the loop is executed a blank
character and the next available character in X$ is concatenated
on the right. When all characters in X have been used the loop
terminates and the resulting string Y$ is printed. Note that
the input word must contain at least one character.

c) Another commonly used string operation is accomplished
using the SREP$ (string replace) function. This function
permits the programmer to replace all occurrences of a substring
within a given string by a new substring. For example

```
X$ = 'C A T'
Y$ = SREP$(X$,' ','***')
PRINT Y$
```

will produce the output

```
C***A***T
```

This is because the SREP$ function selects the string X$ (the
first argument) searches for every occurrence of a blank (the
second argument) and replaces it with '***', (the third
argument).

```
10        ! EXAMPLE 7.4
13
15        OPTION NOPROMPT
18
20        PRINT 'PLEASE ENTER A SHORT SENTENCE'
30        INPUT SENTENCE$
35
40        SHORT_SENTENCE$ = SREP$(SENTENCE$,'A','')
50        NUMBER_OF_A = LEN(SENTENCE$) -  &
51    &              LEN(SHORT_SENTENCE$)
55
60        PRINT'THE LETTER A OCCURS',NUMBER_OF_A,'TIMES'
65
70        STOP
```

Example 7.4 is a realistic application of the SREP$
function. Here the user is asked to input a short sentence and
the program is to determine the number of occurrences of the
letter A. This is done by replacing all A's with the null
string, and assigning the resulting string to a new variable
called SHORT_SENTENCE$. It is clear that the difference in
lengths between SHORT_SENTENCE$ and SENTENCE will be the number
of A's in the original sentence.

NOTE: The statement in line 50 is too long to be placed on a
        single line, so is <u>continued</u> to line 51. The ampersand
        (&) character is placed as the last non-blank character
        in line 50 and is a signal that the statement is

continued on the following line. The continuation line
51 begins with another ampersand after the line number.
Using this method, a statement can be continued to as
many lines as necessary.

d)   Sometimes the programmer would like to include a numeric
constant as part of a character string. Consider the example:

```
N = 256
Y$ = 'TRY '+N + ' TIMES'
PRINT Y$
```

Here the desire is to print the message

```
TRY 256 TIMES
```

However an error occurs because the string expression contains
both string constants and a numeric variable N. The numeric
expression N can be <u>converted</u> to a string expression using the
VALUE$ function as follows:

```
N = 256
Y$ = 'TRY ' + VALUE$(N) + ' TIMES'
PRINT Y$
```

Now the desired result is achieved.   A similar function
VALUE permits the programmer to convert a string constant
containing a properly formed numeric constant so it can be
processed in arithmetic expressions. Consider the example

```
X$ = '123.4'
Y = VALUE(X$)*2
PRINT Y
```

Here the string constant '123.4' is converted to a numeric
constant 123.4 using the VALUE function. It is then multiplied
by 2, and the final result is printed.

```
10        ! EXAMPLE 7.5
13
15        OPTION NOPROMPT
18
20        PRINT 'PLEASE ENTER A SHORT SENTENCE'
30        INPUT SENTENCE$
35
40        SHORT_SENTENCE$ = SREP$(SENTENCE$,'A','')
50        NUMBER_OF_A = LEN(SENTENCE$) - &
51    &             LEN(SHORT_SENTENCE$)
55
60        PRINT 'THE LETTER A OCCURS ' + &
61    &         VALUE$(NUMBER_OF_A) + ' TIMES'
65
70        STOP
```

Example 7.5 shows a realistic situation in which you may want to use the VALUE$ function. This program is identical to that of Example 7.4, except that the PRINT statement has been altered to use the function. Note that only one string is printed; thus avoiding the "windows" problem, and provides a better looking output. Try the programs and observe the results in each case.

e) The RPT$ (repeat) function permits the programmer to create a new string which repeats a given string a specified number of times. For example, suppose we wish to print a line of 72 asterisks. This could be accomplished as follows:

```
X$ = RPT$ ('*', 72)
PRINT X$
```

The asterisk ('*') is repeated 72 times to form the string X$, which is subsequently printed. Of course, the same result could also be achieved as follows:

```
X$ = RPT$('**', 36)
PRINT X$
```

7.7 SUMMARY

The reader is encouraged to study the rest of the available string functions as they are all useful. Note that when a string function returns a string as its value, the function name always ends in a $, for example RPT$. However, when the function returns a numeric result (such as LEN) the function name does not end with a $. Properly speaking, the function LEN is not a string function at all, but is a numeric function. However, it is included in this chapter because its use is associated with strings.

7.8 EXERCISES

7.1 a) Write a program which inputs a three character string such as CAT and prints the three letters vertically as follows:

       C
       A
       T

b) Modify the program in a) so that the string can be of any reasonable length.

7.2 a) Write a program which inputs a collection of words one at a time at a terminal, and determines the total number of words of various lengths. The output will be a table as follows:

```
Number of Words of one character  = 3
Number of Words of two characters = 2
Number of Words of three characters = 6
Number of Words of more than three characters = 12
```

b) Modify the program for part a) so that several words can be entered on a single line with each word separated by one or more spaces.

7.3 With reference to the Exercise 7.2, modify the output to appear as follows:

NUMBER OF CHARACTERS

```
             1            ***
             2            **
             3            ******
MORE THAN 3               ************
```

The number of asterisks corresponds to the number of occurrences of a word of the size indicated.

7.4 Write a program which has the following characteristics:

a) Words are read one at a time using the key-board at the terminal.

b) These words are arranged into lines for printing. Each line contains at most 40 characters. The first word in a line is printed left-justified in the line. All subsequent words in a line are separated from other words by exactly one blank character. If there is not enough space at the end of a line to print the next word, this space should be left blank, with the next word appearing as the first word in the following line.

c) When a period (.) is read at the terminal the program terminates.

7.5 Write a program that accepts two integers as input at the terminal. The program then must print a rectangle with the two integers as the length and width, using an asterisk (*) as the character to outline the rectangle. For example, if 5 and 8 are read the output should appear as follows:

```
* * * * * * * *
*             *
*             *
*             *
* * * * * * * *
```

7.6 Write a program which reads a message containing only letters and blank spaces. This message is to be coded into a "secret message" using the following coding rules:

(i) Any letter is replaced by its successor in the alphabet. For example, A is replaced by B and S by T. The letter Z is replaced by A.

(ii) Blanks are to remain unchanged.

Note: You will find the built-in functions ORD and CHR$ useful for solving this problem. They are described in the Reference Manual.

CHAPTER 8

SIMPLE INPUT, OUTPUT AND FILES

In all examples introduced to this point, the BASIC program caused printing to take place at the terminal in 18-character "windows". Also, data has been read into the computer using the INPUT command and the terminal keyboard. The purpose of this chapter is to generalize these ideas, and specifically to introduce the concept of a file.

8.1 OUTPUT AT THE TERMINAL

Several examples have been introduced where a number of quantities are printed at the user terminal. For example, the statement

    PRINT X$, 'CAT', Y, 6.47

will cause four values to be displayed in four 18-character windows. First the current value of X$ is printed in the first window, assuming it has a length of 18 or less. The string CAT is printed in the second window, the value of Y in the third, and the numeric constant 6.47 in the fourth. All quantities are left-justified in each window. If the length of X$ exceeds 18 characters, as many windows as necessary are used. If there are not enough windows on the printed line, the terminal continues printing on the next and subsequent lines until all the quantities are printed.

The list of items following the keyword PRINT is referred to as the output list. The elements of the list are separated by commas and are referred to as output-list items, or list items for brevity.

Each list item can be a variable name, string constant, numeric constant or expression. If we execute the statement

    PRINT (X+2)*6.3

the expression (X+2)*6.3 is evaluated and the result is printed.

8.2 INPUT AT THE TERMINAL

The INPUT keyword has been used in many examples. When the statement

INPUT X

is executed, a ? appears at the terminal, and the user is expected to type some valid numeric constant. If the user types an invalid quantity, such as CAT or 12,346 an error message is issued and the program ceases to operate.

It is possible to input a list of quantities as follows:

INPUT X, Y$, T

Here the terminal prints the ? and the user normally is expected to type three quantities, separated by commas. A typical response might be

26.49, CAT, 16

in which case X will be assigned the value 26.49, Y$ the string value 'CAT', and T the value 16. It is important to observe that the input quantities must match the input list items in both number and type. String constants do not require the quotes on input; however, if the string to be assigned to Y$ contains a comma, then it must be typed surrounded by quotes. Thus the response

26.49, 'JONES,HENRY',16

will assign the string value JONES,HENRY to the variable Y$.

It is not absolutely necessary to type all three items of data on one line, separated by commas. They could be placed on three separate lines, or two on one line and one on the other. However, when more than one data item appears on a line, the items on that line must be separated by commas.

8.3 FILES IN WATERLOO BASIC

It is frequently desirable to store data on an external device such as disk. For example, a file could be created which contains the names of all the students in a class. This file would contain several records, one for each student. The file is given a name such as STUDENT. This file name can contain up to eight letters or digits, and must begin with a letter.

The files are stored on disk in a form similar to that used to place music on a tape for use with a tape recorder. Magnetic impulses are written which are coded to represent the various characters.

```
1110,STEVENS      ,M,17,065,063,085,056,076
1297,WAGNER       ,M,15,065,086,085,084,074
1317,RANCOURT     ,F,16,075,072,070,068,065
1364,WAGNER       ,M,16,070,058,090,064,083
1617,HAROLD       ,M,17,085,080,080,075,074
1998,WEICKLER     ,M,16,072,074,075,075,075
2203,WILLS        ,F,16,073,072,072,073,084
2232,ROTH         ,M,17,072,070,070,074,072
2234,GEORGE       ,M,18,070,070,071,058,069
2265,MAJOR        ,M,16,065,065,068,068,069
2568,POLLOCK      ,M,17,089,088,085,092,063
2587,PEARSON      ,F,15,055,050,049,061,060
2617,REITER       ,M,17,100,068,069,075,089
3028,SCHULTZ      ,M,18,069,068,075,074,053
3036,BROOKS       ,M,18,065,068,069,070,065
3039,ELLIS        ,M,17,085,085,085,085,085
3049,BECKER       ,F,15,065,065,065,068,069
3055,ASSLEY       ,M,16,065,063,060,063,065
3087,STECKLEY     ,M,15,056,053,085,084,072
9999,ZZZZ         ,M,99,000,000,000,000,000
```

Figure 8.1

Consider Figure 8.1 which is a listing of a file called STUDENT. This file contains 20 records. Each record contains several _fields_ of information about a student. These fields are student-number, name, sex, age, and the marks obtained in 5 courses, namely Algebra, Geometry, English, Physics and Chemistry. Note that each field quantity terminates with a comma (except for the last one). This comma is used as a delimiter to separate the fields.

Another thing to observe is that the 20th record is a _sentinel_ record which is used to define the end of the file. This record contains a special student number, namely 9999. The entire record is a "dummy" which exists only to indicate that no further records follow in the file. It will not be processed normally, but will be used as a signal to terminate processing when the file is being read.

8.4 READING A FILE

Example 8.1 is a BASIC program which reads the STUDENT file and prints out a list of the students' names.

```
10 ! EXAMPLE 8.1
20
30     OPEN #3,'STUDENT',INPUT
40
50     LOOP
60         INPUT #3,NUMBER,NAME$,SEX$,AGE,ALG,GEOM, &
61     &                           ENG,PHYS,CHEM
70         IF NUMBER = 9999 THEN QUIT
80         PRINT NAME$
90     ENDLOOP
100
110    CLOSE #3
115
120    STOP
```

In statement 30 the STUDENT file is OPENed for INPUT. This causes the computer to search for the file named STUDENT, and position it at the beginning, to be read later using INPUT statements. Files cannot be used unless they first are opened, so all programs will contain one OPEN statement for each file to be used.

The #3 is called a <u>file</u> number (or <u>unit</u> number) and is used as an abbreviated name for the file throughout the rest of the program. It must always be used, and can be any number ranging from 2 to 9999 inclusive. It is not permanently associated with the file, and can be a different number each time the file is used.

Line 60 contains an INPUT statement similar to those used in other examples. The difference is that the file number is used to indicate that input is to be obtained from the STUDENT file instead of the keyboard. Also a comma must follow this number.

Line 70 is used to cause the loop to be terminated. Each time through the loop one record is read from the STUDENT file. This record is always printed unless the student number is 9999, which indicates the sentinel record. Thus the loop is repeated 20 times, with 20 records read sequentially; the first 19 of these are used to print the students' names. This process is referred to as <u>sequential</u> reading of the file. Chapter 16 introduces other ways to access records in a file.

Line 110 causes the STUDENT file to be CLOSEd. It is always necessary to close a file when the program has finished processing it.

NOTES: 1. The sequence of items in the OPEN statement must be as indicated. Thus, it is not correct to write

       OPEN #3, INPUT, 'STUDENT'

2. The INPUT statement normally contains exactly the number and type of list items to match the fields in each record in the file. However the statement

    INPUT #3, NUMBER,NAME$

would cause a record in the STUDENT file to be read, with values assigned to NUMBER and NAMES$. The rest of the fields would be ignored.

3. It is not possible to OPEN a file with the same unit number when it is already opened. This is one of the reasons the CLOSE statement is needed. If the CLOSE is omitted in error, the program will function but the file will remain open. If you have forgotten to close a file you can do so using an immediate command, by giving the CLOSE without a statement number. An alternative method is to use the immediate command RESET which causes all files to be closed, if they are still open.

4. The keyword INPUT has been used in two contexts in the program. In line 30 it signifies that the file is to be read, in line 60 it causes a record to be read.

8.5 CREATING A FILE

The reader may be wondering what process was used to create the STUDENT file in the beginning. Example 8.2 is a program which will create a file named TELEPHON which contains names and telephone numbers of as many persons as you wish.

```
10        ! EXAMPLE 8.2
20
25        OPTION NOPROMPT
27
30        OPEN #6, 'TELEPHON', OUTPUT
40
50        LOOP
55          PRINT 'ENTER NAME AND TELEPHONE NUMBER'
60          INPUT NAME$,TELEPHONE_NUMBER$
70          IF NAME$ = 'ZZZZ' THEN QUIT
80          PRINT #6, NAME$ + ',',TELEPHONE_NUMBER$
90        ENDLOOP
95
100       PRINT #6,'ZZZZ,' , '999-9999'
110
120       CLOSE #6
125
130       STOP
```

The most important observation to make is that the name and telephone number are written on the file separated by a comma. This is accomplished using the expression

NAME$ + ','

in the output list. This must be done to provide the field separator in the output file.

NOTES: 1. The OPEN statement causes the file named TELEPHON to be initialized for OUTPUT. If a file by that name already exists, it will be destroyed.

2. The loop will terminate when the sentinel name ZZZZ is read. Note that you must also have typed in a sentinel telephone number as well; otherwise the input list will not be satisfied.

3. After the loop is terminated the sentinel record is written in line 100. This is done so that end-of-file can be recognized during later use of the file.

8.6 SUMMARY

This chapter has been included to introduce the reader to the fundamental concepts of input-output using files and the terminal. This subject is a fairly large one, and complete details are beyond the scope of this text. However in subsequent chapters further concepts are introduced. For a complete description of the input-output facilities which are available, the reader is referred to the Reference Manual.

8.7 EXERCISES

8.1 The file called STUDENT must be created before it can be used. The object of this exercise is to write a program which prompts the user for the appropriate data and creates the file as in Figure 8.1. The program can be written to contain a loop as follows:

```
100    LOOP
110       INPUT X$
120       IF X$ = 'QUIT' THEN QUIT
130       PRINT #2, X$
140    ENDLOOP
```

Each time through the loop a single record is entered as a string whose value is assigned to X$. Be sure to include this string in quotes as there are commas in the record. The value of X$ is then written onto the file whose unit number is 2, thus creating the record in the proper format.

Write the rest of the program, run it to create the file, and verify that the file contents are correct by printing the entire file.

8.2   Write a program which reads the file STUDENT and prints the names of the male students.

8.3   Write a program which reads the file called STUDENT and calculates the class average for each course.

8.4   a) The file called STUDENT contains marks for five courses. The teacher decides to add a sixth course, namely history (HIST). Write a program which will copy the STUDENT file into a new file which has this extra field. This new file should be called STUDENTZ. The new field should in each case have a value of zero for the mark.

NOTE: Do not forget to insert the comma to separate the new field from the others.

b) To verify that your program in a) has worked, write a program to print the file, and examine its contents.

c) In order to place the proper history marks into the new file STUDENTZ it will be necessary to write another program. This program should read the file a record at a time and request the new mark with an appropriate prompting message at the terminal. The new "updated" records should be written into another file called STUDENTY. Write this program, run it, and then print the new file to verify that it is correct.

CHAPTER 9

SELECTION

In most programs the instructions to be executed will vary depending on the data being processed. For example in Chapter 3 a program was introduced which converted Centigrade to Fahrenheit, or vice versa, depending on the value of a code which is typed in. This selection is accomplished using a set of BASIC statements, namely IF, ELSE, ENDIF and ELSEIF. This chapter will discuss these statements and their application.

9.1 TERMINATION OF LOOPS

Virtually every program contains one or more loops. Every loop must be terminated, and all examples to this point have accomplished this using a special IF statement. For example, the statement

    IF NAME$ = 'ZZZZ' THEN QUIT

is used to terminate the loop in Example 8.2. This IF statement is referred to as the IF-THEN, as both the keywords IF and THEN are necessary. It is used in this text only for terminating loops and always has the format

    IF relational expression THEN QUIT

If the relational expression is "true" the loop is terminated; if it is false the next instruction is executed and the loop continues.

The IF-THEN combination is therefore a special-purpose mechanism. This chapter discusses another type of IF combination which has more general application.

9.2 THE IF-ENDIF COMBINATION

Consider the program illustrated in Example 9.1

```
10   ! EXAMPLE 9.1
15
20   OPEN #8,'STUDENT',INPUT
25
30   FEMALE_TOTAL = 0
40   NUMBER_OF_FEMALES = 0
45
50   LOOP
60     INPUT #8,NUMBER,NAME$,SEX$,AGE,ALG
70     IF NUMBER = 9999 THEN QUIT
80     IF SEX$ = 'F'
90       NUMBER_OF_FEMALES = NUMBER_OF_FEMALES + 1
100      FEMALE_TOTAL = FEMALE_TOTAL + ALG
110    ENDIF
120    PRINT NUMBER,NAME$,SEX$,ALG
130  ENDLOOP
135
140  FEMALE_AVERAGE = FEMALE_TOTAL/NUMBER_OF_FEMALES
145
150  PRINT 'FEMALE AVERAGE IS',FEMALE_AVERAGE
155
160  CLOSE #8
165
170  STOP
```

The IF used on line 80 is followed by the relational expression SEX$ = 'F'. If this expression is "true" the block of statements between the IF and ENDIF are executed, namely statements 90 and 100. If the relational expression yields a value which is false, this block of two statements is not executed.

The effect in Example 9.1 is to calculate the aggregate algebra mark for females only, as well as the total number of females. When the loop has terminated the average algebra mark for females is computed and printed. The number and name of each student is printed, as statement 120 is not in the range of the IF-ENDIF block.

To summarize, the IF and ENDIF statements are meant to work together to define a group or block of statements which may or may not be executed, depending on the value of the relational expression associated with the IF statement. The statements in the block are sometimes referred to as the range of the IF-ENDIF.

NOTE: Only the first five fields in each record are read. The others are automatically skipped, as they are not included on the list associated with the INPUT statement.

9.3 THE IF-ELSE-ENDIF COMBINATION

```
10   ! EXAMPLE 9.2
15
20   OPEN #8,'STUDENT',INPUT
25
30   FEMALE_TOTAL = 0
35   MALE_TOTAL = 0
40   NUMBER_OF_FEMALES = 0
45   NUMBER_OF_MALES = 0
48
50   LOOP
60     INPUT #8,NUMBER,NAME$,SEX$,AGE,ALG
70     IF NUMBER = 9999 THEN QUIT
80     IF SEX$ = 'F'
90       NUMBER_OF_FEMALES = NUMBER_OF_FEMALES + 1
100      FEMALE_TOTAL = FEMALE_TOTAL + ALG
110    ELSE
112      NUMBER_OF_MALES = NUMBER_OF_MALES + 1
114      MALE_TOTAL = MALE_TOTAL + ALG
116    ENDIF
120    PRINT NUMBER,NAME$,SEX$,ALG
130  ENDLOOP
135
140  FEMALE_AVERAGE = FEMALE_TOTAL/NUMBER_OF_FEMALES
145  MALE_AVERAGE = MALE_TOTAL/NUMBER_OF_MALES
148
150  PRINT 'FEMALE AVERAGE IS', FEMALE_AVERAGE
155  PRINT 'MALE AVERAGE IS', MALE_AVERAGE
158
160  CLOSE #8
165
170  STOP
```

Example 9.2 is a slight variation of Example 9.1. Here the algebra average is calculated for males as well as females. This is accomplished by incorporating the ELSE statement within the range of the IF-ENDIF. This separates the range of statements into two blocks or sub-ranges, namely the statements between the IF and the ELSE, and the ones between the ELSE and the ENDIF. The former block is referred to as the true range and the latter as the false range. When the relational expression (which must always follow the IF keyword) is true, the statements in the true range are executed; if it is false those in the false range are executed. Thus the computer is able to select between two choices of action, depending on the current value of SEX$.

9.4 THE IF-ELSEIF-ELSE-ENDIF COMBINATION

Suppose it is required to count the number of students in the various age categories, namely ages 15, 16, 17 and 18. Example 9.3 is a program which accomplishes this using another BASIC statement, namely ELSEIF.

```
10   ! EXAMPLE 9.3
15
20   OPEN #8,'STUDENT',INPUT
25
30   TOTAL15 = 0
40   TOTAL16 = 0
50   TOTAL17 = 0
60   TOTAL18 = 0
65
70   LOOP
80     INPUT #8,NUMBER,NAME$,SEX$,AGE
90     IF NUMBER = 9999 THEN QUIT
100    IF AGE = 15
110      TOTAL15 = TOTAL15 + 1
120    ELSEIF AGE = 16
130      TOTAL16 = TOTAL16 + 1
140    ELSEIF AGE = 17
150      TOTAL17 = TOTAL17 + 1
160    ELSEIF AGE = 18
170      TOTAL18 = TOTAL18 + 1
180    ELSE
190      PRINT 'BAD RECORD'
200    ENDIF
210    PRINT NUMBER, NAME$, SEX$, AGE
220  ENDLOOP
222
224  PRINT ' '
225  PRINT 'TOTAL15','TOTAL16','TOTAL17','TOTAL18'
230  PRINT TOTAL15, TOTAL16, TOTAL17, TOTAL18
235
240  CLOSE #8
245
250  STOP
```

In this example, the range of the IF (the statements between the IF and ENDIF) is separated into five sub-ranges. The first sub-range, contained between the IF and the first ELSEIF, is executed only if AGE = 15. The next sub-range, contained between the first and second ELSEIFs, is executed if AGE = 16. This pattern follows until all the ages are considered, providing one block of statements for each age. The last block of statements, between the ELSE and ENDIF, will be executed only if none of the others is selected. This prints an error message because the file contains no ages other than 15 to 18 inclusive.

This IF combination of statements is sometimes referred to as a <u>case</u> <u>construct</u> because only one of several "cases" is selected for processing.

9.5 <u>GENERAL</u> <u>RULES</u> <u>CONCERNING</u> <u>IF-COMBINATIONS</u>

1. Every IF statement contains a relational expression following the keyword IF.

2. Every IF combination ends with the ENDIF statement. All statements between the IF and ENDIF are referred to as the range of the IF, regardless of which of the three IF combinations is being considered.

3. Each of the statements in the range of the IF can be any BASIC statement. This means that the programmer can use other IF combinations <u>within</u> the range of an IF. These are referred to as <u>nested</u> IF's, and BASIC allows complete flexibility to nest IF's of all combinations, to any depth of complexity. It should be pointed out that such nesting makes the program difficult to read and it is generally advisable to avoid this type of programming if at all possible.

4. The indentation of statements is used only to make the program more readable.

5. When an IF combination has selected and executed the appropriate block of code, the processor always proceeds to the statement following the ENDIF statement associated with that IF combination.

6. The IF-THEN-QUIT combination discussed at the beginning of the chapter, and used extensively to terminate loops, can also be used to terminate IF constructs. For example, if this statement is executed within any of the sub-ranges or blocks within the range of any IF combination, and if it's relation evaluates as "true", the next statement to be executed will be the one immediately following the ENDIF statement associated with that combination. In other words the processing will exit from the range of the IF, just as it exited from the range of the LOOP in the case of termination of loops.

9.6 <u>EXERCISES</u>

9.1 a) Using the file called STUDENT as input, list the names of all students who have a mark of 80 or more in at least one course.

b) Using the file called STUDENT as input, list the names of all students who have a mark of 80 or more in at least two courses.

9.2 Using the file called STUDENT as input, list the name and marks for each of the nineteen students. Each mark is to have an asterisk (*) beside it, if the mark exceeds 79.

9.3 Using the file called STUDENT as input, list the name and grade for each of the nineteen students. The grade is A if the average mark is 80 or above. The grade is B if the average mark is between 70 and 79 inclusive; otherwise the grade is Z.

9.4 Print the file STUDENT so that the females are printed first followed by the males. Use the following method:

Read the file, and write the males into MFILE and the females into FFILE. Then close the files, reopen them and print FFILE followed by MFILE.

9.5 Write a program which reads a positive integer number at the terminal. This number is to be printed using 12 positions, filling all high-order positions with asterisks (*) as follows:

```
If the input is   123 print   *********123
If the input is 12345 print   *******12345
etc.
```

CHAPTER 10

In virtually every BASIC program it is necessary to repeat blocks or groups of statements. This has been illustrated in many examples using the LOOP - ENDLOOP combination of statements. This chapter summarizes some of the rules for loops, and introduces several other looping statements in BASIC.

10.1 SIMPLE LOOPS

Suppose it is required to calculate the sum of the digits in a given integer. For example, if the integer is 2749, the sum of the digits is

$$2 + 7 + 4 + 9 = 22$$

This type of computation is often useful for calculating a check digit to be added to a part number, student number, etc.

```
10        ! EXAMPLE 10.1
15
20        INPUT   X$
25
30        LENGTH = LEN(X$)
35        I = 1
45        TOTAL = 0
50
55        LOOP
60          IF I > LENGTH THEN QUIT
65          TOTAL = TOTAL + VALUE (STR$ (X$,I,1))
70          I = I + 1
75        ENDLOOP
80
85        PRINT TOTAL
90
100       STOP
```

Example 10.1 is a program which reads a string of digits at the terminal and assigns it to a string variable X$. (We use a string variable in order to be able to use string functions to simplify the computations.) The length of the string is determined, and a loop is repeated LENGTH times to add up the digits, one digit for each time through the loop. Finally the sum is printed.

The group of statements between the LOOP and ENDLOOP statements is said to be a block which is the range of the loop. All statements contained in this block are said to be "within" the loop, or "contained" in the loop.

Provision for the loop to be terminated is accomplished with the special IF-THEN-QUIT combination of keywords. Note that, since this statement is placed at the beginning of the range, the computation in the loop will not occur if the null string is entered at the key-board.

The loop is initialized by reading in the number, determining its length and setting I and SUM to their initial values.

NOTES: 1. Normally much of the data to be used in a loop must be initialized before entering the loop.

2. The statements between any LOOP and ENDLOOP statements will be repeated endlessly, unless some mechanism such as the IF-THEN-QUIT causes termination. This mechanism can occur anywhere within the simple loop, to recognize the condition at the appropriate time.

3. All statements in the range of the loop are indented for readability.

10.2 NESTED LOOPS

```
5       ! EXAMPLE 10.2
15
19      LOOP
20         INPUT   X$
21         IF X$ = 'QUIT' THEN QUIT
30         LENGTH = LEN(X$)
35         I = 1
45         TOTAL = 0
55         LOOP
60            IF I > LENGTH THEN QUIT
65            TOTAL = TOTAL + VALUE (STR$ (X$,I,1))
70            I = I + 1
75         ENDLOOP
85         PRINT TOTAL
90      ENDLOOP
100
110     STOP
```

Example 10.2 is similar to Example 10.1 except that several numbers can be read in, one at a time, with the sum of the digits computed and printed. The program is terminated when the string QUIT is entered at the key-board.

The reader will notice that there is a loop within a loop. The inside loop is said to be a _nested_ loop, because it is contained in the range of the outside loop. This inside loop has its own range, which is a sub-range of the range of the outside loop. The statements in the inner loop are further indented to make it easier to read the program.

The range of the inside loop is a separate block of statements which is part of the outside loop but is considered to be at a lower level than the other statements in the outside loop. When the inside loop terminates, the rest of the statements in the outside loop continue to function until it also terminates.

Another way of stating the previous paragraph is to say that the statement

    IF I > LENGTH THEN QUIT

makes provision for only the inside loop to terminate. After it terminates the statement

    PRINT TOTAL

is executed, and then the outside loop is repeated. This outside loop is finally terminated when the string QUIT has been entered, and the statement

    IF X$ = 'QUIT' THEN QUIT

is executed.

NOTES: 1. Each loop usually has its own mechanism for termination.

2. Each loop usually has some initialization statements. In this example, the outside loop has no explicit initialization statements.

3. The loops can be nested to any desired level. However, such nesting can make the program more difficult to read and debug. When several levels of looping are required it is usually advisable to use functions (Chapter 13) to repackage the program to improve readability.

4. Because of the indentation, it is clear which ENDLOOP statement belongs to each of the LOOP statements;

however the rule is as follows:

a) Find all LOOP-ENDLOOP combinations which have no intervening LOOP or ENDLOOP statements in their range. These particular combinations are said to be <u>correctly paired</u>, or more briefly, paired.

b) Find all LOOP-ENDLOOP combinations which have no intervening unpaired LOOP or ENDLOOP statements in their range. These are then paired.

c) Step b) is repeated until all LOOP-ENDLOOP combinations have been paired.

d) If there are any LOOP or ENDLOOP statements remaining which have not been paired, the loops are incorrectly nested.

10.3 <u>LOOPS</u> <u>WITH</u> <u>THE</u> <u>WHILE-ENDLOOP</u> <u>COMBINATION</u>

```
10        ! EXAMPLE 10.3
15
20        INPUT   X$
25
30        LENGTH = LEN(X$)
35        I = 1
45        TOTAL = 0
50
55        WHILE I <= LENGTH
65           TOTAL = TOTAL + VALUE (STR$ (X$,I,1))
70           I = I + 1
75        ENDLOOP
80
85        PRINT TOTAL
90
100       STOP
```

Example 10.3 is identical to Example 10.1 except that a new BASIC statement has been used, namely

WHILE I <= LENGTH

The WHILE statement can only be used to start a loop, and is an alternative to the LOOP statement. The keyword WHILE is always followed by a relational expression. This expression is always calculated at the beginning of the loop, and the statements in the range of the loop are executed only if its value is "true".

The WHILE statement provides no additional function for the programmer. It is never necessary, but is used to make the program more readable in some cases. It functions in precisely the same manner as if the following two statements were used as in Example 10.1.

```
LOOP
  IF I > LENGTH THEN QUIT
```

10.4 LOOPS WITH THE LOOP-UNTIL COMBINATION

```
10         ! EXAMPLE 10.4
15
20         INPUT    X$
25
30         LENGTH = LEN(X$)
35         I = 1
45         TOTAL = 0
50
55         LOOP
60           IF I > LENGTH THEN QUIT
65           TOTAL = TOTAL + VALUE (STR$ (X$,I,1))
70           I = I + 1
75         UNTIL I > 5
80
85         PRINT TOTAL
90
100        STOP
```

Example 10.4 is identical to Example 10.1 except for an extra provision. The sum consists only of the first 5 digits in the number. If the number has fewer than 5 digits, the sum includes all of the digits.

Here a new statement has been introduced, namely

UNTIL I > 5

The UNTIL statement can only be used to end a loop, and is an alternative to the ENDLOOP statement. The keyword is always followed by a relational expression. This expression is always calculated at the end of the loop, and the loop is terminated if its value is "true".

Just as is the case with the WHILE statement, the UNTIL provides no additional function for the programmer. It is never necessary, but is used to make the program more readable under the appropriate circumstances. It functions in precisely the same manner as if the following two statements were used in its place.

```
    IF I > 5 THEN QUIT
ENDLOOP
```

10.5 LOOPS WITH THE WHILE-UNTIL COMBINATION

```
10        ! EXAMPLE 10.5
15
20        INPUT   X$
25
30        LENGTH = LEN(X$)
35        I = 1
45        TOTAL = 0
50
55        WHILE I <= LENGTH
65          TOTAL = TOTAL + VALUE (STR$ (X$,I,1))
70          I = I + 1
75        UNTIL I > 5
80
85        PRINT TOTAL
90
100       STOP
```

Example 10.5 is another version of Example 10.4 which uses the WHILE at the beginning and the UNTIL at the end of the loop. Note that the WHILE relational expression is evaluated before each iteration of the loop; the UNTIL relational expression is evaluated after each iteration of the loop.

10.6 LOOPS WITH THE FOR-NEXT COMBINATION

Suppose it is required to calculate the sum of the integers from 1 to 8. The computation to be performed is

$$1 + 2 + 3 + 4 + 5 + 6 + 7 + 8$$

Example 10.6 is an illustration of a program which uses the FOR-NEXT combination of statements for solving this simple problem.

```
10        ! EXAMPLE 10.6
15
25        TOTAL = 0
28
30        FOR I = 1 TO 8
35          TOTAL = TOTAL + I
40        NEXT I
45
50        PRINT TOTAL
55
60        STOP
```

The loop is contained between the FOR and the NEXT statements. In this case the range of the loop consists of only one statement, namely

```
TOTAL = TOTAL + I
```

The loop is repeated for all integer values beginning with 1, up to and including 8.

The FOR statement always contains an <u>index</u> <u>variable</u>, in this case I. This variable is set to the <u>initial</u> <u>value</u> (in this case 1) before the loop is executed the first time. Then the index is checked to be sure its value is not greater than the <u>terminal</u> <u>value</u> (in this case 8). If the index value satisfies this test, the statements in the range of the loop are executed.

The end of the loop is recognized with the NEXT statement. This keyword is always followed by the index variable name, in this case I. When this statement is executed the value of the index variable I is increased by one, and control returns to the FOR statement at the beginning of the loop.

NOTE: When the FOR loop is completed I has a value of 9.

Example 10.7 calculates the sum of the odd integers from 1 to 99 inclusive. Notice we have introduced the STEP keyword in the FOR statement. This causes the NEXT statement to increment I by two rather than one.

```
10        ! EXAMPLE 10.7
15
25        TOTAL = 0
28
30        FOR I = 1 TO 99 STEP 2
35           TOTAL = TOTAL + I
40        NEXT I
45
50        PRINT TOTAL
55
60        STOP
```

Example 10.8 illustrates the nested FOR loop. Here a table of the sum of the integers from 1 to N, for all N ranging from 5 to 20 is calculated and printed. Note that the terminal value of the index-variable for the inner loop is itself a variable, namely J.

```
10        ! EXAMPLE 10.8
20
25        FOR J = 5 TO 20
30           TOTAL = 0
35           FOR I = 1 TO J
40              TOTAL = TOTAL + I
45           NEXT I
50           PRINT J,TOTAL
55        NEXT J
60
75        STOP
```

NOTES: 1. The FOR statement has the general form

FOR index-variable = A TO B STEP C

A, B, and C are all numeric expressions, and their values can be any real constants. Thus it is permissible to have a statement such as

FOR K = 63.5 TO 21.5 STEP -.5

which causes K to begin with a value of 63.5, and be reduced by .5 each time through the loop, with a terminal value of 21.5.

2. When the STEP keyword is used the value of the increment could be positive or negative. When negative, the index value is compared to the terminal value to determine whether or not the statements within the loop are to be executed; if the index value is less than the terminal value the loop is terminated.

3. Under certain circumstances the statements in a FOR loop are not executed at all. For example in the statement

FOR I = 6 TO 4 STEP 2

the increment is 2 and therefore positive. When executed for the first time the index variable I is assigned the value 6. This already exceeds the terminal value 4, so the FOR loop is immediately terminated.

4. Any BASIC statement can be placed within the range of the FOR loop.

5. A FOR loop can be terminated prematurely using the IF-THEN-QUIT construct which is used with other types of loops.

10.7 SUMMARY

The only looping mechanism required to solve any computing problem is the LOOP-ENDLOOP used in previous chapters. The other statements introduced in this chapter are an enrichment providing convenience to the programmer, and enhanced readability in appropriate circumstances.

10.8   EXERCISES

10.1   Write a program which uses the file STUDENT as   input   and
       prints each record in the following approximate format:

       1110   STEVENS
                        65
                        63
                        85
                        56
                        76
                        ──
              AVERAGE   69

10.2   Write a program which has the file STUDENT   as   input   and
       prints the names of the students, with three names on each
       line. As there are 19 students, the last line   will   have
       only one name.

10.3   Write a program which prints a calendar page for   a   given
       month.   The   program   accepts   as   input   the name of the
       month, number of days in the month, and   the   day   of   the
       week on which the month begins.

10.4   a) Write a program which prints a   triangle   of   asterisks
       (*) which is similar to the following:

              *
              **
              ***
              ****

       The input to the program is the size of the   triangle,   in
       this   case   4, which is the number of rows in the vertical
       side of the triangle.

       b) Write a program   which   produces   triangles   which   are
       similar to the following:

                 *
                **
               ***
              ****

c) Write a program which produces triangles which are similar to the following:

```
* * * *
 * * *
  * *
   *
```

10.5 a) Write a program which prints all possible three-letter sequences involving the five letters A, C, E, T and W. Print these sequences five-to-a-line.

b) Modify the program in a) so that each three-letter sequence has at least one vowel.

CHAPTER 11

RELATIONAL EXPRESSIONS

Relational expressions have been introduced informally in
earlier chapters. The purpose of this chapter is to give
further examples and introduce the logical operators AND, OR and
NOT.

11.1 SIMPLE RELATIONAL EXPRESSIONS

Relational expressions are used in IF, ELSEIF, WHILE and
UNTIL statements, and have been included in most programs.
Examples are:

```
(i)      SEX$ = 'F'
(ii)     NUMBER = 9999
(iii)    NUMBER < 0
(iv)     AGE <> 19
(v)      16 > 14
(vi)     'CAT' = ' CAT'
(vii)    'CAT' = 'CAT '
(viii)   'CAT' < 'DOG'
```

Each of these expressions has a value "true" or "false".
In example (i) the current value assigned to the string variable
SEX$ is compared to the string constant 'F'. If they are
identical, the expression has a value of true, otherwise it is
false.

In Example (iii) the expression will be true only if the
current value of NUMBER is negative.

Example (iv) illustrates the use of the symbols <> to mean
"not equal to". Thus if AGE is not equal to 19, the expression
is true.

Example (v) is a special case because no variables are
involved. Since 16 is greater than 14 the expression is always
true.

Example (vi) points out an important point. The two string
constants 'CAT' and ' CAT' are not equal because the latter has
4 characters beginning with a blank. It is always good policy
when comparing strings to have them the same size, with leading
blank spaces removed. It is also true that 'CAT' and 'CAT '

(example vii) are not equal, even though the blank is on the
right. For two strings to be equal they must be of the same
length. In Example (viii) the expression is true because
strings can be compared, and the usual ordering between letters
of the alphabet applies here.

The reader may be wondering why examples (i) and (ii) are
not assignment statements. In fact, they could be assignment
statements, but for purposes of this discussion they are assumed
to be the relational expression component of the IF, ELSEIF,
WHILE or UNTIL statement. The computer detects that they are
relational expressions by examining the <u>context</u> in which they
are used.

11.2 RELATIONAL OPERATORS

As has been mentioned in Chapter 1, there are six
relational operators as follows:

```
=   equals
>   greater than
<   less than
>=  greater than or equal
<=  less than or equal
<>  not equal
```

These operators are <u>binary</u>, which means that there are
always two operands one on each side of the operator. Thus in
example (iv) AGE and 19 are operands and the operator is <>.
The two operands are always of the same kind, either string
expressions or numeric expressions. It would make no sense to
try to compare a string of characters to a number. When the
operands are expressions they are evaluated before the
relational expression is computed. Thus with the relational
expression

    AGE-14 >= TEST+1

the two numeric expressions AGE-14 and TEST+1 are computed and
then the relational operator >= is applied to the two values,
yielding a result of either true or false.

11.3 COMPOUND RELATIONAL EXPRESSIONS

Relational expressions can be combined using the logical
operators AND, OR, and NOT to produce other relational
expressions. Consider the following examples:

    (i)   (SEX$ = 'F') AND (AGE > 17)

    (ii)   (SEX$ = 'F') AND ((AGE = 17) OR (AGE < 10))

    (iii)   NOT (SEX$ = 'F')

The compound relation in example (i) will be true only if SEX$ = 'F' and AGE > 17 are both true.

In example (ii) the sub-expression

(AGE = 17) OR (AGE < 10)

is evaluated first, because of the use of parentheses. The sub-expression result will be true if either of the relational expressions has a true value. This value is used along with the result of sub-expression SEX$ = 'F' to produce "true" only if both values are true.

In example (iii) the NOT is used to reverse the value of SEX$ = 'F'. If SEX$ = 'F' is true, then NOT(SEX = 'F') is false, and vice versa.

11.4 LOGICAL OPERATORS

The three logical operators are defined as follows:

(i)   AND is a binary operator whose two operands are relational expressions. If the two expressions are true, the resulting operation is true. Otherwise it is false.

(ii)   OR is a binary operator whose two operands are relational expressions. If either of the two expressions is true the result of the operation is true. O⁺herwise it is false.

(iii) NOT is a unary operator whose operand is a relational expression. If the value of the operand is true, the result of the operation is false; if the value of the operand is false, the result is true.

The operators have the following priority with respect to each other:

NOT
AND and OR

For example, a NOT operation takes precedence over an AND or OR, provided there are no parentheses. Of course the usual conventions with respect to parentheses are used, with inner-most parentheses being evaluated first.

Three levels of operators have been used in this text. In order of decreasing priority they are

(i)   arithmetic operators or string operators
(ii)   relational operators
(iii)   logical operators

Therefore in an example such as

NOT X + 3 > 6

the numeric expression X+3 is calculated. Then the relational
expression X+3 > 6 is evaluated. Finally the result is operated
upon with the logical operator NOT. Incidentally the whole
expression should have been written with parentheses for greater
readability, as follows

NOT((X+3) > 6)

11.5 SUMMARY

Relational expressions play an indispensible role in any
realistic computer program. The logical operators AND, OR and
NOT provide considerable flexibility in the construction of
compound relational expressions. However, the reader should be
warned that large, complex relational expressions are a hazard
to readability, and make debugging difficult. Therefore they
should be used with discretion. Clarity is often introduced by
using parentheses, even when they are not strictly required
because of the priority rules.

11.6 EXERCISES

11.1 Using the file STUDENT as input, write a program which
      prints the names of all the male students who are age 17
      and have received a mark of less than 80 in algebra.

11.2 Using the file STUDENT as input, write a program which
      prints the names of the male students who are not age 17,
      and who have an average mark exceeding 79.

11.3 Using the file STUDENT as input, write a program which
      prints the names and marks of both the male and female
      students with the highest average mark.

11.4 Using the file STUDENT as input, write a program which
      prints the names and marks of both the male and female
      students with the highest average mark, and who are less
      than or equal to sixteen years of age.

CHAPTER 12

TABLES

Many applications require the use of tables or matrices (also called arrays or vectors) to store data in a convenient form. This chapter introduces several BASIC features which make this type of processing convenient to program.

The various features are illustrated with a series of examples to progressively introduce and demonstrate the ideas.

12.1 EXAMPLE 12.1

Suppose it is required to read a list of words into the computer and print the entire list in reverse order of input. All of the words would have to be stored in a table in the computer, because the first output line cannot be printed until the last word has been read in.

A table of variables can be formed using the DIM statement, as in Example 12.1.

```
10   ! EXAMPLE 12.1
15
20   OPTION NOPROMPT
30   OPTION BASE 1
35
40   DIM NAME$(4)
45
50   PRINT 'TYPE FIRST NAME'
60   INPUT NAME$(1)
70   PRINT 'TYPE SECOND NAME'
80   INPUT NAME$(2)
90   PRINT 'TYPE THIRD NAME'
100  INPUT NAME$(3)
110  PRINT 'TYPE FOURTH NAME'
120  INPUT NAME$(4)
130  PRINT 'THE NAMES IN REVERSE ORDER ARE'
140  PRINT NAME$(4)
150  PRINT NAME$(3)
160  PRINT NAME$(2)
170  PRINT NAME$(1)
175
180  STOP
```

Statement 40 uses the DIM keyword to declare a table which has four _entries_ or _elements_. These elements are BASIC variables which can be individually referenced as NAME$(1), NAME$(2), NAME$(3) and NAME$(4). The integer contained in parentheses is often called a _subscript_. It is also referred to as the _index_ of the table entry.

Example 12.1 is designed to read four names and store them in turn in the four elements of the table. Then the elements are selected in reverse order, and printed.

NOTES: 1. The table contains four elements which have indices 1, 2, 3, and 4. The _range_ of indices is said to be 1 to 4 inclusive.

2. The statement

OPTION BASE 1

is used in most examples in this text. If it were omitted, the table NAME$ would actually have _five_ elements with the indices ranging from 0 to 4 inclusive.

3. The table defined in the DIM statement can have as many elements as required.

4. If several tables are needed to solve a problem they can be declared in separate DIM statements; alternatively one DIM statement can be used as follows:

DIM NAME$(4), MARK(5)

5. Each table can have elements which are string variables or numeric variables, but not both.

6. The index or subscript always has an integer value which must be within the appropriate range. If the index is a non-integer value, the BASIC system will automatically convert it to an integer using rounding.

7. The quantities within parentheses in a DIM statement denote the number of entries in the tables. These quantities are always positive integers.

8. DIM statements are usually placed near the beginning of the program to improve readability.

12.2   EXAMPLE 12.2

Example 12.1 is obviously a very cumbersome way of writing the program, especially if a large table were involved. Example 12.2 is an improved version which takes fewer statements to write, and produces similar output.

```
10   ! EXAMPLE 12.2
15
20   OPTION NOPROMPT
30   OPTION BASE 1
35
40   DIM NAME$(4)
45
50   FOR I = 1 TO 4
60      PRINT 'NAME PLEASE'
70      INPUT NAME$(I)
80   NEXT I
85
90   PRINT 'THE NAMES IN REVERSE ORDER ARE'
95
100  FOR I = 4 TO 1 STEP -1
110     PRINT NAME$(I)
120  NEXT I
125
130  STOP
```

In this example the index is a variable I which is assigned appropriate values as the loops are executed. In fact, this index can be any numeric expression.

12.3 EXAMPLE 12.3

```
10   ! EXAMPLE 12.3
15
20   OPTION NOPROMPT
30   OPTION BASE 1
35
40   DIM NAME$(4)
45
50   PRINT 'PLEASE TYPE 4 NAMES'
60   PRINT ' SEPARATED BY COMMAS'
65
70   INPUT MAT NAME$
75
80   PRINT 'THE NAMES IN REVERSE ORDER ARE'
90   FOR I = 4 TO 1 STEP -1
100     PRINT NAME$(I)
110  NEXT I
115
120  STOP
```

In this example the new keyword MAT is introduced in line 70. This keyword is followed by the table name NAME$, and is a signal to BASIC to process all entries in the table in ascending sequence of the index. In other words the program processes NAME$(1) followed by NAME$(2) then NAME$(3) and so on. In this case, INPUT will require the user to enter four names. These names will normally be entered on one line, separated by commas. However they can be entered one at a time or 2 on one line and 2 on the next, or any combination provided exactly 4 names are entered.

The keyword MAT is short form for matrix, which is a mathematical term having the same meaning as table. Thus the statement

INPUT MAT NAME$

requests the user to enter the entire table, in order, at the terminal.

12.4   EXAMPLE 12.4

```
10   ! EXAMPLE 12.4
15
20   OPTION NOPROMPT
30   OPTION BASE 1
35
40   DIM NAME$(4)
45
50   PRINT 'PLEASE TYPE 4 NAMES'
60   PRINT ' SEPARATED BY COMMAS'
70   INPUT MAT NAME$
80   PRINT MAT NAME$
85
90   STOP
```

This example uses the MAT keyword in the statement

PRINT MAT NAME$

This causes the entire table to be printed in ascending sequence by index. However, all 4 entries are printed in separate windows on one line.

NOTE: Consider the following BASIC statement:

PRINT A, MAT B, C, D, MAT E

The value of variable A will be printed on line one in the first window. The table B will be printed with its first element appearing on a new line. As many lines as needed are used to print the elements of this table. Then the values of C and D are printed beginning on a new line. Finally table E is printed, once again starting with a new line. The general rule is that when tables are printed, each new table encountered causes a new line to begin.

12.5 UNDERLINE EXAMPLE 12.5

```
10   ! EXAMPLE 12.5
15
20   OPTION BASE 1
25
30   OPEN #6,'STUDENT',INPUT
35
40   DIM MARK(5)
45
50   LOOP
60      INPUT #6,NUMBER,NAME$,SEX$,AGE,MAT MARK
70      IF NUMBER = 9999 THEN QUIT
80      AGGREGATE = 0
90      FOR I = 1 TO 5
100        AGGREGATE = AGGREGATE+MARK(I)
110     NEXT I
120     AVERAGE = AGGREGATE/5
130     PRINT NUMBER,NAME$,AVERAGE
140  ENDLOOP
145
150  CLOSE #6
155
160  STOP
```

In this example all records in the STUDENT file are read in turn. For each record the 5 marks are read into a table called MARK, and the average is computed; then the students' number, name, and average is printed. The output appears at the terminal as follows

1110	STEVENS	69
1297	WAGNER	78.8
1317	RANCOURT	70
1364	WAGNER	73
1617	HAROLD	78.8
1998	WEICKLER	74.2
2203	WILLS	74.8
2232	ROTH	71.6
2234	GEORGE	67.6
2265	MAJOR	67
2568	POLLOCK	83.4
2587	PEARSON	55
2617	REITER	80.2
3028	SCHULTZ	67.8
3036	BROOKS	67.4
3039	ELLIS	85
3049	BECKER	66.4
3055	ASSLEY	63.2
3087	STECKLEY	70

12.6   EXAMPLE 12.6

```
10   ! EXAMPLE 12.6
15
20   OPTION NOPROMPT
30   OPTION BASE 1
35
40   DIM X(100)
45
50   J = 0
60   LOOP
70      PRINT 'NUMBER PLEASE'
80      INPUT NUMBER
90      IF NUMBER < 0 THEN QUIT
100     J = J + 1
110     X(J) = NUMBER
120  ENDLOOP
125
130  AGGREGATE = 0
140  FOR I = 1 TO J
150     AGGREGATE = AGGREGATE + X(I)
160  NEXT I
165
170  AVERAGE = AGGREGATE/J
175
180  PRINT 'THE FOLLOWING ARE ABOVE AVERAGE'
190  FOR I = 1 TO J
200     IF X(I) > AVERAGE
210        PRINT X(I)
220     ENDIF
230  NEXT I
235
240  STOP
```

In this example a table X of 100 entries is defined. Then up to 100 positive numbers are read at the terminal and stored in the table. The average is computed and then all entries whose value exceed this average are printed. Note that the variable J is used to store the current size of the table. Even though the table can have up to 100 entries, only J of them are used when the program is run.

12.7   EXAMPLE 12.7

```
10  ! EXAMPLE 12.7
15
20  OPTION BASE 1
25
30  OPEN #6,'STUDENT',INPUT
35
40  DIM AGE_COUNT(4)
45
50  FOR I = 1 TO 4
60     AGE_COUNT(I) = 0
70  NEXT I
75
80  LOOP
90     INPUT #6,NUMBER,NAME$,SEX$,AGE
100    IF NUMBER = 9999 THEN QUIT
110    INDEX = AGE - 14
120    AGE_COUNT(INDEX) = AGE_COUNT(INDEX) + 1
130 ENDLOOP
135
140 PRINT '15','16','17','18'
150 PRINT MAT AGE_COUNT
155
160 CLOSE #6
165
170 STOP
```

Suppose it is desired to count the number of students in the STUDENT file for each of the ages 15, 16, 17 and 18. In Example 12.7 the table AGE_COUNT is defined to accumulate the four totals as the computation proceeds. Thus AGE_COUNT (1) will contain a running total for all students who are age 15; AGE_COUNT(2) will be used for age 16, AGE_COUNT(3) for age 17 and AGE_COUNT(4) for age 18. In line 110 the INDEX of the table is computed by subtracting 14 from AGE. Thus the ages 15, 16, 17, 18 are "translated" to index values 1, 2, 3, 4 respectively so they will be in the proper range.

12.8   TWO DIMENSIONAL TABLES

Sometimes it is useful to have tables which contain rows and columns. For example the following table indicates the number of females and males in each of the four age groups for records in the STUDENT FILE

	FEMALES	MALES
AGE15	2	2
AGE16	2	4
AGE17	0	6
AGE18	0	3

This table has four rows and two columns, and contains 8

entries.   Example   12.8   is a program which produces this table
without the row headings.

```
10   ! EXAMPLE 12.8
15
20   OPTION BASE 1
25
30   OPEN #6,'STUDENT',INPUT
35
40   DIM COUNT(4,2)
45
50   FOR I = 1 TO 4
60     FOR J = 1 TO 2
70       COUNT(I,J)=0
80     NEXT J
90   NEXT I
95
100 LOOP
110    INPUT #6,NUMBER,NAME$,SEX$,AGE
120    IF NUMBER = 9999 THEN QUIT
130    AGE_INDEX = AGE - 14
140    IF SEX$ = 'F'
150      SEX_INDEX = 1
160    ELSE
170      SEX_INDEX = 2
180    ENDIF
190    COUNT(AGE_INDEX,SEX_INDEX) =      &
191    & COUNT(AGE_INDEX,SEX_INDEX) + 1
200 ENDLOOP
205
210 PRINT 'FEMALES','MALES'
220 PRINT MAT COUNT
225
230 CLOSE #6
235
240 STOP
```

The two-dimensional table COUNT is defined in line   40   as
follows

```
40 DIM COUNT(4,2)
```

The eight entries are referenced in the program using two
indices, which are called AGE_INDEX and SEX_INDEX. The age
index is calculated in line 130 and will have a value between 1
and 4 inclusive.   In the IF block between lines 140 and 180
inclusively the sex value 'F' is translated to 1 and the sex
value of 'M' to 2, thus calculating the SEX_INDEX in the proper
range of 1 or 2.

When the table is printed in line 220 the output is
automatically produced as 4 lines, one line for each row. Of
course each row contains two numbers, one for each sex.   The

general rule is that when two-dimensional tables are being printed, a new line is initiated for each new row of the table.

If it is required to print row headings, the MAT keyword cannot be used in the PRINT statement. Instead the table must be printed a row at a time as indicated in Example 12.9.

```
10   ! EXAMPLE 12.9
15
20   OPTION BASE 1
25
30   OPEN #6,'STUDENT',INPUT
35
40   DIM COUNT(4,2)
45
50   FOR I = 1 TO 4
60     FOR J = 1 TO 2
70       COUNT(I,J) = 0
80     NEXT J
90   NEXT I
95
100 LOOP
110   INPUT #6,NUMBER,NAME$,SEX$,AGE
120   IF NUMBER = 9999 THEN QUIT
130   AGE_INDEX = AGE - 14
140   IF SEX$ = 'F'
150     SEX_INDEX = 1
160   ELSE
170     SEX_INDEX = 2
180   ENDIF
190   COUNT(AGE_INDEX,SEX_INDEX) =        &
191   &       COUNT(AGE_INDEX,SEX_INDEX) + 1
200 ENDLOOP
205
210 PRINT '','FEMALES','MALES'
220 FOR I = 1 TO 4
230   AGE = I + 14
240   PRINT 'AGE'+VALUE$(AGE),COUNT(I,1),COUNT(I,2)
250 NEXT I
255
260 CLOSE #6
265
270 STOP
```

12.9 MULTI-DIMENSIONAL TABLES

The BASIC system permits the use of tables with up to 255 dimensions. While such large dimensions are seldom practical it is useful to have the facility available if needed. To declare a table of 5 dimensions you could write

    DIM TABLE (20, 40, 6, 8, 2)

This will create a table of 20 x 40 x 6 x 8 x 2 = 76800 entries! When using such large tables remember that the computer is of limited size, and you could easily exhaust the space available.

12.10 SUMMARY

In many practical programming situations, one or more tables will be necessary. It is therefore important to learn this facility of BASIC thoroughly. The following exercises will provide the necessary practice.

12.11 EXERCISES

12.1   Write a program which reads the 19 records in the file STUDENT and stores them in a table. The program then determines the student with the highest mark in algebra and prints that record.

12.2   a) Write a program which reads several words at the terminal and stores them in a table. The program then chooses the smallest word in the alphabetic sequence and prints it.

b) Expand on the program so that each of the words is printed in sequence, thus producing an alphabetic listing of all the words.

c) Use the program in b) to enter each of the characters on the key-board as single-character "words". In this way a complete listing of all of the available characters will be produced in "alphabetical order". This order is known as the collating sequence of the character set, and may differ from computer to computer.

12.3   A cryptogram is a common form of puzzle which presents a string of text (message) in a coded form to the reader. The object is to decode the message so it makes sense. In a cryptogram each letter is replaced by a different letter of the alphabet. For example the word CAT might be written as ZTB where C, A and T are encoded as Z, T and B respectively. This correspondence can be set up as a table within the computer.

a) Write a program which permits the user to input the

characters as an encoding table. Then a sentence should be read at the terminal, and the encoded sentence subsequently printed.

b) Modify the program so that the encoded sentence can be read at the terminal to produce the original sentence.

12.4 Write a program which reads the 19 records in the file STUDENT and stores them in a table. The program then prints the entries in the table one at a time but in descending sequence by algebra mark, the highest algebra mark first. You might consider finding the entry containing the largest algebra mark, printing that entry, replacing it by zero and repeating the process for all entries in the table.

12.5 Remove the OPTION BASE 1 command from Example 12.7; rewrite the rest of the program so that it will operate correctly.

CHAPTER 13

In previous chapters there are many examples of built-in functions which have been provided as part of the Waterloo BASIC system. This chapter explains how the programmer can construct other functions which may be useful for the particular problem being considered. Functions can also be used as a means of packaging the program into meaningful units, making it more readable and easier to maintain.

13.1 AN INTRODUCTION TO FUNCTION DEFINITIONS

The reader is requested to review Example 12.5 which is a program to read the STUDENT file, calculate the average of the five marks for each of the 19 students in the file, and print a listing of the student number, name and average for each student. Example 13.1 is another version of the same program.

```
10   ! EXAMPLE 13.1
15
20   OPTION BASE 1
25   DIM MARK(5)
30   OPEN #6,'STUDENT',INPUT
40
50   LOOP
60      INPUT #6,NUMBER,NAME$,SEX$,AGE,MAT MARK
70      IF NUMBER = 9999 THEN QUIT
80      AVERAGE = FN_AVERAGE
90      PRINT NUMBER,NAME$,AVERAGE
100  ENDLOOP
105
110  CLOSE #6
120  STOP
140
600  DEF FN_AVERAGE
605
610  AGGREGATE = 0
620  FOR I = 1 TO 5
630     AGGREGATE = AGGREGATE + MARK(I)
640  NEXT I
650  FN_AVERAGE = AGGREGATE/5
655
660  FNEND
```

Example 13.1 introduces two new BASIC keywords, namely DEF and FNEND, located at lines 600 and 660 respectively. These two keywords define a block of code which is a _function_. In the example, the function consists of the 5 statements between lines 610 and 650 inclusive. The _name_ of the function is FN_AVERAGE. The function name always follows the keyword DEF, and must begin with the letters FN. The function name is a variable which is assigned a value when the function is executed. In this case, the function calculates the average of the 5 marks, and assigns its value to FN_AVERAGE in line 650.

The statements contained at the beginning of the program, namely those between line 10 and 120 inclusive, are referred to as the _mainline_ program and the function is called a _subprogram_. When the program is RUN, it begins to execute at the first statement in the mainline program. When the statement in line 80, namely

AVERAGE = FN_AVERAGE

is executed, the computer encounters the function name FN_AVERAGE. This causes the statements between lines 610 and 650 inclusive to be executed, thus assigning a value for the variable FN_AVERAGE. The execution resumes at line 90 and the mainline program continues. The mainline program is said to have _called_ or _invoked_ the function subprogram.

The purpose of this example has been to describe how a simple function is defined, and explain the mechanics of its operation. In the following sections we explain some of the reasons functions are used, and describe their other properties.

13.2 SEGMENTING A PROGRAM USING FUNCTIONS

Most real-life programs are quite large, and can contain hundreds or thousands of statements. The program becomes difficult to read and understand. One of the most important uses of function subprograms is to _package_ the program into smaller segments, each of which performs a specific well-defined operation or function.

```
10   ! EXAMPLE 13.2
15
20   OPTION NOPROMPT
30   OPTION BASE 1
40   DIM X(100)
45
50   INVOKE = FN_READ_NUMBERS
60   INVOKE = FN_CALCULATE_AVERAGE
70   INVOKE = FN_PRINT_NUMBERS
80   STOP
100
500  DEF FN_READ_NUMBERS
505
510  J = 0
520  LOOP
530    PRINT 'NUMBER PLEASE'
540    INPUT NUMBER
550    IF NUMBER < 0 THEN QUIT
560    J = J + 1
570    X(J) = NUMBER
580  ENDLOOP
595
600  FNEND
620
800  DEF FN_CALCULATE_AVERAGE
805
810  AGGREGATE = 0
820  FOR I = 1 TO J
830    AGGREGATE = AGGREGATE + X(I)
840  NEXT I
850  AVERAGE = AGGREGATE / J
865
870  FNEND
890
900  DEF FN_PRINT_NUMBERS
901
905  PRINT 'THE FOLLOWING ARE ABOVE AVERAGE'
910  FOR I = 1 TO J
920    IF X(I) > AVERAGE
930      PRINT X(I)
940    ENDIF
950  NEXT I
965
970  FNEND
```

Example 13.2 is another version of Example 12.6 which demonstrates this "repackaging" of a program.

The program has been packaged into four components — the mainline program and three functions.

(i)   The function FN_READ_NUMBERS causes several numbers to be read at the terminal and stores them in a table called X. The value of the variable J will indicate the number of entries which have been read and stored in the table after the function has been invoked.

(ii)   The function FN_CALCULATE_AVERAGE uses entries in the table X, and the value of J, as data and calculates the average of the values in the table. This is assigned to the variable AVERAGE.

(iii)   The function FN_PRINT_NUMBERS uses the entries in the table, the value of J, and the value of AVERAGE as input and prints a list of the entries which have a value which is above average.

(iv)   The mainline program is used to invoke the three functions, in the proper sequence. This happens when the following three statements are executed:

```
50 INVOKE = FN_READ_NUMBERS
60 INVOKE = FN_CALCULATE_NUMBERS
70 INVOKE = FN_PRINT_NUMBERS
```

For example, when line 50 is executed, the function name FN_READ_NUMBERS is encountered. This causes the statements numbered 510 to 580 to be executed. This is the only purpose of line 50; there is no meaningful value assigned to the variable INVOKE. This technique is used, whenever appropriate, to cause a function to be executed (invoked). Thus in line 60 and 70 the functions FN_CALCULATE_NUMBERS and FN_PRINT_NUMBERS are invoked.

NOTES: 1. The line-number range for each of the three functions has been chosen to start with an artificially high statement number. This is to separate the functions from one another, and to permit the programmer to easily increase the number of statements within the function, if the need should arise.

2. The functions are separated from each other, and from the mainline by null statements. This is to cause a separation in the listing, thus making the program easier to read.

13.3 SOME RULES ABOUT FUNCTIONS

1.   All variables used in the two example programs have a global definition. For example, assume a variable X has been assigned a value 6 in the mainline program. When a function subprogram is executed, this variable can be used, and if desired it can be altered using an assignment statement. As well, any variable introduced in the subprogram is "known", and therefore can be used by all other subprograms, as well as the mainline program.

2. In the examples, function subprograms have been invoked by the mainline program. In fact, function subprograms may invoke other function subprograms. In special circumstances to be described later, it will be shown that functions can call themselves, and are said to be recursive.

3. In the examples, all function names have been numeric variables. They also can be string variables, and under these circumstances would end with the $ character.

13.4 FUNCTIONS USING PARAMETERS

Many examples have been introduced which use built-in functions. This is especially the case in the chapter on string manipulation, where such functions were used to analyse the nature of strings, and convert them into other related strings.

As a general rule, these built-in functions had one or more arguments. For example SQR(X) has one argument and SREP$(A$,B$,C$) has three arguments. It is possible to define further functions of this nature using the subprogram mechanism introduced in this chapter.

```
10   ! EXAMPLE 13.3
15
20   OPTION NOPROMPT
25
30   LOOP
40      PRINT 'WHAT STRING IS TO BE REPEATED?'
50      INPUT X$
60      IF X$ = 'QUIT' THEN QUIT
70      PRINT 'HOW MANY TIMES?'
80      INPUT NUMBER
90      PRINT FN_RPT$(X$,NUMBER)
100  ENDLOOP
105
110  STOP
120
130
400  DEF FN_RPT$(A$,N)
405
410  NEW_STRING$ = ''
420  FOR I = 1 TO N
430     NEW_STRING$ = NEW_STRING$ + A$
440  NEXT I
450  FN_RPT$ = NEW_STRING$
455
460  FNEND
```

As a simple illustration, suppose that the built-in function RPT$(A$,N) did not exist. Example 13.3 incorporates a function subprogram called FN_RPT$ which accomplishes the purpose. The mainline program requests the user to type a string and the number of times it is to be repeated. Then the function FN_RPT$ is invoked in the print statement to produce the desired result.

Notice that the DEF keyword is followed by the function name, which in turn is followed by a parameter list contained in parentheses. These parameter variables A$ and N are temporary variables which are used only when the function is invoked. They are assigned the values in the argument list each time the function is used. In other words when the PRINT statement is executed, the function is called; at that time the parameter variable A$ is assigned the value of the argument X$, and the parameter variable N is assigned the value of the argument NUMBER. The statements in the range of the function definition are then executed, with the result that the variable FN_RPT$ becomes a long string, repeating X$ as many times as required.

Obviously the parameter list and the argument list must have exactly the same number of items, separated by commas. Also, these items must correspond according to type. This means that parameters which correspond to a number can only be assigned a number, and parameters which correspond to a character can only be assigned a character.

NOTES: 1. When the function has been completed the values of the parameter variables "disappear" so are not available to the invoking program.

2. Any other variable used in the range of this function definition is a global variable, known to the mainline and all subprograms.

13.5 ANOTHER EXAMPLE

Example 13.4 illustrates another important point about parameter variables.

```
10   ! EXAMPLE 13.4
15
20   OPTION NOPROMPT
25
30   LOOP
35     A$ = 'IS THE NEW STRING'
40     PRINT 'WHAT STRING IS TO BE REPEATED?'
50     INPUT X$
60     IF X$ = 'QUIT' THEN QUIT
70     PRINT 'HOW MANY TIMES?'
80     INPUT NUMBER
90     PRINT FN_RPT$(X$,NUMBER)
95     PRINT A$
100  ENDLOOP
105
110  STOP
120
130
400  DEF FN_RPT$(A$,N)
405
410  NEW_STRING$ = ''
420  FOR I = 1 TO N
430    NEW_STRING$ = NEW_STRING$ + A$
440  NEXT I
450  FN_RPT$ = NEW_STRING$
455
460  FNEND
```

Note that the variable A$ in the mainline program has been assigned a value 'IS THE NEW STRING'. This value is printed just after the new string has been printed. The important observation to make is that one of the parameter variables is also called A$. When the function is invoked, the current value of the global variable A$ is "saved" automatically by the computer. Then A$ is assigned the current value of X$ and is used as a temporary variable during execution of the function subprogram. When the function is completed, the variable A$ is "restored" to its former value.

This feature is important because it permits the parameter variables of functions to be defined independently of the variables used in the calling program. This allows pre-written "library" functions to be created since the programmer can use any names for the parameters.

13.6 <u>RECURSIVE</u> <u>FUNCTION</u> <u>CALLS</u>

The fact that parameter variables are temporary variables
which do not affect the values of other variables in the calling
program can be used when invoking a function <u>recursively</u>.
Consider Example 13.5, which invites the user to type any
integer N. Then N! (factorial N) is calculated using the
function FN_FACT (N), and this value is subsequently printed.

```
10   ! EXAMPLE 13.5
15
20   OPTION NOPROMPT
25
30   LOOP
40      PRINT 'PLEASE ENTER AN INTEGER'
50      INPUT INTEGER
60      IF INTEGER < 0 THEN QUIT
70      PRINT INTEGER,FN_FACT(INTEGER)
80   ENDLOOP
85
90   STOP
100
200
300 DEF FN_FACT(N)
305
310 IF N = 0
320    FN_FACT = 1
330 ELSE
340    FN_FACT = N * FN_FACT(N-1)
350 ENDIF
355
360 FNEND
```

The thing to observe is that the function FN_FACT is re-invoked
within its own definition. The current value of N is saved, and
a new temporary variable N is established each time the function
is invoked. These saved values are automatically restored as
each recursive call has been completed.

The reader should also note that the arguments of a
function can be expressions. Within the function definition,
the function is called using the argument N-1.

13.7 SINGLE STATEMENT FUNCTION DEFINITIONS

Sometimes it is possible to compute the value of a function using a single assignment statement. When this is the case, only the DEF keyword need be used as in Example 13.6.

```
10   ! EXAMPLE 13.6
15
20   OPTION NOPROMPT
25
30   LOOP
40      PRINT 'PLEASE ENTER THREE NUMBERS'
50      INPUT A$,B,C
60      IF A$ = 'QUIT' THEN QUIT
70      A = VALUE(A$)
80      PRINT A,B,C,FN_AVG(A,B,C)
90   ENDLOOP
95
100  STOP
105
110
300  DEF FN_AVG(X,Y,Z) = (X + Y + Z) / 3
```

This program computes the average of three numeric values, and prints the result. The function definition consists of the single statement

DEF FN_AVG(X,Y,Z) = (X + Y + Z) / 3

The assignment of FN_AVG takes place after the expression to the right of the = has been evaluated.

13.8 SUMMARY

Large programs should always be written as a collection of modules, each of which performs a specific task. The BASIC facility to define functions provides a useful mechanism for creating these modules.

13.9 EXERCISES

13.1 a) Please refer to Example 7.5 in Chapter 7. This program computes the number of occurrences of the letter A in a given sentence. Repackage this program so it becomes a function. The function should return the number of occurrences as its value.

b) Generalize the function in part a) so that it will determine the number of occurrences of any given character in any given string. Do this by including two parameters in the function definition.

c) Use the function of part b) to write a program which computes the total number of vowels in a given sentence.

13.2 Write a function which determines the lowest entry in an array of string constants. Use this function to print a list of the names of students in the file called STUDENT, in alphabetical sequence.

13.3 a) In problem 12.4 the program repeatedly finds the entry with the highest algebra mark. Write this part of the program as a function which returns as its value the position of the entry in the table.

b) Modify the function in a) so that it will work for any one of the marks in the entry. The parameter of the function is the position of the mark in the entry.

13.4 The nth Fibonacci number is defined by the formula $f(n) = f(n-1) + f(n-2)$ where $f(0) = f(1) = 1$. Write a recursive function which computes the nth Fibonacci number and prepare a main line program which reads n from the terminal and displays the answer.

CHAPTER 14

FORMAT

       To this point the concept of print "windows" has been used
to explain the format of output when using the PRINT statement.
These windows are always of fixed size, and provide virtually no
flexibility in the organization of fields in the output record.
The use of format specifiers permits considerably more
flexibility.   They are also important when reading records from
files, particularly where the various fields have not been
separated by commas.

       This chapter will introduce the concept of formatted input
and output using a simple subset of the formatting capabilities
of Waterloo BASIC. A more comprehensive description of the
format features available is provided in the Reference Manual.

14.1 SOME EXAMPLES

       A convenient way to describe the use of format specifiers
is to introduce a series of examples which illustrate their use.
The following examples are all of a trivial nature, meant to
make their point as briefly as possible.

a)   Example 14.1 uses the simplest form of a format specifier.

```
10   ! EXAMPLE 14.1
15
20   FORM$ = '#######'
30   X$ = 'CAT'
35
40   PRINT USING FORM$,X$
45
50   STOP
```

Here the format specifier is the string '#######' which is
assigned to the variable FORM$. This variable appears in the
PRINT statement following the keyword USING.   When the PRINT
statement is executed the value of the variable X$ is printed in
the "centre" of a window of size 7, determined by the seven #'s
which form the format specifier. Thus the word CAT would be
printed in columns 3, 4, and 5 in the output.

b)   Example 14.2 introduces the symbol < at the beginning of
the format specifier.   This means that the word CAT will be

left-justified in the seven-position print window, and so would
be printed in columns 1, 2, and 3.

```
10   ! EXAMPLE 14.2
15
20   FORM$ = '<#######'
30   X$ = 'CAT'
35
40   PRINT USING FORM$,X$
45
50   STOP
```

c)   Example 14.3 introduces the symbol > at the beginning
of the format specifier. This means that the word CAT
will be right-justified in the seven-position print window,
so would be printed in columns 5, 6, and 7.

```
10   ! EXAMPLE 14.3
15
20   FORM$ = '>#######'
30   X$ = 'CAT'
35
40   PRINT USING FORM$,X$
45
50   STOP
```

d)   Example 14.4 illustrates how two format specifiers can be
concatenated to describe two adjacent print windows of different
sizes in the output line. The resulting string is called a
format string.   The word CAT is left-justified in the first
window, and DOG is right-justified in the second. Thus CAT is
printed in columns 1, 2, and 3 and DOG is printed in columns 9,
10 and 11.   Columns 4 to 8 inclusive contain blanks.

```
10   ! EXAMPLE 14.4
15
20   FORM$ = '<#######' + '>####'
30   X$ = 'CAT'
35
40   PRINT USING FORM$,X$,'DOG'
45
50   STOP
```

e)   Example 14.5 is identical to Example 14.4, except the two
format specifiers are separated by an asterisk (*) character.
This causes the * to be printed in the output line in position 8
between the windows, so the string DOG is shifted right one
column and appears in positions 10, 11, and 12.

```
10  ! EXAMPLE 14.5
15
20  FORM$ = '<#######*>####'
30  X$ = 'CAT'
35
40  PRINT USING FORM$,X$,'DOG'
45
50  STOP
```

As a general rule, any characters contained in the string specifier in the USING clause, and which are not part of a string specifier are printed as literal constants in the output record. This means that if FORM$ had been defined as follows

```
FORM$ = '<#######' + 'JUNK' + '>####'
```

the word JUNK would print in columns 8, 9, 10, and 11 between the two windows.

f) Example 14.6 illustrates the use of format specifiers with numeric quantities. The integer 5 is printed centered in the first window; the value 4.62627 is printed so that the decimal place <u>coincides</u> with the decimal contained in the format specifier. Also the numeric constant is automatically rounded to 4 decimal places as required in the format specifier.

```
10  ! EXAMPLE 14.6
15
20  FORM$ = '####### ###.####'
25
30  PRINT USING FORM$,5,4.62627
35
40  STOP
```

g) In Example 14.7 there is only one format specifier in the format string. However, we are printing two items. The first item is printed and the format string is completely used. When the second item is printed the format string is repeated using a new line. Thus CAT and DOG print underneath one another on 2 lines. The general rule is that the format string will continue to be repeated until the output list is exhausted, using one specifier per variable or expression in the list; for each repetition a new output record is created.

```
10  ! EXAMPLE 14.7
15
20  FORM$ = '#######'
25
30  PRINT USING FORM$,'CAT','DOG'
35
40  STOP
```

h)   Example 14.8 is identical to Example 14.7 except that both CAT and DOG are printed on the same line. This is because the semi-colon (;) is used as a separator in the list of output variables. This causes the two records to be concatenated together into a single record.

```
10   ! EXAMPLE 14.8
15
20   FORM$ = '#######'
25
30   PRINT USING FORM$,'CAT';'DOG'
35
40   STOP
```

14.2   GENERAL OBSERVATIONS

1.   There is nothing special about the variable name FORM$. It could be any string variable name.

2.   The variable FORM$ need not be used at all. For example, the statement

PRINT USING '***>####', 'CAT'

would cause three asterisks to be printed in columns 1, 2, and 3, with the word CAT printed in columns 5, 6, and 7. Thus the format string appears as a literal string constant following the keyword USING.

3.   It is not possible to print two character strings centered in two adjacent windows, using the format specifiers described, because it would be impossible to individually identify the two format specifiers in a single format string. For example, if the first field is of width 5 the specifier would be '#####'; if the second field is of width 4 the specifier would be '####'. When they are concatenated the string '#########' would be produced. To accomplish this objective two separate PRINT statements could be used as follows

PRINT USING '#####', 'CAT';
PRINT USING '####', 'DOG'

The use of the semi-colon (;) causes the two output records to be concatenated together in one line.

Other means of printing adjacent, centered character strings are provided by the extended format specifiers described in the Reference Manual. For example, such format specifiers can be separated by at-symbol pairs (@@). The objective of the example above could be accomplished as illustrated below.

```
PRINT USING '#####@@####', 'CAT', 'DOG'.
```

4. Recall that when using a table name in the print list, a
    new record is started when that item is encountered. This
    happens even when format is used if output is directed to
    the user's terminal. It follows that there is very little
    format control provided to the programmer when displaying
    tables. Normally when such control is required the
    individual elements must be printed.

    When output is directed to a file or device other than the
    user's terminal, the table's contents are displayed
    according to the format specified as if the individual
    elements appeared in the list.

14.3 USING FORMAT WITH INPUT

```
            1110STEVENS     M17 65 63 85 56 76
            1297WAGNER      M15 65 86 85 84 74
            1317RANCOURT    F16 75 72 70 68 65
            1364WAGNER      M16 70 58 90 64 83
            1617HAROLD      M17 85 80 80 75 74
            1998WEICKLER    M16 72 74 75 75 75
            2203WILLS       F16 73 72 72 73 84
            2232ROTH        M17 72 70 70 74 72
            2234GEORGE      M18 70 70 71 58 69
            2265MAJOR       M16 65 65 68 68 69
            2568POLLOCK     M17 89 88 85 92 63
            2587PEARSON     F15 55 50 49 61 60
            2617REITER      M17100 68 69 75 89
            3028SCHULTZ     M18 69 68 75 74 53
            3036BROOKS      M18 65 68 69 70 65
            3039ELLIS       M17 85 85 85 85 85
            3049BECKER      F15 65 65 65 68 69
            3055ASSLEY      M16 65 63 60 63 65
            3087STECKLEY    M15 56 53 85 84 72
            9999ZZZZ        M99  0  0  0  0  0
```

Figure 14.1

        Consider Figure 14.1 which is a listing of the records
contained in a file called CLASS. A careful study of the data
indicates that it is identical to that contained in the file
called STUDENT, except that there are no commas to separate the
various fields in each record. The only way to identify each
field is by knowing the columns at which it starts and ends.

        It is not possible to read the file CLASS using the INPUT
statement with a list of variable names unless a format string
is used. In Example 14.9 each of the records in the file CLASS
is read; student number and name is printed for each of the

records. The format string is called FORM$ and consists of 9
format specifiers, one for each of the fields in each record.
Each of the specifiers is precisely the correct size to match
the fields in turn.

```
10   ! EXAMPLE 14.9
15
20   FORM$='<####<###############<#<##<###' + &
25   &    '<###<###<###<###'
28
30   OPEN #3,'CLASS',INPUT
35
40   LOOP
50      INPUT#3 USING FORM$,NUM,NAME$,SEX$,AGE,A,B,C,D,E
60      IF NUM = 9999 THEN QUIT
70      PRINT NUM,NAME$
80   ENDLOOP
85
90   CLOSE #3
95
110  STOP
```

NOTES: 1. The format specifiers described are used merely to
determine the size of the field on input. Thus the use
of < in the specifiers in Example 14.9 is merely to act
as a separator for format specifiers; the program would
have worked equally well if the > symbol had been used as
the separator.

2. Since these format specifiers are only used to
determine field size, there is no need to include the
decimal point in numeric fields. However, if it is used,
it is counted as part of the length of the field being
defined.

3. The position of the format specifier in the format
string must match the relative position of the field
within the record being read. If the format string
includes non-format characters, they are ignored, but are
counted in the length of the string. Consider the format
string assignment

    FOR"$ = 'CATS<###DOG<##'

If used on input, the first four columns of the input
record would be ignored because of the non-format
character string 'CATS'. The first format specifier
defines a 3-position field located at position 5, 6, and
7 in the input record. Then 8, 9, and 10 are ignored
because of 'DOG' and position 11 and 12 are fields
defined by the second format specifier.

4. If the format string is too short, it is re-used

until the INPUT list is complete. However, a new record
is read each time the format string is re-started. You
can override this by using the ; between the appropriate
list items in the INPUT statement.

14.4 SUMMARY

Format control provides a convenient mechanism for
organizing data on the printed page. However it has equally
important applications when writing and reading files. It is a
nuisance to have to include commas between fields within
records; the only way to overcome the difficulty is to use
format control. Thus input-output operations using files will
almost always involve the USING clause.

Advanced format facilities are described in the Reference
Manual. These include features for formatting financial
documents and reports, as well as various means of storing
numeric data compactly in file records.

14.5 EXERCISES

14.1 The following series of problems will provide the reader
with a simple means of obtaining considerable practice
using format strings.

a) Enter the following BASIC program into the computer.

```
10    OPTION NOPROMPT
20    PRINT 'ENTER A FORMAT SPECIFIER'
30    INPUT FORM$
40    LOOP
50      PRINT 'ENTER A NUMERIC QUANTITY'
60      INPUT X
70      PRINT USING FORM$,X
80    ENDLOOP
90    STOP
```

When this program is run, the user is requested to enter a
format specifier such as <####, for example. Then the
program begins to loop, each time requesting a numeric
quantity, which is subsequently printed using the format
specifier.

b) Run this program using several different format
specifiers with various numeric input to observe the
effect.

c) Modify the program so that it accepts an alphabetic
string as input, and repeat the exercise suggested in b).

d) Modify the program so that it prints several quantities
in the PRINT statement, and try various types of format

strings.

e) Try reading and printing several tables using various format specifiers.

14.2 Use format strings to print all of the records in the student file with approximately the following format.

```
          STUDENT NUMBER:  1110
                    NAME:  STEVENS

          MARKS:   ALG     65
                   GEOM    63
                   ENG     85
                   PHYS    56
                   CHEM    76

          AVERAGE:         69
```

CHAPTER 15

FILE CONCEPTS

In order to use files in a practical application it is important to be aware of precisely what is happening when statements such as OPEN, CLOSE, INPUT, and PRINT are used. The purpose of this chapter is to provide a general understanding of the concepts used. Complete details are available in the Reference Manual.

15.1 FILES AND RECORDS

Files are normally stored on disks, diskettes or magnetic tapes. The storage medium used depends on the hardware configuration of the computer installation. Each file is referred to by its name, which appears as one of the items in the OPEN statement. File names in this text have been limited to 8 alphabetic or numeric characters. However a file can have a more complex name depending upon the machine or operating system being used, and upon whether or not the user has a special "privileged" status. To learn more about these implementation-dependent aspects of file names, the reader should refer to the Reference Manual.

Files consist of several records of a specified size. These file attributes are referred to as "number of records in the file" (file-size) and "number of characters in each record" (record-size) respectively. When your BASIC system has been set up, default values have been assigned to these attributes. Typically file-size in a teaching environment will be approximately 100 records, and record-size will be 80 characters. Files are "defined" when they are OPENed for OUTPUT. It is possible in the OPEN statement to override the default attributes by including new specifications as part of the file name. Consider an example which applies to the IBM Series/1 with the CPS operating system.

OPEN #6, 'STUDENT/RECSIZE:100', OUTPUT

Here a file called STUDENT is defined. It has a record-size of 100 characters. It is not necessary to specify a file-size attribute when creating a file since space for storing records is automatically allocated to a file as records are written. (Please note that the maximum record-size permitted with Waterloo BASIC on the Series/1 is 32000 characters.)

Obviously it is necessary to include specifications for the file attributes in any realistic application program. Seldom would the default attribute values be suitable, except for classroom or learning applications. It is important therefore that a serious user of a particular Waterloo BASIC system study the Reference Manual to discover how these attributes are assigned for his or her particular system.

15.2 WRITING RECORDS

Generally speaking, each time a PRINT statement is executed a record is written. However, sometimes more than one record is written as will become evident in subsequent paragraphs.

Each PRINT statement has associated with it a print-list which contains one or more items separated by commas; these items are either expressions or constants. When the PRINT statement is executed, all expressions in the print-list are evaluated, and you can imagine that the system organizes the results into an "internal record" using the sequence in which the items appear in the print-list. This organization takes place using a format string, if it is present, or into "windows" as described in Chapter 2. If the size of this internal record is less than or equal to the record-size attribute of the file, the record is written, padding on the right with blanks if necessary. If the size exceeds the record-size attribute, more than one file record is written. It would be simple if the internal record was written as "bursts" of characters of record-size in length. However the rules are more complex, depending on whether or not a format string is being used. These rules are beyond the scope of this chapter, and once again the reader is referred to the Reference Manual for details. The best strategy is to avoid this complexity by making sure the record being written is within the size specification given in the record-size attribute.

NOTES: 1. When the print-list is terminated with a semi-colon (;) the internal record is not written on the file. When the next PRINT statement is encountered its print-list values are concatenated to the right of the existing internal record. The internal record is not written onto the file until the print-list is terminated by a blank or end-of-line. However, see notes 2 and 3 for special circumstances related to this point.

2. Recall that when the format string is too short to accommodate all the items in the print-list, it is re-used. For each repetition of the format string a new record is written on the file. However, this record is saved in the internal record area if the ; appears in the print-list at the point at which the format string is to be repeated.

3. When printing two-dimensional tables or matrices using the MAT keyword without format strings, a separate file record is written for each row of the table. This becomes somewhat more complicated when using multi-dimensional tables; the details are given in the Reference Manual.

4. It is generally advisable to write all records under format control. This will save space in the file because data is not written in windows; it also greatly simplifies the reading of the record when that is required.

15.3   READING RECORDS

Assume that a file has been created by writing the data under format control. The simplest way to read the file is to use the same format string in the INPUT statement, with the same items in the print-list. Under these circumstances the data will be read from the file, regardless of the complexity of its organization.

If for some reason the foregoing suggestion is inappropriate, it is necessary to have a thorough knowledge of the field layout of each record being read so an appropriate format string can be used. Some general observations made in the notes which follow will be useful.

NOTES: 1. When the INPUT statement is executed, a record is read into an "internal buffer". Then this buffer is scanned left-to-right under format-string control, and various fields are selected and assigned to the items in the input-list. If the buffer is exhausted before the input-list has been completed, another record is read into the buffer and the scanning continues.

2. If the input-list is terminated by a semi-colon (;) the current position in the buffer is noted. When the next INPUT statement is encountered a record is not immediately read. Instead, data is selected from the buffer beginning at the current position.

3. If the format string does not have sufficient specifiers to match the number of items in the input-list, it will be re-used. However, a new record is read into the buffer for each repetition of this format string. If a semi-colon (;) appears in the input-list at the point where the format string is about to be repeated, a new record is not read into the buffer.

4. If the user tries to read a record without using a format string, the fields in the input record must be separated by commas. The record is read into the buffer,

and the input-list items are assigned values according to
the data recorded between two consecutive commas.

15.4 THE TERMINAL AND PRINTER

Each time the PRINT keyword is used without a unit number,
a   record   or   records   are   written   to   the   terminal.   This
record-size is typically 80 characters because   the   screen   is
usually 80 characters wide.   All rules pertaining to the writing
of records apply to the screen, as if it were a file,   with   the
exception   of   tables   printed   under   format   control.   This
exception is noted in the chapter dealing with format.

The same sort of comment applies to   the   keyboard   of   the
terminal.   Each time a line is entered it can be thought of as a
record.   These   records   are   usually 80   characters   in   size,
because   the screen is 80 characters wide.   Generally, all rules
pertaining to the reading of records apply   to   the   reading   of
lines at the terminal.

To obtain hard-copy output you can prepare   a   file   to   be
printed   on   a hard-copy printer.   These printers usually have a
line-width of 132 characters, so it is appropriate   to   organize
the   file with   132-character   records.   Then   the file can be
printed using a special utility program which   prints   the   file
placing one record on each printed line.   Often the printer is a
"privileged" device and cannot be used   by   the   ordinary   user,
except   by   employing such a utility program.   The reader should
consult his or her installation manager for details.

15.5 USING RECORD INPUT MODE

Sometimes you are presented with a file which contains data
in a format which is unknown.   When this happens the file can be
listed using a program similar to Example 15.1.

```
10        ! EXAMPLE 15.1
15
20        OPEN #6,'CLASS',INPUT
25
30        LOOP
40           LINPUT #6, X$
50           PRINT X$
60        ENDLOOP
65
70        CLOSE #6
75
80        STOP
```

When the keyword LINPUT is encountered an entire record   is
read,   regardless   of its size, and it is assigned to the string
variable X$.   Then the value of X$ is printed at   the   terminal.
Since   no   loop   control   is included, the program will terminate

with an error message. However its purpose will have been accomplished, namely, to list the content of the file for study. Note that the file will remain open, so should be closed with an immediate command such as RESET.

The LINPUT mode of input is very powerful when scanning records in a file using immediate mode operation. As a debugging aid it is indispensable when analysing errors in input-output.

15.6 END OF FILE

In each of the examples a special "sentinel" record was used at the end of a file so that the program could recognize when "end of file" occurred. In actual fact, the computer system always writes its own special sentinel record onto the file when it is CLOSEd after being OPENed for OUTPUT. This record will be referred to as the "end-of-file record".

When a file is being read sequentially this record will eventually be encountered. When this happens a particular non-zero value is assigned to a built-in function called IO_STATUS(N). This can be tested as shown in Example 15.2.

```
10        ! EXAMPLE 15.2
15
20        ON EOF IGNORE
25
30        OPEN #6,'CLASS',INPUT
35
40        LOOP
50           LINPUT #6, X$
60           IF IO_STATUS(6) <> 0 THEN QUIT
70           PRINT X$
80        ENDLOOP
85
90        CLOSE #6
95
100       STOP
```

In line 60 the built-in function IO_STATUS(6) is used. The argument 6 refers to the unit number. The function returns the value of IO_STATUS to be non-zero when the end of file record has been read. Note that the statement on line 20, namely

       20 ON EOF IGNORE

must also be included to prevent the system from automatically displaying an error message when the end-of-file record is read.

15.7 SUMMARY

Generally speaking, the rules for using input-output are numerous and cumbersome. However they become straight-forward if the following restrictions can be accepted.

a)   Always read and write records using format control.

b)   Always use format strings which are long enough to satisfy the input or output list without repetition.

c)   Always declare record-size to match the size of the output record as it will be composed by the format string.

d)   Always use a sentinel record, rather than the system end-of-file record to recognize end of file.

15.8 EXERCISES

15.1   a) Write a program which creates a file of marks for a new course, namely History. Each record contains only student number and mark. The file should have only 20 records, and the record-size should be just large enough to hold the two fields. The marks should be entered using the terminal with appropriate prompting messages. Be sure to enter the sentinel record, and insert a comma between the fields.

b) Read the new file to be sure it was created correctly.

15.2   Write a program which reads the file STUDENT using LINPUT to read each record into a string variable X$. Then print the value of this string to verify that the records are as expected, including commas.

15.3   Use LINPUT to read and print the records that were created in Exercise 15.1.

15.4   Using the end-of-file method described in Section 15.6, print the file STUDENT, including the sentinel record.

CHAPTER 16

SEQUENTIAL AND RELATIVE FILE PROCESSING

Many of the mechanical aspects of creating and processing
files have been discussed in previous chapters. In this chapter
these concepts are applied to further examples to illustrate the
fundamental notions of the sequential and relative processing of
records in a file.

16.1 INTRODUCTION

All files in BASIC have a name, and contain a number of
records of fixed size. The number of records can be zero, in
which case the file is said to be empty. The size of a record
is never zero, as then the record could never exist, and the
file would be useless. Depending on the type of computer and
its operating system, the records can have an upper limit on
size. On the IBM Series/1 with CPS, the record size has a
maximum of 32000 characters (bytes).

All files have a special record at the end, referred to as
the end-of-file record. This record is written automatically
when the file is CLOSEd after having been OPENed for OUTPUT.
This record cannot be read for processing purposes. It is used
by the system to automatically recognize that the file has
terminated. This is accomplished when the end-of-file record is
read by an INPUT or LINPUT statement; at that time the system
transfers control to the ON EOF statement which should be in the
program. If this statement is absent, the program is terminated
with an appropriate error message.

The records in a file are numbered in order from 0 to N-1,
where N is the number of records in the file. The end-of-file
record is not a processable record and is therefore not
numbered. Thus the first record is numbered 0, the second is
numbered 1, etc.

16.2 SEQUENTIAL FILE PROCESSING

In every example to this point in the text, files are read
or written sequentially. To read a file sequentially it must
first be OPENed for INPUT. This "positions" the file to the
first record, giving the record-pointer a value of 0. When
INPUT is executed, records are read starting with the record
pointed to by the record-pointer. When each record is read, the

record-pointer is increased by 1. Thus the records are read sequentially in turn, starting at the beginning of the file.

It is not necessary to read all of the records in a file when processing it sequentially. You could read the first few records, decide to terminate use of the file, and CLOSE it. When re-OPENed it will be positioned to the beginning again.

All files must be created sequentially. To create a file it is first OPENed for OUTPUT at which point a file description is established and space is allocated for the file. As each PRINT statement is executed one or more records are written into the file, gradually consuming the allocated space. If an attempt is made to write too many records, the effect may vary depending on the environment. With the Series/1 under RPS, the system will cause BASIC to issue an error message and processing will terminate. With the Series/1 under CPS and the 370 under VM/CMS, extra file space is allocated automatically as new records are written.

When the file is CLOSEd the end-of-file record is written and the file is no longer available for processing until it is OPENed again.

Caution: If you OPEN a file for OUTPUT and it already exists, the existing file is destroyed. Records may be added sequentially to the end of an existing file by OPENing it for APPEND. This type of OPEN positions the record-pointer past the last record of the file so that subsequent PRINTs cause new records to be added following existing records.

16.3 RELATIVE ACCESS

Since the records are all numbered, they can be read in any desired order, provided the record number (also called relative address) is given. Such file processing is referred to as relative access. Example 16.1 is a program which reads the STUDENT file in reverse sequence. Since this file contains 20 records, the records have relative addresses 0 to 19 inclusive. The program uses a FOR loop whose index I begins with 19 and is decremented by 1 each time through the loop. Note that the INPUT statement contains the clause REC=I which specifies the relative address of the record to be read.

```
10        ! EXAMPLE 16.1
15
20        OPEN #4,'STUDENT',INOUT
25
30        FOR I = 19 TO 0 STEP -1
40          INPUT #4, REC = I, NUMBER, NAME$
50          PRINT NUMBER, NAME$
60        NEXT I
65
70        CLOSE #4
75
80        STOP
```

As has been pointed out in preceding chapters, the INPUT statement causes more than one record to be read under various circumstances. When this happens the first record read is given by the relative address in the REC= clause, and the subsequent records are read sequentially. Any subsequent INPUT statement which does not contain the REC= clause will cause the file to continue to be read sequentially.

It is also possible to write a specific record, specifying its relative address with the REC= clause in the PRINT statement. When this is done the file must have been OPENed with the INOUT or O"TIN keyword (see Example 16.3 later). The computer will write a record at the specified relative address, erasing the information already there. This process is referred to as "updating" the record. If more than one record is written by the PRINT, the writing takes place sequentially, replacing the data already located in records with higher relative addresses. If a subsequent PRINT is executed without the REC= clause, records continue to be processed sequentially beginning with the record whose relative address is next in sequence.

NOTE: Recall that all files must be created sequentially. Do not attempt to open a new file for output, and write a record into relative address 23, for example. This will only work if the file already exists, having been created sequentially.

16.4 AN EXAMPLE

The ability to read a record "at random", as is made possible by relative addressing, can be put to many useful purposes. For example, it may be desirable to have a BASIC terminal set up as an "inquiry" station. The program could be set up to access the STUDENT file and would prompt the user for a particular student number. The corresponding record could be "identified", read, and displayed at the terminal. The problem is one of identifying the proper record. For example, student number 1203 is stored at relative address 6 in the file. This identification can be accomplished using a table, commonly called an "index" for the file.

```
10    ! EXAMPLE 16.2
15
20    OPTION NOPROMPT
25
30    DIM STUDENT_INDEX(19)
35
40    INVOKE = FN_CREATE_INDEX
45
50    OPEN #8,'STUDENT',INPUT
55
60    LOOP
70      PRINT 'WHAT IS THE STUDENT NUMBER?'
80      INPUT NUMBER
90      IF NUMBER = 9999 THEN QUIT
100     STUDENT_PTR = FN_LOOKUP
110     IF STUDENT_PTR = LAST_STUDENT
120       PRINT 'THERE IS NO STUDENT WITH THAT NUMBER'
130     ELSE
140       INPUT #8,REC=STUDENT_PTR,     &
145 &           NUMBER, NAME$, SEX$, AGE
150       PRINT NUMBER,NAME$,SEX$,AGE
160     ENDIF
170   ENDLOOP
175
180   CLOSE #8
185
190   STOP
200
210
400   DEF FN_CREATE_INDEX
405
410   OPEN #8,'STUDENT',INPUT
420   LAST_STUDENT = 0
430   LOOP
440     INPUT #8,NUMBER
450     STUDENT_INDEX(LAST_STUDENT) = NUMBER
460     IF NUMBER = 9999 THEN QUIT
470     LAST_STUDENT = LAST_STUDENT + 1
480   ENDLOOP
490   CLOSE #8
500   FN_CREATE_INDEX = 0
505
510   FNEND
520
600   DEF FN_LOOKUP
605
608   I = 0
610   WHILE NUMBER <> STUDENT_INDEX(I)
620     I=I+1
630   UNTIL I >= LAST_STUDENT
640   FN_LOOKUP = I
645
650   FNEND
```

Example 16.2 is a program which first of all creates an index table called STUDENT_INDEX using the function FN_CREATE_INDEX. Then the program proceeds to "inquiry status" in the loop. It prompts the user for a student number. This number is then looked up in the index table usig the function FN_LOOKUP. This function calculates the relative address of the record to be read directly.

This type of file processing is referred to as <u>indexed access</u>, and always uses a table to determine the relative address of the record. In our example, this table is computed during initialization. However, it is more common to store this table in a separate file, and read it into the computer. This will save considerable time when setting up large files for indexed access. The next chapter describes another method of indexed access in which the computer system handles creation, lookup and maintenance of the index used to access specific records.

16.5 <u>UPDATING</u> <u>RECORDS</u> <u>IN</u> <u>A</u> <u>FILE</u>

A common requirement is to change some of the content of some of the records in a file. For example, students often obtain a mark adjustment by negotiation with the teacher. Example 16.3 is a small modification of Example 16.2 which permits the user to change the algebra mark for a given student or students. The adjusted record is re-written into the file. Note that the file CLASS is used rather than STUDENT in order to illustrate format control.

```
10   ! EXAMPLE 16.3
15
20   OPTION NOPROMPT
22
25   FORM$ = '>####<##############<#>##>###'+&
28     &   '>###>###>###>###'
30   DIM STUDENT_INDEX(19),MARK(4)
35
40   INVOKE = FN_CREATE_INDEX
45
50   OPEN #8,'CLASS',INOUT
55
60   LOOP
70     PRINT 'WHAT IS THE STUDENT NUMBER?'
80     INPUT NUMBER
90     IF NUMBER = 9999 THEN QUIT
100    STUDENT_PTR = FN_LOOKUP
110    IF STUDENT_PTR = LAST_STUDENT
120      PRINT 'THERE IS NO STUDENT WITH THAT NUMBER'
130    ELSE
140      INPUT #8, REC=STUDENT_PTR, USING FORM$, &
145        &      NUMBER, NAME$, SEX$, AGE, MAT MARK
148      PRINT 'THE OLD ALGEBRA MARK IS',MARK(0)
150      PRINT 'WHAT IS THE NEW ALGEBRA MARK?'
152      INPUT MARK(0)
154      PRINT #8 REC=STUDENT_PTR, USING FORM$, &
155        &      NUMBER, NAME$, SEX$, AGE, MAT MARK
158      PRINT 'THE RECORD HAS BEEN UPDATED'
160    ENDIF
170  ENDLOOP
175
180  CLOSE #8
190  STOP
```

```
200
300
400 DEF FN_CREATE_INDEX
405
410 OPEN #8,'CLASS',INPUT
420 LAST_STUDENT = 0
430 LOOP
440   INPUT #8,USING FORM$,NUMBER
450   STUDENT_INDEX(LAST_STUDENT) = NUMBER
460   IF NUMBER = 9999 THEN QUIT
470   LAST_STUDENT = LAST_STUDENT + 1
480 ENDLOOP
490 CLOSE #8
505
510 FNEND
520
530
600 DEF FN_LOOKUP
605
608 I = 0
610 WHILE NUMBER <> STUDENT_INDEX(I)
620   I = I + 1
630 UNTIL I >= LAST_STUDENT
640 FN_LOOKUP = I
645
650 FNEND
```

16.6 SUMMARY

Relative addressing of records using the REC= clause introduces considerable flexibility in file processing. The reader is encouraged to complete the exercises to obtain the experience needed to become familiar with the concepts.

16.7 EXERCISES

16.1 Write a program which prompts the user for the relative record number, and prints the corresponding record in the file STUDENT.

16.2 Write a program which first creates an index file for the names of the students in the file STUDENT. Then the program should prompt the user for a student's name, examine the index table to determine the relative address, and print the corresponding record at the terminal.

16.3 Write a program which first creates an index file for the ages of the students in the file STUDENT. Note: Each entry for an age in the index file can contain addresses for up to six records. The program should prompt the user for an age, examine the index to determine the relative addresses of all the records for that age and display the corresponding records at the terminal.

CHAPTER 17

INDEXED OR KEYED FILE PROCESSING

Many applications involve the use of files in which each record contains the data about a specific entity. For example, a student file contains records, each of which has information about a specific student. It is often desirable to access records in these files randomly, using a key value to obtain the record. In the preceding chapter, the student number was used as a key value to read and update a student record.

When the keys for a file are numbers 0,1,2,...,N-1 for the N records in the file, the REC= clause, introduced in the preceding chapter, may be used to access records in the file. When the keys are not a sequential range of integral numbers, some other strategy must be used to obtain a number from 0 to (N-1), given the key. In the preceding chapter, an table of keys was used for this purpose.

As pointed out in the previous chapter, the indexing technique used to illustrate relative access is not practical for large files. If an index was maintained in a separate file, the program would need to be considerably more sophisticated to accommodate addition and removal of records from the file. In addition, the straightforward index organization and lookup technique illustrated provides unacceptably slow access for many applications involving large files.

Because keyed access for files is widely used, a special type of file, known as keyed or indexed file, has been made part of the Waterloo BASIC system.

17.1 INTRODUCTION

An index of 'keys' is maintained for the data records of the file. A key is a unique character string used to identify a data record, such as the student number which identifies records in the examples of the previous chapter. (Note that a key cannot be numeric but may be a character string containing digits.) A particular record of a keyed file may be accessed at random by naming its key value using a KEY clause with INPUT, LINPUT and PRINT statements. Records may be deleted from a keyed file with the REMOVE statement. A sequence of examples follow which illustrate the use of keyed files for an application similar to the examples of the previous chapter.

17.2 CREATING A KEYED FILE

A keyed file is comprised actually of two files, an index and a data file. Both files must be named when creating a keyed file. The name of the data file is stored with the index. Consequently, if an existing keyed file is OPENed with the INPUT, INOUT or OUTIN keywords (see Example 17.2 later), only the index file name is specified. A maximum key length is defined using the KEYLEN clause when a keyed file is created. This information is used to define the internal format of the index file.

In Example 17.1, a keyed file KLASS is created with an associated data file named KLASSDAT. The key length is defined as 4 characters. This is accomplished by the OPEN statement in line 70. Subsequently the sequential file CLASS, used in previous examples, is opened and read. Each record is written to the KLASS file specifying the student number as the record's identifying key. Note that key values must be character strings, hence the digits of the student number are read as a character string.

```
10   !EXAMPLE 17.1
20
30   FORM$ = '>####<###############<#>##>###'+&
40      &  '>###>###>###>###'
50   DIM MARK(4)
60
70   OPEN#7,'KLASS',OUTPUT,DATAFILE='KLASSDAT',KEYLEN=4
80   OPEN#8,'CLASS',INPUT
90
100  LOOP
110    INPUT #8, USING FORM$, &
120    &      NUMBER$, NAME$, SEX$, AGE, MAT MARK
130    IF NUMBER$='9999' THEN QUIT
140    PRINT #7, KEY=NUMBER$, USING FORM$,  &
150    &      NUMBER$, NAME$, SEX$, AGE, MAT MARK
160  ENDLOOP
170
180  CLOSE #8
190  CLOSE #7
200  STOP
```

Note that there is nothing significant about the name KLASS beginning with a K. This serves only to differentiate from the similar file CLASS.

17.3 READING A KEYED FILE

Specific records of a keyed file may be read using the INPUT statement with a KEY clause as illustrated in Example 17.2.

```
10    !EXAMPLE 17.2
20
30    OPTION NOPROMPT
40    ON IOERR IGNORE
50
60    FORM$ = '>####<###############<#>##>###'+&
70      & '>###>###>###>###'
80    DIM MARK(4)
90
100   OPEN#8,'KLASS',INPUT
110
120   LOOP
130     PRINT 'WHAT IS THE STUDENT NUMBER?'
140     INPUT NUMBER$
150     IF NUMBER$='9999' THEN QUIT
160     INPUT#8, KEY=NUMBER$, USING FORM$,  &
170      &    NUMBER$, NAME$, SEX$, AGE, MAT MARK
180     IF IO_STATUS(8) <> 0
190       PRINT 'THERE IS NO STUDENT WITH THAT NUMBER'
200     ELSE
210       PRINT NUMBER$,NAME$,SEX$,AGE,MAT MARK
220     ENDIF
230   ENDLOOP
240
250   CLOSE#8
260   STOP
```

Since lookup of key values in the index is performed by the system, it is not possible to determine whether or not a record exists for a particular key without attempting to read it. In line 180 of Example 17.2, the value of the built-in function IO_STATUS is checked after attempting to INPUT from file number 8. An IO_STATUS value of 13 indicates that the specified key was not found. Note that the statement on line 40, namely

```
40    ON IOERR IGNORE
```

must be included to prevent the system from interrupting the program and displaying an error message when this condition arises.

Keyed files may be read sequentially by omitting the KEY clause from INPUT or LINPUT statements. In this case, records are read in order by ascending key value which may have no relationship to the order in which records were written to the file. Consequently, since keys are character strings, records of the file are read in alphabetical sequence of key value. The KEY clause may not be omitted from PRINT statements, however, since each record must have a specific identifying key value.

```
10   ! EXAMPLE 17.3
20
30   ON EOF IGNORE
40
50   OPEN #8, 'KLASS', INPUT
60
70   LOOP
80      LINPUT #8, RECORD$
90      IF IO_STATUS(8) <> 0 THEN QUIT
100     PRINT RECORD$
110  ENDLOOP
120
130  CLOSE #8
140  STOP
```

The above program reads the records of keyed file KLASS and displays its contents in order of ascending student number. Note that the same program could be used to display the sequential file CLASS if the file name in line 50 were changed. Thus, a file may be read sequentially without knowing whether it is a keyed file or a sequential file.

17.4 UPDATING A KEYED FILE

As discussed in the previous chapter, it is frequently necessary to change the content of some of the records in a file. Records in keyed files may be replaced or re-written in a manner similar to that used with relative access. When a key value specified in a PRINT statement corresponds to an existing record, the contents of that record are replaced by the data in the PRINT list.

Another common requirement is to add new records to a file. When a key value specified in a PRINT is not found in the index, the key is automatically added to the index and a data record is added to the file.

Records may be deleted from a keyed file by executing a REMOVE statement. The statement

REMOVE #8, KEY="3028"

will cause the record, whose key is "3028", to be removed from the indicated file.

```
10    ! EXAMPLE 17.4
20
30    ON IOERR IGNORE
40    DIM MARK(4)
50    FORM$ = '>####<##############<#>##>###'+&
60       &   '>###>###>###>###'
70
80    OPEN #2, 'KLASS', INOUT
90
100   LOOP
110     PRINT 'Enter ADD, CHG, DEL or STOP'
120     LINPUT FUNCTION$
130     IF FUNCTION$ = 'STOP' THEN QUIT
140     IF FUNCTION$ = 'ADD'
150        INVOKE = FN_ADD
160     ELSEIF FUNCTION$ = 'CHG'
170        INVOKE = FN_CHANGE
180     ELSEIF FUNCTION$ = 'DEL'
190        INVOKE = FN_DELETE
200     ELSE
210        PRINT 'Invalid function'
220     ENDIF
230   ENDLOOP
240
250   CLOSE #2
260
270
280   DEF FN_ADD
290
300   INVOKE = FN_READ_STUDENT_RECORD
310   IF STUDENT_NUMBER$ = '9999'
320     INVOKE = FN_GET_NEW_DATA
330     INVOKE = FN_WRITE_STUDENT_RECORD
340   ELSE
350     PRINT 'Record already exists for student number'
360   ENDIF
370
380   FNEND
390
400
410   DEF FN_CHANGE
420
430   INVOKE = FN_READ_STUDENT_RECORD
440   IF STUDENT_NUMBER$ <> '9999'
450     INVOKE = FN_GET_NEW_DATA
460     INVOKE = FN_WRITE_STUDENT_RECORD
470   ELSE
480     PRINT 'Record does not exist for student number'
490   ENDIF
500
510   FNEND
520
530
```

```
540   DEF FN_DELETE
550
560   INVOKE = FN_READ_STUDENT_RECORD
570   IF STUDENT_NUMBER$ <> '9999'
580     REMOVE #2, KEY = STUDENT_NUMBER$
590   ELSE
600     PRINT 'Record does not exist for student number'
610   ENDIF
620
630   FNEND
640
650
660   DEF FN_READ_STUDENT_RECORD
670
680   PRINT 'Enter student number'
690   LINPUT STUDENT_KEY$
700   INPUT #2, KEY=STUDENT_KEY$, USING FORM$, &
710   &     STUDENT_NUMBER$, NAME$, SEX$, AGE, MAT MARK
720   IF IO_STATUS <> 0
730     STUDENT_NUMBER$ = '9999'
740   ENDIF
750
760   FNEND
770
780
790   DEF FN_WRITE_STUDENT_RECORD
800
810   PRINT #2, KEY=STUDENT_KEY$, USING FORM$, &
820   &     STUDENT_KEY$, NAME$, SEX$, AGE, MAT MARK
830
840   FNEND
850
860
870   DEF FN_GET_NEW_DATA
880
890   PRINT 'Enter new data for student record'
900   INPUT NAME$, SEX$, AGE, MAT MARK
910
920   FNEND
```

An interactive update program is shown in Example 17.4. In order to emphasize the features of keyed files, the program has been deliberately simplified. Clearly, much more validation of the input data would be required for such a program to be practical. Marks, for example, should not be negative or exceed a value of 100.

The program illustrates how records may be added to, deleted from, or changed in a keyed file. The program should be studied closely to ascertain how the keyed-file access is used to diagnose logic errors such as deleting or changing non-existent records or adding records with the keys that already exist.

17.5 SUMMARY

Keyed or indexed file access provides a more convenient and effective means of processing files for many applications. This is particularly true in interactive environments where information must be accessed quickly from large files in response to queries at a terminal. Programming such applications can be relatively straightforward if queries may be conveniently made in terms of the keys by which the file is indexed. The exercises which follow should be completed to gain a fuller appreciation for the application of keyed files. More extensive information concerning the capabilities provided with keyed access files is contained in the Reference Manual.

17.6 EXERCISES

17.1 Create a keyed file to be used for defining the words in a dictionary. The data records should contain the definitions of words which are used as keys to index the file. The program should prompt for words and their meanings, and write them to the file.

17.2 Write a program which allows querying of the dictionary. The program should prompt for words and display their meanings.

17.3 Change the program of 17.2 to allow definition of new words if a word queried is not found.

17.4 Write a program which uses the built-in function KEYVAL$(N) and sequential LINPUT to list the dictionary of words alphabetically with their meanings. KEYVAL$(N) returns a character string with the key value for the last record accessed in the keyed file OPENed with number N.

CHAPTER 18

ADDITIONAL TOPICS

The reader, having completed the preceding chapters, will have a general understanding of most capabilities of Waterloo BASIC. A reader intending to make serious use of the language should also read the Reference Manual to obtain a more detailed understanding of the topics already covered. In addition, there are five significant topics not covered in this Primer:

1. An extensive set of program-editing and system commands is available in addition to those introduced in earlier chapters;

2. A number of formatting capabilities provide special features for preparing financial reports or documents, and permit compaction of numeric data in files;

3. SORT and TAGSORT statements provide file-sorting capabilities which may be used under control of a program or directly from the terminal as 'immediate' commands;

4. Many built-in functions are available which are useful in mathematical calculations, character-string manipulation, file management and error-condition handling;

5. The CHAIN statement provides a means whereby one program may invoke another. The first program may optionally communicate data values to the invoked program.

A.   Fundamental Concepts

A-1   Introduction

A BASIC program is a series of statements each of which starts with a line number. The statements occur in the program in ascending order according to these line numbers. Consider the following example:

```
10    XVALUE = 71
20    CUBE = XVALUE * XVALUE * XVALUE
30    PRINT   XVALUE,CUBE
40    STOP
50    END
```

There are five statements in the program. The first two statements are assignment statements which cause values to be assigned to variables when the statements are executed. The third statement, when executed, causes the current values of the two variables, XVALUE and CUBE, to be displayed on the terminal. The fourth statement will stop the execution of the program when it is executed. The final statement is included according to the rules of BASIC to signal the end of a program.

Once the program has been entered into the computer, (see Section B for how this is accomplished) the program may be executed by issuing the RUN command. This will cause execution of the statements starting with the first one in the program. In the preceding sample program, four statements would be executed in the following sequence:

Statement (10):   The value 71 will be assigned to the variable XVALUE.

Statement (20):   The value (71) of the variable XVALUE is multiplied together three times to produce a result (357911). This resultant value is assigned to the variable CUBE.

Statement (30):   The execution of this statement causes the current value of XVALUE (71) and CUBE (357911) to be displayed at the terminal.

Statement (40):   This statement causes execution of the program to stop.

The following output will be displayed on the user's terminal:

```
EX-00: EXECUTION BEGINS
   71                 357911
EX-01: EXECUTION ENDS
```

The first message signals that program execution has started and the last message signals that execution has completed.

It should be noted that the sample program performed a simple manipulation (computation of a cube) of numeric data. In subsequent sections we will describe in detail numeric data and numeric variables.

Additional Rules About Programs

(1) Line Numbers:

Line numbers must be specified for each line in a BASIC program. These numbers must be integral values in the range 1 to 65535. Leading zeros are ignored in line numbers; i.e., 100, 0100, and 00100 are all treated as the same line number.

(2) Continued Statements:

A statement can be entered on more than one line. This is accomplished by placing an '&' as the last non-blank character on a line containing a statement which is continued. The next line in the program must contain an '&' as the first non-blank character following the line number.

```
020   CUBE =  &
021   & XVALUE *  &
022   & XVALUE * XVALUE
```

The preceding three lines could be substituted for line (20) in the sample program. Elements of a statement, such as variable names or constant values, cannot be continued across lines of a program.

(3) Use of Spaces:

Spaces should be used in statements to clarify the program. Spaces cannot occur inside variable names, numeric constants, operators which are composed of more than one character, keywords or line numbers. Spaces are required to separate keywords from variable names or numeric constants.

(4) Null Lines:

It is permissible to enter a line containing only a line number. These null lines may be used to increase the readability of programs.

(5) Comments:

Comments may be placed at the end of most lines. A comment
starts with a '!' character. The comment character, '!',
causes the remainder of the line to be treated only as
documentation and to be ignored by the BASIC system (the
last non-blank character is still significant for
continuation purposes).

In addition, comments may be entered into a program with
the REMARK statement. When a statement starts with the
keyword REM, the remainder of that line is treated as a
comment.

(6) Multiple Statements Per Line:

It is possible to enter multiple statements on a single
line by separating the statements with a '%' character.
This practice is generally considered to be a poor
programming technique as it tends to produce unreadable
programs.

(7) END Statement:

The strict rules of BASIC require that every program have
an END statement as the last statement in a program. The
program will, however, execute properly if the END
statement is missing. It is an error to place an END
statement anywhere in the program except as the last
statement.

A-2 Assignment or LET Statement

    Syntax: variable = expression
                   LET variable = expression

    Examples: X = 493 * 4 + 2
                   TITLE$ = 'ABC' + PAGE$

    The assignment statement specifies an expression which is
used to calculate a resultant value to be assigned to the
variable on the left of the '=' operator. The LET keyword is
optional. In the succeeding sections we will discuss in detail
the rules for specifying variables and expressions.

    The expression is evaluated and assignment occurs when the
statement is executed. This means that a different result could
be assigned each time the statement is executed since the values
of variables on the right hand side of the '=' operator could
have different values at each execution of the statement.

A-3 Numeric Constants and Variables

Numeric constants and variables may be used interchangeably in numeric expressions. In a succeeding section, we will specify the rules for programming numeric expressions. In this section, we will indicate the rules for numeric constants and variables.

A numeric variable is written as a sequence of alphabetic characters, digits, and '_' characters. The variable must start with an alphabetic character. The name may have as many characters as desired as long as it is entered on a single line. It is a good idea to use names which clearly indicate the use of the variable. Examples of numeric variables are as follows:

```
SUM_OF_SQUARES
PAGE_NUMBER
LINE_COUNTER
STUDENT_AVERAGE
```

Note that the names can be used to clearly define the usage of a variable.

At any time there is one value associated with a variable. When the variable is initially defined, it is automatically assigned a value of zero. Other values may be assigned to the variable by execution of BASIC statements such as assignment statements.

Programs should not be written with the assumption that variables are initially assigned zero values. Not only is this considered to be a poor programming practice, but erroneous results may be obtained since variables are not automatically assigned zero each time the program is executed.

Numeric constants are entered in BASIC programs in a number of formats, as illustrated below:

```
7194632      (integer value)
 400.37      (decimal value)
 .36945      (decimal value)
-63          (integer value)
-.00395      (decimal value)
```

Each constant has an optional integer part followed by an optional decimal part. Commas may not be used in a numeric constant:

```
7,194,632.79
7,432
6.479.321,437
```

The preceding specifications are all incorrect and will cause error messages to be displayed if they are entered.

Numeric constants may also be entered in scientific notation. In this situation, the integer or decimal value is followed by an 'E' and a second integer value.

Scientific Notation	Value
7.36E2	736
21.437E-6	.000021437
-.098E+4	-980

In the preceding example, the first column illustrates numeric constants in scientific notation and the second column gives the corresponding values. The actual value to be represented is determined by taking the number preceding the 'E' and multiplying it by ten raised to the power of the integer following the 'E'. This number preceding the 'E' is called the mantissa and the integer following the 'E' is called the exponent. Scientific notation is commonly used when the magnitude of numbers is either very large or very small.

There are no rules in BASIC which specify where scientific notation should or should not be used. A programmer should use whichever format makes the program easier to understand by another person.

Additional Rules About Numeric Data

(1)   The largest absolute numeric value is approximately 7.237005E+75. When values larger than this are calculated, an OVERFLOW condition is generated and the maximum value is substituted for the result (see ERROR HANDLING).

(2)   The smallest absolute value, other than zero, is approximately 5.397961E-79. When non-zero values smaller than this are calculated, an UNDERFLOW condition is generated and zero is substituted for the result (see ERROR HANDLING).

(3)   Numeric values are stored in the computer in a format which is approximate for many values. The values are kept in a format which ensures that the amount of error is normally quite small. When a numeric constant is converted to this internal format, it will be correct to a specified number of significant digits (sixteen digits in long precision or six digits in short precision - see OPTION LPREC/SPREC). The evaluation of an expression may cause this error to be larger than the amount indicated when the initial conversion occurs. It is beyond the scope of this manual to thoroughly discuss this phenomenon. In most cases the amount of error is too small to impact the computations in a program.

(4) <u>Keywords</u>: Certain names are reserved for use as BASIC keywords. These names cannot be used as variable names. A list of these reserved names is found in a separate chapter (see RESERVED WORDS).

A-4 <u>Character</u> <u>Constants</u> <u>and</u> <u>Variables</u>

Character data is a sequence of 0 to 65535 characters. Character constants may be used in character expressions to specify character data. Examples of character constants are as follows:

```
'HI THERE'
'Report Title'
"WATERLOO BASIC -- Version 2.0"
"I CAN'T LEAVE NOW"
' '
" "
```

The last two constants are character strings of length zero, called null strings. Each constant is enclosed by a pair of either single or double quotation characters. The same character must be used to start and terminate the constant. Thus, to include one of the quotation characters in the constant, the other quotation character must be used to mark the start and the end of the constant.

A character variable is written using the same rules as apply to a numeric variable, except that the last character of the name must be a '$' character.

```
TITLE_PAGE$
CUSTOMER_NAME$
DATA_RECORD$
```

As with numeric variables, it is a good idea to use names that clearly indicate the use of the variable.

At any time there is a character string associated with a variable. When the variable is first defined it is assigned a null string. Other values may be assigned to the variable by execution of BASIC statements such as assignment statements. As with numeric variables, it is considered poor programming practice to assume that null strings have been assigned to all character variables when a program starts execution.

Additional <u>Rules</u> <u>About</u> <u>Character</u> <u>Data</u>

(1) When a character string with more than 65535 characters is generated, the character string is truncated to 65535 characters and the STRING OVERFLOW condition is raised (see ERROR HANDLING).

(2) As with numeric variables, certain names are reserved. These reserved names are found in a separate chapter (see RESERVED WORDS).

A-5 <u>Expressions</u>

Expressions are combinations of operators, variables, constants and function references which specify a computation to be performed. The order in which this computation is performed is determined by parentheses in the expression and the priority of the operators involved. The following table gives the priority of the operators involved in Waterloo BASIC:

<u>Priority</u>	<u>Operator</u>
1	enclosed in parentheses
2	** or ^ (exponentiation)
3	unary +, unary -
4	* (multiply), / (divide)
5	+ (addition), - (subtraction), + or & (concatenation)
6	comparison operations: =,>,<,<>, >=,<=,=>,=<,><
7	NOT (logical complement)
8	AND (logical AND), OR (logical OR)

Operations enclosed in parentheses are performed before any other operations. Operations with a lower priority are performed before those with a higher priority. When two operations have the same priority, the left one is performed first. In the evaluation, the current value of a variable is used in the computation.

The evaluation of an expression can be viewed as a number of successive reductions of sub-expressions, according to the priorities, until only a single value (the result) is left. Consider the expression,

$$-A**((2+B)/C)*2.5*C.$$

where the variables A,B and C have values of 4, 6 and 2 respectively. The first step is to substitute the values for the variables used in the expression:

$$-4**((2+6)/2)*2.5*2$$

The evaluation then proceeds according to the priority of the
operations:

Expression	Operator Applied
-4**((2+6)/2)*2.5*2	(start)
-4**({8} /2)*2.5*2	(+)
-4** {4} *2.5*2	(/)
-{256} *2.5*2	(**)
{-256} *2.5*2	(-)
{-640} *2	(*)
{-1280}	(*)

In the preceding example, each evaluation result is shown in
special brackets, { and }. The second column shows the
operation performed at each step. In the next section, precise
definitions of the BASIC operators are specified.

A-6 BASIC Operators

     In this section, each of the BASIC operators is defined.
Each operation involves one or two operators which are indicated
by NUMB for a numeric datum and by CHAR for a character datum.

Exponentiation: NUMB ** NUMB , or
                  NUMB ^ NUMB

     The first number is raised to the power of the second
number. Thus, a square root of 19 can be specified as 19**.5
and the reciprocal of 2.6 can be specified as 2.6**-1. It is an
error if the first number is a negative number and the second
number is not an integer. Any number, including zero, raised to
a power of zero produces a result of one. Zero raised to a
positive power produces a result of zero and zero raised to a
negative power produces a result which is the largest
representable number in BASIC (approx. 7.237005E+75).

Multiplication: NUMB * NUMB

     The result is the product of the two numeric operands.

Division: NUMB / NUMB

     The result is the quotient of the two numbers; the second
is divided into the first. When the second number is zero, the
ZERODIVIDE error condition is raised (see ERROR HANDLING);   if
no special action has been specified for the ZERODIVIDE
condition, the result will be the largest representable number
in BASIC (approximately 7.237005E+75).

<u>Addition</u>:   NUMB + NUMB

The result is the sum of the two numeric operands.

<u>Subtraction</u>:   NUMB - NUMB

The result is the difference between the two numeric operands; the second operand is subtracted from the first.

<u>Unary</u> <u>Minus</u>:   - NUMB

The result has the same magnitude as the operand and is given the opposite sign.

<u>Unary</u> <u>Plus</u>:   + NUMB

The result is identical to the numeric operand. This operation has no effect and is included only to aid in writing readable programs.

<u>Numeric Comparison</u>   NUMB = NUMB   (equal)
                      NUMB > NUMB   (greater)
                      NUMB < NUMB   (less)
                      NUMB >= NUMB (greater, equal)
                      NUMB <= NUMB (less, equal)
                      NUMB => NUMB (greater, equal)
                      NUMB =< NUMB (less, equal)
                      NUMB >< NUMB (not equal)
                      NUMB <> NUMB (not equal)

The two numeric operands are compared to determine a result of one (relationship is true) or zero (relationship is false). The relationship to be tested is indicated by the comparison operator.

Care should be exercised when comparing two numbers for equality or for non-equality. Because the internal numeric representation is accurate to, at most, sixteen decimal places, two values which are algebraically equal may be computed as unequal; i.e., 5*.1 does not equal .5; the difference between the values is 2.7755576E-17.

<u>Character Comparison</u>   CHAR = CHAR   (equal)
                      CHAR > CHAR   (greater)
                      CHAR < CHAR   (less)
                      CHAR >= CHAR (greater, equal)
                      CHAR <= CHAR (less, equal)
                      CHAR => CHAR (greater, equal)
                      CHAR =< CHAR (less, equal)
                      CHAR <> CHAR (not equal)
                      CHAR >< CHAR (not equal)

The two character operands are compared to determine a numeric result of one (relationship is true) or zero (relationship is false). The relationship to be tested is indicated by the comparison operator.

When the two character strings are of different lengths, the comparison is first made using the shorter length. If the strings have identical contents over this shorter length, then the longer string is greater than the shorter string.

Concatenation   CHAR + CHAR   or
               CHAR & CHAR

The result of this operation is a character string composed of the contents of the first operand followed by the contents of the second operand; i.e.,

'WATERLOO' + ' BASIC'

results in a character string

'WATERLOO BASIC'

This operation is used to build up large character strings from small character strings.

Logical AND   NUMB AND NUMB

The result of this operation is a numeric value of zero or one. If both the operands are non-zero, the result is one; otherwise, the result is zero.

Logical OR   NUMB OR NUMB

The result of this operation is a numeric value of zero or one. If either operand is non-zero, the result is one; otherwise, the result is zero.

Logical NOT   NOT NUMB

The result of this operation is a numeric value of zero or one. If the operand is zero, the result is one; otherwise, the result is zero.

A-7 Examples of Expressions

In this section, several examples of expressions are given in order to illustrate the BASIC operations. Suppose that the following assignment statements have been executed in order to assign values to variables:

```
A  = 2
B  = 3
C  = 3
D  = 4
A$ ='AAA'
B$ ='BBBB'
C$ ='CCCCC'
```

These preceding values will be used in the following examples. In each case the successive reductions to the final result are illustrated.

Example: (A+B)*-(D+C**2)

```
(2+3)*-(4+3**2)
 {5} *-(4+3**2)
 {5} *-(4+{9})
 {5} *- {13}
 {5} * {-13}
   {-65}
```

Example: A$ & B$ & C$

```
'AAA' & 'BBBB' & 'CCCCC'
 {'AAABBBB'} & 'CCCCC'
   {'AAABBBBCCCCC'}
```

Example: A=B OR C<>D

```
2=3  OR   3<>4
{0}  OR   3<>4
{0}  OR  {1}
     {1}
```

Example: NOT (A+C=B+D)

```
NOT (2+3 = 3+4)
NOT ({5} = 3+4)
NOT ({5} = {7})
NOT  {0}
     {1}
```

A-8   Immediate Mode

     When BASIC statements are entered, without line numbers   at
the start of the line, they are immediately executed.

     X = 17
     READY
     Y = X * X
     READY
     PRINT X,Y
      17   289
     READY

Three lines were entered by the user. Each statement, as it was
entered,   was   executed.   The message 'READY' is displayed
following execution of the statement.

     Immediate-mode of execution is useful when   debugging
programs.   Statements   can   be   immediately executed while a
program is in a suspended state (because of an error or   because
of the execution of a PAUSE statement). In this way the values
of variables can be displayed (using the PRINT statement) or
altered (using an assignment statement).

     Not all BASIC statements are acceptable for immediate-mode
execution.   Non-executable statements (e.g., END) and certain
other statements which are not meaningful by themselves (e.g.,
LOOP) cannot be executed. Waterloo BASIC will display an error
message when one of these statements is entered in immediate
mode.

A-9   Attention Key

     Most BASIC terminals have a special key marked 'ATTN',
'ATTENTION' or 'BREAK'. If this key is pressed while a program
is executing, it causes the execution to be suspended. Waterloo
BASIC will display an error message specifying the number of the
line at which this suspension occurred.   The program can be
resumed from this point by entering the CONTINUE command.

     While a program is suspended, immediate-mode execution of
statements can be used to determine the current state of the
program. In addition, the program may be modified by using
editing   commands. Thus, a program with an infinite loop may be
interrupted, corrected, and resumed.

B. Editing A BASIC Program

B-1 Introduction

Editing a program means the process of initially entering a program into the computer and the process by which it may be modified once it exists in the BASIC system. Broadly speaking, these processes may be categorized as adding lines to an existing program, changing lines in an existing program and deleting lines from an existing program. There also exist commands to save and to load programs (described in the next chapter) or to display BASIC statements at the terminal.

At any one time there is a single program associated with a terminal. Immediately after signing onto the system, this program is the empty program consisting of no lines. At any other time, this "initial state" may be obtained by issuing the CLEAR command.

Programs can be changed between executions or while execution is in the suspended state as a result of an error, as a result of the execution of a PAUSE statement, or as a result of the user interrupting the program with an attention key. This ability, combined with immediate-mode execution, provides an effective environment for debugging programs. A suspended program can be resumed after editing from the point of interruption by entering the CONTINUE command.

Some commands may be abbreviated. The format used for command syntax shows the minimum form of each command to the left of the angle brackets. A subset or all of the text enclosed in angle brackets may be entered if desired. For example, the LIST command is shown as LI<ST> and may be entered as LI, LIS or LIST. New commands introduced in other sections will be described using the same format.

B-2 Adding Lines

New lines can be added to the current program by entering a new line exactly as it will appear in the program. The line number is used to determine the position in the program to place the new line. If there exists a line in the program with the same line number as the new line, then the new line replaces the old line. When a line is entered that replaces an existing line in the program, a message is displayed warning that a line has been replaced. The text of the replaced line is also displayed.

If a number of lines are to be added in a sequence, it is convenient to use the automatic line numbering facility.

Syntax: A<UTOLINE> line-number, increment

Examples: AUTO
            AUTO   1000
            AUTO   50,50

This command generates a five-digit line number, followed by a blank, at the terminal and leaves the cursor positioned on the same line awaiting entry of a program line. When a line has been entered, the next line number in sequence is generated. Automatic line number generation is terminated when an empty line is entered. Null lines for program spacing may be added with AUTOLINE by entering one or more blank characters. Lines entered with AUTOLINE are added to the program in the position designated by the line number in the same manner as lines with manually entered line numbers. Similarly, old lines are replaced by new ones with the same line number.

A line number specified in the AUTOLINE command indicates the starting number to be generated. If this is not specified, line numbers begin with ten (00010) and are incremented by ten. The increment specifies the amount to be added to generate each new line number. If no increment is specified, generated line numbers increase by ten.

A space may be used in place of a comma to separate line number and increment.

B-3 <u>Line</u> <u>Ranges</u>

Several editing commands refer to a consecutive sequence of
lines in the current program by a "line range". A line range
specifies the starting and ending lines in the sequence. Thus,
a line range indicates a consecutive portion of a program since
the source lines are in ascending order according to the line
numbers.

A single line can be specified by entering only the line
number of that line. Alternatively, two line numbers separated
by a '-' can be used to refer to all lines, starting with the
first line indicated, up to and including the second line
indicated. When a '-' is given in the line range and the first
line number is omitted, the range starts with the first line in
the program. When the second line number is omitted and a '-'
is given, the range ends with the last line in the program. The
entire program can be specified by a range consisting only of a
'-'.

Consider the following program:

```
100    X = 1
110    Y = 2
120    Z = 3
130    A = 5
150    STOP
```

The following example illustrates several line ranges for the
preceding program:

Line Range	Lines In Range
120	120
110-0130	110,120,130
-120	100,110,120
110-	110,120,130,150
-	100,110,120,130,150

B-4 <u>Listing</u> <u>Lines</u>

Syntax: L<IST>
           L<IST>   line-range
           L<IST>   file-name
           L<IST>   line-range file-name

Examples: LIST   'SAMPLER'
           LIST   100-999   'LISTPGM'
           LIST   100-999

This command displays on the terminal the lines indicated in the line range (second form). If no line range is given, the entire program is displayed. When a file-name is present, the lines are written to the file indicated rather than the terminal.

If a LIST command will cause more lines to be displayed than will fit on the terminal's screen, listing will pause with each screenful. Listing will continue when an empty line is entered. If a command, program line or immediate statement is entered while listing is paused, listing terminates and the specified action is performed. Refer to the description of the SCREENSIZE command for suppressing pauses or altering the number of lines to be displayed between pauses.

B-5 Deleting Lines

    Syntax: DEL<ETE>   line range

This command removes the lines in the line range from the program. It is an error to not specify a line range.

B-6 Changing Lines

    Syntax: C<HANGE> line range   /string1/string2/occurrence
              C<HANGE> /string1/string2/occurrence

This command is used to change a sequence of lines. For each line to be changed, the first occurrence of "string1" is changed to be "string2" if "occurrence" is not specified. All lines that are changed are displayed on the terminal.

When no line range is specified, the "current line" is changed. This current line is the last line referenced in an editing operation; i.e., the last line displayed in a LIST command, the line following the last line deleted with the DELETE command, or the last line inspected by the CHANGE or SEARCH commands.

It is not necessary to use the '/' character to delimit the substitution strings in the CHANGE command. Symbols '=' and '(' cannot be used as string delimiters to avoid confusion with immediate-mode assignment of values to variables or elements of matrices with names such as C, CH or CHANGE. Any other delimiter, which cannot be mistaken as part of the line range, can be used:

```
CHANGE  100-500    /TLT/TOTAL/
CH      100-500    $TLT$TOTAL$
C       100-500    ;TLT;TOTAL;
```

All three of the preceding commands are equivalent.

The CHANGE command cannot change the line number at the start of a line. It only operates on the part of a line following the line number.

The third delimiting character of the substitution strings is optional, unless the second string ends with one or more space characters or an occurrence is specified.

```
CH   -    /CUST_NO/CUST_NUMB/
CH   -    /CUST_NO/CUST_NUMB
```

The preceding two commands are equivalent.

An occurrence number or asterisk may follow the third delimiting character. This may be used to specify which occurrence of string1 is to be replaced by string2 in each line. An asterisk indicates that all occurrences of string1 are to be replaced by string2 in each line.

The following command would substitute the string 'TOTAL' for the second occurrence of string 'SUM' in line 30:

```
CH   30 /SUM/TOTAL/2
```

The next example command would substitute the string 'TOTAL' for all occurrences of string 'SUM' in all lines of the program:

```
CH   - /SUM/TOTAL/*
```

B-7 CLEAR Command

Syntax: CLEAR

This initializes the environment associated with a terminal to be the empty state such as exists when a user first signs onto the BASIC system. This means that the current program is erased, all data items are erased and all files are closed with two possible exceptions. If active, the terminal input/output log (LOGIO) file and the current EXECUTE command file are not closed and remain active.

B-8 CONTINUE Command

Syntax: CONT<INUE>

The CONTINUE command can be used to resume the execution of a program which has been suspended. It provides a method of resuming execution without knowing the line number at which the program was suspended. It is often employed while debugging programs. A program cannot be CONTINUEd if it is not in the suspended state.

A program may become suspended for a number of reasons. Often it is because an unrecoverable error has occurred, resulting in an error message being displayed. It may also occur because the attention key was pressed or because a PAUSE statement was executed.

When a program is suspended because of the execution of a PAUSE statement, the statement following the PAUSE statement receives control when the CONTINUE command is entered. In all other cases, the statement to receive control is the statement at which the program was suspended.

It is possible to edit a suspended program and then resume execution with a CONTINUE command. In those cases where the statement normally CONTINUEd to has been deleted, the statement following the deleted statement(s) will receive control.

B-9 BYE Command

Syntax: BYE

The BYE command is used to sign off the Waterloo BASIC system. It causes all open files to be closed and the current program is erased.

B-10 <u>SEARCH</u> <u>Command</u>

    Syntax: S<EARCH>   line-range/string/occurrence

    The line range is examined for a line containing the specified string. If no line range is specified, lines are examined which follow the "current line". This current line is the last line accessed in an editing operation; i.e., the last line displayed in a LIST command, the line following a line which was deleted, or the last line inspected by the CHANGE or SEARCH commands.

    Occurrence may be a number which indicates how many lines containing the specified string must be found before the last one is displayed and the search stopped. If occurrence is not specified, the first line found to contain the string is displayed. An asterisk may be used in place of an occurrence number to indicate that all lines found to contain the string are to be displayed.

    Similar to the CHANGE command, string delimiter characters other than '/' may be used. These should not include '=' or '(' that could be mistaken as part of an immediate-mode assignment of a value to a variable or matrix element with a name such as S, SEA or SEARCH. In addition, characters that could form part of a line-range cannot be used as a delimiter. The second string delimiter character is optional unless an occurrence is specified or the string ends with one or more space characters.

    Examples of valid SEARCH commands follow:

SEARCH /SUM/
   (find the next line containing 'SUM')

SEARCH 100-500/SUM
   (find the first line containing 'SUM' between lines
   100 and 500 inclusive)

SEARCH SUM4
   (find the fourth line containing 'SUM' following the
   "current line")

SEARCH - /SUM/*
   (find all lines in the program containing 'SUM')

B-11 <u>RENUMBER</u> <u>Command</u>

    Syntax: RENUM<BER> line-number, increment

    Line numbers of a program may be replaced by numbers generated using the specified starting line number and increment. This command is particularly useful when it is necessary to add more statements between existing lines than unused line numbers permit. In addition to line numbers at the left of each program line being changed, all referencing line numbers in statements such as QUIT or GOTO are suitably updated. The existing order of the program is preserved.

    Line numbers are generated starting with the specified line number and adding the increment value for each new line. If a line number is not specified, generated numbers begin with ten and are incremented by ten. If the increment is not specified, new numbers begin with the specified line number and are incremented by ten. A space may be used instead of a comma to separate line number and increment.

    The following are examples of valid RENUMBER commands:

```
RENUM
RENUM   100,20
RENUM   2000
```

C. System Commands

C-1 Introduction

Programs can be saved for later use by using either the SAVE command, the STORE command, or the STOREOBJ command. The SAVE command places only a copy of the source statements in a file. The STORE command saves the entire environment associated with a terminal; i.e., the values of variables are stored in addition to the source statements. The STOREOBJ command is identical to the STORE command, except the source lines are not saved.

A SAVEd program is loaded into memory using the OLD command. A STORE or STOREOBJ program is loaded into memory by using the LOAD command. In either case, the system does an implicit CLEAR before loading the program.

Because the SAVE command saves only the source statements, the storage requirements to keep a copy of the program will be lower than if STORE were used. The OLD command causes each statement to be analyzed and processed as if it was entered from a terminal. Consequently, it takes longer to "OLD" a program than to "LOAD" it.

Programs are saved in files. Because each different computing system has a different method of naming files, we will specify the full details of these conventions in the chapters on specific systems (see FILE names).

C-2 SAVE Command

```
Syntax:     SAVE      'filename'
            SAVE      line-range 'filename'

Examples:   SAVE      'EDITOR'
            SAVE      3000-4000  'EDSUBS'
```

This command causes a copy of the current program to be saved in the file named in the command. Only the source statements are saved in this file. The program may be loaded into memory at some subsequent time by using the OLD command. When a line-range is specified, only the lines in the line-range are saved in the file.

C-3   <u>OLD</u> Command

      Syntax: OLD   'filename'

     This command causes the source statements in the specified file to be used as the current program. Before these statements are processed, an implicit CLEAR command is issued by the system. Thus, the new program replaces whatever program was previously associated with the terminal.

C-4   <u>STORE</u> Command

      Syntax: STO<RE>   'filename'

     This command saves a copy of the environment associated with a terminal. For example, the following information is saved:

- the source statements
- values of all variables
- the current execution state
- options in effect

     The one part of the environment that is not saved is file information. The STORE command does not save the current positions in files and whether or not the files were open.

C-5   <u>STOREOBJ</u> Command

      Syntax: STOREO<BJ> 'filename'

     This command is identical to the STORE command, except that the source statements are not saved. The source statements should be saved in some other way, because when the file created by the STOREOBJ command is LOADed, it cannot be modified or inspected. This form of the command is often used when storing programs into the program library. The execution of statements in immediate-mode is inhibited when the STOREOBJ program is loaded.

C-6 LOAD Command

Syntax: LOAD   'filename'

This command reloads into memory a program that was previously saved using the STORE or STOREOBJ command. In effect, it restores the environment that existed immediately before that STORE command was issued, except that all open files have been closed. Before the LOAD is performed, an implicit CLEAR command is issued by the system. Thus, the LOADed program replaces the environment that was present before the command was issued.

C-7 RUNLIB Command

Syntax: RUNL<IB>   'name'

This command causes a program to be LOADed from the system library and placed into execution. The name of the program to be run is specified in the command.

C-8 MERGE Command

Syntax: MERGE   'filename'

This command merges lines from a file with the lines in the current program associated with a terminal. This process is equivalent to entering each of the lines in the merge file using the terminal. Thus, if the same line number occurs on a line in both the current program and the file being merged, the line from the merge file will replace the line in the program.

The merge command can be used to add commonly used subroutines or functions to a program. This may be accompanied by establishing a convention that line numbers in the merge files start at some large number and by coding programs with line numbers less than any line numbers in the merge files.

A file to be used as a merge file can be created with the SAVE command. It is an error to attempt to merge a file containing a program created with the STORE or STOREOBJ command.

C-9 <u>RUN</u> <u>Command</u>

    Syntax: RUN
                  RUN   'filename'

    The RUN command is used to place a program into execution.
Program execution starts with the first statement in the
program. When a file name is specified, the program is LOADed
into the computer memory and then placed into execution. Such
programs must have been saved with the STORE or STOREOBJ
command.

C-10 <u>RESET</u> <u>Command</u>

    Syntax: RESET

    This command is used to close all opened files in a
program.

C-11 <u>DIRECTORY</u> <u>Command</u>

    Syntax: DI<RECTORY>
                  DI<RECTORY> 'filename'

    The DIRECTORY command causes a list of all files associated
with a terminal to be displayed at the terminal, if no filename
is specified. When a filename is specified, the DIRECTORY
command lists all files associated with that name. Refer to the
chapters concerning system dependencies for information
concerning the latter form of this command.

    If a DIRECTORY command will cause more lines to be
displayed than will fit on the terminal's screen, listing will
pause with each screenful. Listing will continue when an empty
line is entered. If a command, program line or immediate
statement is entered while listing is paused, DIRECTORY listing
terminates and the specified action is performed. Refer to the
description of the SCREENSIZE command for suppressing of pauses
or altering the number of lines to be displayed between pauses.

C-12 <u>SCREENSIZE</u> Command

    Syntax: SC<REENSIZE>   number
               SC<REENSIZE>

    This command allows resetting or displaying of the value of the internal system parameter that controls the number of lines to be displayed between screenful pauses for LIST, DIRECTORY and TYPE commands. The value of this parameter is set to 22 when the user signs on with the Series/1 CPS system. Each user may reset this value to suit a particular terminal. Screenful pauses may be suppressed by specifying a number of 0 (zero). Zero is the initial value of this parameter with the VM/CMS system for reasons outlined in the chapter concerning VM/CMS dependencies.

    If a number is not specified with the SCREENSIZE command, the current value of this parameter is displayed at the terminal.

C-13 <u>HELP</u> Command

    Syntax: H<ELP>   ED<ITOR>   command
               H<ELP>   FU<NCTION> function name
               H<ELP>   ST<ATEMENT> statement keyword

    The HELP command displays a brief description of the various commands, built-in functions and programming-language statements supported by the system. Use of the HELP command is self-descriptive. Enter HELP or HELP HELP to get started. Editing and system commands are grouped together in the HELP categories.

C-14 <u>TYPE</u> Command

    Syntax: T<YPE>   'filename'

    The TYPE command may be used to display the contents of a file at the terminal. If the records of a file are longer than the width of a terminal line, they are truncated. This command is useful only for displaying the contents of files stored in character format, such as SAVEd programs, EXECUTE files and data files containing character data. It is recommended that this command not be used with STOREd files or other files containing binary data. Displaying of arbitrary binary data to a terminal may result in special characters being transmitted which can lock out the keyboard or put the terminal into other undesirable modes. Use of the TYPE command with keyed files or files with records larger than 256 characters is not supported and may give unexpected results.

If a TYPE command will cause more lines to be displayed than will fit on the terminal's screen, listing will pause with each screenful. Listing will continue when an empty line is entered. If a command, program line or immediate statement is entered while listing is paused, TYPE listing terminates and the specified action is performed. Refer to the description of the SCREENSIZE command for suppressing of pauses or altering the number of lines to be displayed between pauses.

C-15 <u>EXECUTE</u> <u>Command</u>

      Syntax: EX<ECUTE> 'filename'

This command allows processing of commands from a file rather than the terminal. All commands which may be entered at the terminal may also be used in EXECUTE files with the exception of AUTOLINE. If a BASIC program is RUN from an EXECUTE file, data that the program would normally read (INPUT) from the terminal is read instead from the EXECUTE file. EXECUTE files may contain EXECUTE commands which invoke other EXECUTE files. When the end of an EXECUTE file is reached, commands and program input continue from the invoking EXECUTE file where it was suspended. When all active EXECUTE files are processed, control returns to the terminal. Control will return directly to the terminal if an error is encountered opening an EXECUTE file.

C-16 <u>ASSIGN</u> <u>Command</u>

      Syntax: AS<SIGN> 'name' to 'filename', mode

    where mode is INPUT, INOUT, or OUTIN

This command allows the definition of a pseudo-name for a filename or filename subset. The ASSIGN command can only be used with the Series/1 CPS version of Waterloo BASIC.

A filename subset must consist of a valid filename prefix. A pseudo-name can be referenced as part of, or in place of, a filename in BASIC statements or commands. In such a reference, the pseudo-name is recognized if it appears as a prefix and its ASSIGNed filename (subset) is substituted. For example, if the following ASSIGN command has been issued, filename '.LIB.CLASSDAT' is interpreted as '.WFL0.BASLIB.CLASSDAT'.

    ASSIGN 'LIB' TO '.WFL0.BASLIB', INPUT

A mode of INPUT restricts file access through the pseudo name in question to read-only. That is, file contents may be examined but not modified. If no mode is specified, INPUT is assumed. INOUT and OUTIN modes provide read-write access to files through the pseudo name in question. That is, files may be examined or modified.

Privileged users may find this a convenient method of abbreviating names of files accessed from outside their default or personal file area. The most significant use, however, is in providing unprivileged users with limited and specific access to files or sets of files. ASSIGN commands may be issued from an unprivileged user's sign-on EXECUTE file to define access to files outside personal file space. The content of the sign-on EXECUTE file is determined by the system manager, giving him control over file security. Unprivileged users may not use the ASSIGN command.

Note that pseudo-names cannot be used for files in the default personal file area unless the assigned filename is fully qualified (i.e., the default prefix explicitly specified). This is because the pseudo-name prefix overrides the default prefix.

C-17 DEASSIGN Command

Syntax: DEAS<SIGN> 'name'

This command removes a pseudo-name which was ASSIGNed to a filename or filename subset. For example, if the pseudo-name, 'LIB', was ASSIGNed to the file prefix '.WFL0.BASLIB', this definition may be undone by the following command. This command can only be issued by a privileged user and is only available with the Series/1 CPS version of Waterloo BASIC.

DEASSIGN 'LIB'

C-18 SHOW Command

Syntax: SH<OW>

This command displays all pseudo-names that have been ASSIGNed to filenames or filename subsets. For each ASSIGNment, the pseudo-name, access mode and filename (subset) are displayed. In addition, the user's default file prefix is shown as the first entry. This entry has DEFAULT in the access-mode column to distinguish it from ASSIGNed pseudo names. The SHOW command is only available with the Series/1 CPS version of Waterloo BASIC.

C-19 LOGIO Command

Syntax: LOG<IO>   'filename'

This command causes all terminal input and output to be
copied to the specified file or device. Terminal lines in the
LOGIO file are preceded by an 'I:' or 'O:' designating input or
output. In educational environments, students can use this
facility to record interactive testing of programming
assignments for marking by their instructors. Other uses
include recording examples of program bugs and keeping audit
trails of file updates.

C-20 ENDLOG Command

Syntax: ENDL<OG>

This command terminates recording of terminal input and
output and closes the LOGIO file.

C-21 FINISH Command

Syntax: FINISH

This command terminates Waterloo BASIC so that another
system or program may be used at the terminal. This command can
only be issued by a privileged user.

D-1 What Is Meant By Control

"Control" means the manner in which BASIC statements are selected for execution. Normally, statements are executed one at a time in the order in which they occur in a program. Thus, after one statement is executed, the next statement to be executed is normally the statement on the line with the next higher line number.

A program can be placed into execution with the RUN command. In this case, the first statement to be executed is the one with the lowest line number in the program. Execution of a program is terminated whenever an unrecoverable error (see ERROR HANDLING) occurs or when a STOP or PAUSE statement is executed, or when the attention key is pressed.

Certain BASIC statements cause the normal sequential progression of control to be altered. These statements specify another statement in the program to be the next statement to be executed. The normal sequential flow of control then proceeds from this new point in the program. Consider the following program to print the squares of integers from 10 to 20.

```
1000    INTEGER = 10
1020    WHILE INTEGER < 21
1030        PRINT INTEGER, INTEGER*INTEGER
1040        INTEGER = INTEGER + 1
1050    ENDLOOP
1060    STOP
1070    END
```

When this program is executed, statements 1030 and 1040 will be repeated 11 times. For each repetition, the variable INTEGER will have a different value, starting at 10 and increasing by 1. Thus, when statement 1030 is executed each time, the current value of INTEGER and the square of that value is printed.

The sample program illustrates a loop. The bounds of the loop are defined by the statements at 1020 and 1050. The WHILE statement at line 1020 specifies that the statements inside the loop are to be executed while the value of INTEGER is less than 21. As long as this condition is evaluated as true, control will pass to the statement following the WHILE statement. When the condition is evaluated as false, control will pass to next statement following the ENDLOOP statement. Whenever the ENDLOOP statement is executed, control passes to the WHILE statement in order to test if the loop is to be repeated for another iteration.

The preceding example was intended to illustrate how the
normal sequential flow of execution can be altered by certain
BASIC statements. The remainder of this chapter describes some
of the statements which can be used in this way. We have
classified these statements as Structured Control Statements.

It has been theoretically proven that the only necessary
constructs required to write programs are the normal sequential
flow of control, a way to program loops and a way to select
different sequences of statements for execution. The first two
mechanisms have already been illustrated in part. Programs that
are written using only these mechanisms are usually called
"Structured Programs". Consequently, we have termed the
statements which are used to control program execution in this
manner, "Structured Control Statements".

There also exist, primarily for historical reasons, other
methods of altering control from the next sequential statement.
Although they are not strictly required in the BASIC language,
they have been included in Waterloo BASIC in order that existing
programs written in BASIC can be executed. These statements are
called "Unstructured Control Statements" (See chapter J).

D-2 Structured Loops

         Syntax: WHILE   expression , or
                      LOOP
                      ......(body of loop)
                      ENDLOOP , or
                      UNTIL   expression

Loops have three parts: a statement (WHILE or LOOP) to
mark the start of the loop; a number of BASIC statements to
form the body of the loop; and a statement (ENDLOOP or UNTIL)
to mark the end of the loop. The body of the loop is repeated
while the numeric expression is non-zero at the start of the
loop (WHILE statement) and/or the numeric expression is zero at
the end of the loop (UNTIL statement).

In the preceding section we have already seen an example of
a loop using a WHILE statement to start a loop and an ENDLOOP
statement to terminate the loop. An equivalent program is as
follows:

```
1000    INTEGER = 10
1020    LOOP
1030       PRINT INTEGER,INTEGER*INTEGER
1040       INTEGER = INTEGER + 1
1050    UNTIL INTEGER > 20
1060    STOP
1070    END
```

In this case the loop was programmed with a LOOP statement to start the loop and an UNTIL statement to terminate it.

Depending on the data involved in the expression associated with the WHILE statement, a WHILE-ENDLOOP loop may have the body of the loop executed zero times. This will be the situation when the expression associated with the WHILE statement is initially false (zero). A LOOP-UNTIL loop, however, will always execute the body of the loop at least once. This is because the WHILE statement is executed at the start of each iteration of a loop and because the UNTIL statement is executed at the completion of each iteration of a loop.

It is also possible to program WHILE-UNTIL loops. These loops are controlled by both the WHILE statement at the start of the loop and the UNTIL statement at the end of the loop. Consider the following program:

```
10000     TOTAL = 0
10100     INTEGER = 0
10200     WHILE INTEGER < 100
10300         INTEGER = INTEGER + 1
10400         TOTAL = TOTAL + INTEGER
10500     UNTIL TOTAL > 1000000
10600     PRINT INTEGER, TOTAL
10700     STOP
10800     END
```

The preceding program may be used to determine the first two-digit integer for which the sum of the positive integers to that number exceeds one million. If no such integer exists, the sum of the integers from one to ninety-nine is printed.

It is also possible to program LOOP-ENDLOOP loops. In this case a statement in the body of the loop must be used to terminate the loop (see QUIT statement).

The body of a loop may itself contain a loop. In this case the inner loop is said to be nested inside the outer loop. Consider the following program:

```
0080    RATE = .015
0090    PRINCIPAL = 1.00
0100    YEAR = 1
0200    WHILE YEAR <=2
0300        PRINT 'YEAR = ', YEAR
0400        MONTH = 1
0500        WHILE MONTH <=12
0600            PRINCIPAL = PRINCIPAL*(1+RATE)
0700            PRINT MONTH, PRINCIPAL
0750            MONTH = MONTH + 1
0800        ENDLOOP
0900        YEAR = YEAR + 1
1000    ENDLOOP
1100    STOP
1200    END
```

The preceding program shows how a principal of one dollar appreciates in value at a rate of 1.5% computed monthly over a two-year period. Note the inner loop (500-800) nested inside the outer loop (200-1000).

It is considered good programming practice to indent the body of loops. In this way, the program becomes more readable as the repeated sequences of statements are clearly marked by the indentation level.

D-3   IF,ELSEIF,ELSE,ENDIF   Statements

Syntax:	IF	expression	
	....		
	ELSEIF	expression	(optional)
	....		(optional)
	ELSEIF	expression	(optional)
	....		(optional)
	ELSE		(optional)
	....		(optional)
	ENDIF		

The IF statement and its associated statements are used to execute different sequences of statements, depending upon the alternatives in the data. Consider the following sequence of BASIC statements:

```
5000      IF   COLOUR_CODE = 19
5010             COLOUR$ = 'RED'
5020      ELSEIF   COLOUR_CODE = 23
5030             COLOUR$ = 'BLUE'
5040      ELSE
5050             COLOUR$ = 'UNKNOWN COLOUR'
5060      ENDIF
```

The execution of this sequence will cause a variable COLOUR$ to be assigned a value of 'RED', 'BLUE', or 'UNKNOWN COLOUR' depending on the value of the variable COLOUR_CODE. Thus, the example illustrates a three-way choice, based upon the current value of the variable COLOUR_CODE.

The general form of an IF-group is shown by the syntax at the start of this section. An IF-group must start with an IF statement and must be terminated with an ENDIF statement. The simplest form is illustrated in the following example:

```
3020      IF   SEX_CODE$="MALE"
3030             MALE_COUNT=MALE_COUNT+1
3040             MALE_WAGES=MALE_WAGES+SALARY
3050      ENDIF
```

In this case, the expression associated with the IF is evaluated. If the result is true (non-zero), then the statements following the IF are executed. Otherwise, control passes to the statement following the ENDIF statement.

A second form of the IF may be used to distinguish between two alternatives.

```
5010      IF   SALARY > 50000
5015             TYPE$ = 'EXECUTIVE'
5020             MANAGEMENT_COUNT=MANAGEMENT_COUNT+1
5025      ELSE
5030             TYPE$ = 'WORKER'
5040             WORKER_COUNT=WORKER_COUNT+1
5045      ENDIF
```

In this situation one of two sequences of code is selected. When the expression in the IF statement evaluates as true (non-zero), the first sequence (5015-5020) is selected and then control passes to the statement following the ENDIF statement. When the expression in the IF statement is false (zero), the second sequence of code (5030-5040) is selected and then control passes to the statement following the ENDIF statement.

When several alternatives are possible, the ELSEIF statement can be used to select one of a number of alternatives.

```
500    IF   CODE$ = 'ADD'
          ....statements for add processing
600    ELSEIF   CODE$ = 'CHG'
          ....statements for change processing
700    ELSEIF   CODE$ = 'DLT'
          ....statements for deletion processing
800    ELSE
          ....statements for error processing
900    ENDIF
```

The preceding example illustrates a selection of one of four alternatives. The actual statements to do the processing for each of the alternatives has been omitted for clarity. The value of the variable CODE$ is used to select which of the alternatives is to be executed:

- when the expression in statement 500 is true (non-zero), the statements between statements 500 and 600 are executed and then control passes to the statement following the ENDIF statement.

- otherwise, if the expression in statement 600 is true (non-zero), the statements between statements 600 and 700 are executed and then control passes to the statement following the ENDIF statement.

- otherwise, if the expression in statement 700 is true (non-zero), the statements between 700 and 800 are executed and then control passes to the statement following the ENDIF statement.

- otherwise, the statements between 800 and 900 are executed and then control passes to the statement following the ENDIF statement.

As many ELSEIF statements as required can be associated with an IF statement. The ELSE statement, if present, must follow the ELSEIF statements for an IF group. When the ELSE statement is not included and all the expressions in the IF statement and all ELSEIF statements are false, then none of the alternative sequences of statements are executed and control continues at the statement following the ENDIF statement.

It is a good idea to use the same indentation for each of the IF, ELSEIF, ELSE and ENDIF statements and to indent the alternative sequences of code. In this way the program becomes more readable.

D-4 <u>Nesting</u> <u>Loops</u> <u>And</u> <u>IF-Groups</u>

A program in Waterloo BASIC may be viewed as a number of "blocks" of statements. A block can be defined to be a program, the body of a loop, the alternatives in an IF-group, the body of a function definition (see FUNCTIONS), or the alternatives in a GUESS group (see GUESS/ADMIT).

A block can be nested inside another block, but cannot overlap only part of another block. Thus, loops can be nested inside loops, an IF group can be nested inside a loop, and a loop can exist inside one of the alternatives of an IF group. Consider the following example:

<u>Nest-level</u>

100	WHILE	1
	....	2
200	IF	2
	....	3
300	ELSE	2
	....	3
400	LOOP	3
	....	4
500	UNTIL	3
	.....	3
600	ENDIF	2
	.....	2
700	WHILE	2
	....	3
800	ENDLOOP	2
	....	2
900	ENDLOOP	1

The example illustrates a loop (100-900) which contains an IF group (200-600) and another loop (700-800). One of the alternatives (300-600) of the IF group contains a loop (400-500).

The following examples illustrates an illegal nesting of blocks:

100	IF
	.....
200	LOOP
	.....
300	ELSE
	.....
400	UNTIL
	.....
500	ENDIF

The loop (200-400) neither contains or is contained in the two alternatives (100-300, 300-500) of the IF group (100-500). In such situations, Waterloo BASIC will display error messages diagnosing the error.

E.   Functions

E-1   Introduction

A function is used to compute a value to be used in an expression. When an expression containing a function reference is evaluated, control is passed to the function to compute a value which is then used in the expression. Consider the following assignment statement:

```
SIZE = LEN(STRING1$) + LEN(STRING2$)
```

The example contains two function references to the LEN function which computes the length of a string. The first reference will return the length of the string assigned to the variable STRING1$ and the second reference will return the length of the string assigned to the variable STRING2$. Thus, the execution of the assignment statement will assign to the variable SIZE the sum of the lengths of the strings assigned to the variables STRING1$ and STRING2$.

A function may be passed values as parameters. For example, the LEN function requires one parameter, the string whose length is to be returned. Some functions have no parameters and others may require a number of parameters. In a function reference, each parameter is an expression which is evaluated before the function is invoked. The results of these evaluations are then made available to the function in order to perform the computation indicated in the function.

There are two kinds of functions in Waterloo BASIC - those supplied with the system (built-in functions) and those which can be coded in a program (user-supplied functions). Built-in functions are described in the next chapter.

User-defined functions have names which start with FN. A numeric function is named according to the same rules as are used for numeric variables and a character function is named according to the rules for character variables i.e., the names start with FN and have one or more characters that are letters, underscore characters, or digits. The last letter of a character function must be the $ character. Numeric functions return numeric values and character functions return character values.

E-2 Defining One-Line Functions

    Syntax: DEF   function-name (parameters) = expression

        A one-line function defines a computation which is executed
when an expression containing a reference to that function is
executed. Consider the following example:

        500   CTEMP = FN_FAH_TO_CEN (FTEMP)
                .....
        10100   DEF FN_FAH_TO_CEN (DEG) = (DEG-32)*5/9

Statement 10100 is a one-line definition of a function to return
a value representing a Celsius temperature for the corresponding
temperature in Fahrenheit. The definition specifies that there
is one parameter (symbolically named DEG). This parameter is
used in the expression which defines the computation to
calculate the return value. When the assignment statement in
line 500 is executed, the function referenced will be invoked to
compute a value. This value is then assigned to the variable
CTEMP.

        When a function is invoked, the values of the parameters in
the function reference are calculated and assigned to the
symbolic parameters named in the function definition. The
expression in the function definition is then evaluated to
compute the result to be returned to the place from which the
function was invoked. The symbolic parameters in the function
definition are ordinary variables. Before these variables are
assigned values from the function reference, the existing values
for these variables are saved. The saved values are restored to
these variables after the expression in the function definition
has been evaluated.

        The expression in a function definition is an ordinary
expression in Waterloo BASIC. Consequently, it may contain
constants, variables, or references to other functions.

Additional Rules About One-Line Function Definitions

(1) It is legal syntactically to reference the function being
     defined in the expression defining that function. If such
     a function is ever invoked, an infinite loop will result as
     the function recursively invokes itself.

(2) Parameters that are passed to a function must be of the
     same type (numeric or character) as the symbolic parameters
     in the function definition. There must be the same number
     of parameters in both cases.

(3) A function cannot be defined within the body of another
     function definition.

E-3 Multi-line Function Definitions

Syntax: DEF   function-name (symbolic parameters)
             .....body of definition
             FNEND

A multi-line function defines a body of statements which
are executed when an expression containing a reference to that
function is executed. Consider the following example:

```
40230  AMNT = BILL + FN_TAX (BILL)
.....
51000  DEF FN_TAX (AMOUNT)
51010    IF AMOUNT > 3.00
51020       FN_TAX = 0.15 * AMOUNT
51030    ELSE
51040       FN_TAX = 0
51050    ENDIF
51060  FNEND
```

The multi-line function FN_TAX computes 15% tax on amounts
greater than three dollars and no tax otherwise. The body of
the function (51010-51050) is executed when the function is
invoked.

When an expression containing a function reference is
evaluated, the result of the function is determined as follows:

   - the expressions for parameter values are evaluated
   - the values of the symbolic parameters are saved
   - the parameter values are assigned to the symbolic
     parameters
   - the body of the function definition is executed until the
     FNEND statement is encountered
   - the values of the saved parameters are restored to the
     symbolic parameters
   - the return value is now whatever has been assigned to the
     function name

Note in the example that the return value is assigned in lines
51020 and 51040.

The value to be returned by a function is assigned to the
function name within the body of the function. When the
function is initially invoked, this return value is set to be
zero (numeric functions) or to be the null string (character
functions).

Functions may be used in a recursive manner. Consider the
following example to compute a factorial value (the factorial of
a positive integer is the product of all the positive integers
less than or equal to the integer in question).

```
20100 DEF    FN_FACTORIAL (NUMB)
20200    IF  NUMB > 1
20300         FN_FACTORIAL = NUMB*FN_FACTORIAL (NUMB-1)
20400    ELSE
20500         FN_FACTORIAL = 1
20600    ENDIF
20700 FNEND
```

The function is said to be recursive since it can invoke itself
(line 20300). Suppose the following statement is executed:

```
5159    PRINT   FN_FACTORIAL (3)
```

In this case, the following sequence of statements would be
executed:

```
5159      invoke FN_FACTORIAL (3)
   20100      save current NUMB, NUMB = 3
   20200
   20300      invoke FN_FACTORIAL (2)
     20100      save current NUMB; NUMB = 2
     20200
     20300      invoke FN_FACTORIAL (1)
       20100      save NUMB; NUMB = 1
       20200
       20500      FN_FACTORIAL = 1
       20700      restore NUMB = 2; return (1)
     20300      FN_FACTORIAL = 2
     20700      restore NUMB = 3; return (2)
   20300      FN_FACTORIAL = 6
   20700      restore NUMB; return (6)
5159      print 6
```

Indentation has been used to illustrate the levels of function
activation.   The   comments   briefly   describe   the   actions
performed.

One consequence of recursion is that each time a function
name occurs to the right of the '=' character in an assignment
statement, the function will be invoked.   Thus, the function
name cannot be used in an expression in the same way a variable
is used.

```
20100   DEF   FN_FACTORIAL (NUMB)
20200    FN_FACTORIAL = 1
20300    WHILE (NUMB > 1)
20400      FN_FACTORIAL = FN_FACTORIAL * NUMB
20500      NUMB = NUMB - 1
20600    ENDLOOP
20700    FNEND
```

The preceding example would be diagnosed as containing an error in line 20400 since the usage of FN_FACTORIAL in the expression to the right of the '=' sign implies another invocation of the function and since there are no parameters in that function reference.

Additional Rules About Multi-line Function Definitions

(1)   Parameters that are passed to a function must be of the same type (numeric or character) as the symbolic parameter in the function definition. The number of parameters must also match the number in the definition.

(2)   A function cannot be defined within the body of another function definition.

F.   Built-In Functions

F-1   Introduction

Waterloo BASIC includes a number of built-in functions to return values for commonly used calculations. These system functions can be invoked in any BASIC expression where a value of the corresponding type can be used.

These functions can be classified into a number of different classes. Some of these classes are explained in the different sections of this chapter. Functions related to error status and detection are described in the chapter dealing with Error Handling. Functions related to the characteristics of files are described in the chapter on Input/Output Statements.

F-2   Trigonometric Functions

These functions return values for the common trigonometric functions. It is beyond the scope of this manual to describe the actual meaning of such functions. The functions are described in most texts about Trigonometry.

ACOS (X)

This function returns the arc COSINE (in radians) of the real number X where $-1 < X < 1$ and $0 < ACOS(X) < PI$.

ASIN (X)

This function returns the arc SINE (in radians) of the real number X where $-1 < X < 1$ and $-(PI/2) < ASIN(X) < (PI/2)$.

ATN (X)

This function returns the arc TANGENT (in radians) of the real number X where $-(PI/2) < ATN(X) < (PI/2)$.

ATN2 (X,Y)

This function returns the arc TANGENT (in radians) of the quotient X/Y where $(-PI) <= ATN2(X,Y) <= PI$.

COS (X)

This function computes the COSINE of the real number X, where X is in radians.

COSH (X)

This function computes the hyperbolic COSINE of the real number X.

COT (X)

This function computes the COTANGENT of the real number X, where X is in radians.

CSC (X)

This function computes the COSECANT of the real number X, where X is in radians.

DEG (X)

This function computes the number of degrees for the real number X, where X is in radians.

RAD (X)

This function computes the number of radians for the real number X, where X is in degrees.

SEC (X)

This function computes the SECANT of the real number X, where X is in radians.

SIN (X)

This function computes the SINE of the real number X, where X is in radians.

SINH (X)

This function computes the hyperbolic SINE of the real number X.

TAN (X)

This function computes the TANGENT of the real value X, where X is in radians.

TANH (X)

This function computes the hyperbolic TANGENT of the real value X.

F-3 Numeric Functions

ABS (X)

  This function returns the absolute value of the parameter X.

CEIL (X)

  This function returns the smallest integer that is not less than the value of X.

CEN (X)

  This function returns the number of degrees in Celsius (Centigrade) corresponding to the temperature of X degrees Fahrenheit.

EPS

  This function returns the smallest positive number representable in BASIC.

EXP (X)

  This function returns the value of the mathematical constant e raised to the power X. If no parameter is specified, the mathematical constant e is returned.

FAH (X)

  This function returns the number of degrees in Fahrenheit corresponding to the temperature of X degrees Celsius (Centigrade).

FP (X)

  This function returns the fractional part of the number X. The returned value has the same sign as X.

GALI

  This function returns a constant representing the number of litres in a U.S. gallon.

INCM

  This function returns a constant representing the number of centimetres in an inch.

INF

The function returns the largest positive number representable in BASIC.

INT (X)

This function returns the largest integer which is not greater than the real number X.

IP (X)

This function returns the integer part of the real number X. The returned value has the same sign as the number X.

LBKG

This function returns a constant representing the number of kilograms in a pound.

LINE

This function returns the line number of the last line where a program was interrupted, where an error occurred, or where execution was suspended.

LOG (X)

This function returns the natural logarithm (base e) of the real value X. The parameter X must be a positive number.

LOG10 (X)

This function returns the logarithm (base 10) of the real value X. The parameter X must be a positive number.

LOG2 (X)

This function returns the logarithm (base 2) of the real value X. The parameter X must be a positive number.

MAX (X1,X2...,Xn)

This function returns the maximum value from the list of numbers X1,X2,....,Xn. At least two parameters must be specified.

MIN (X1,X2,...,Xn)

This function returns the minimum value from the list of numbers X1,X2,....,Xn. At least two parameters must be specified.

MOD (X,Y)

This function returns the modulus of the value X for range Y. The calculation is equivalent to specifying X-Y*INT(X/Y).

PI

This function returns the value of the mathematical constant PI (approximately 3.141593).

REM (X,Y)

This function returns the remainder when the value X is divided by the value Y. It is equivalent to specifying X-Y*IP(X/Y).

RND (X)

This function returns a pseudo-random number in the range (0,1), according to a uniform distribution over this interval. When no parameter is specified, the value is computed from the last value according to a fixed algorithm. When a parameter X is specified, the random number generator is reset using the parameter X (seed) as a starting point. Thus, a reproduceable sequence of random numbers can be generated by initially using a seed and then successively invoking the RND function without a parameter. An unpredictable starting point may be set by using the RANDOMIZE statement.

SGN (X)

This function returns a value based upon the sign of the parameter X: if X<0 the value returned is (-1); if X=0, the value returned is (0); and if X>0, the value returned is (+1).

SQR (X)

This function returns the square root of the real number X. It is an error if X has a negative value.

F-4 Character Functions

These functions are used in conjunction with character strings.

CHR$ (X)

This function returns a single character representing the character in position (X) of the possible characters available on the computer. X is rounded to an integer value and used as a number modulus the number of characters available, usually zero to 255.

HEX (A$)

This function returns a number obtained by converting the hexadecimal digits (base 16) of the character string A$ to a decimal number (base 10) in internal numeric format. Hexadecimal digits are represented as the characters 0-9 and A-F. For example, the value of HEX('2A0F') is 10767 (i.e., $2*4096 + 10*256 + 0*16 + 15*1$).

HEX$ (M)

This function returns a character-string of hexadecimal digits (base 16) representing the value of the number M. HEX$ performs the inverse of the conversion provided by the HEX function.

IDX (A$,B$)

This function returns a number representing the position (BASE 1) at which the character string B$ first occurs in the character string A$. If B$ is not found in A$, zero is returned.

LEN (A$)

This function returns a number representing the number of characters in the string A$.

LPAD$ (A$,M)

The value M is rounded to an integer value. If the length of A$ is greater than M, then A$ is the return value; otherwise, the return value is a character string of M characters produced by padding space characters in front of the value of A$.

LTRM$ (A$)

This function returns a character string identical to A$ with all space characters removed from the left of the value.

LWRC$ (A$)

This function returns a character string identical to A$ except all upper case letters have been changed to the corresponding lower case letters.

MAX$ (A1$,A2$,....,An$)

This function returns a character string equal to the largest character-string value in the list of character values A1$, A2$,....,An$.

MIN$ (A1$,A2$,....,An$)

This function returns a character string equal to the smallest character-string value in the list of character values A1$, A2$,...,An$.

OCT (A$)

This function returns a number obtained by converting the octal digits (base 8) of the character string A$ to a decimal number (base 10) in internal numeric format. Octal digits are represented as the characters 0-7. For example, the value of OCT('25017') is 10767 (i.e., 2*4096 + 5*512 + 0*64 + 1*8 + 7*1).

OCT$ (M)

This function returns a character-string of octal digits (base 8) representing the value of the number M. OCT$ performs the inverse of the conversion provided by the OCT function.

ORD (A$)

This function returns a number, called the ordinal value, representing the position of A$ in the set of characters for the computer. A$ must have a length of 1 character.

RPAD$ (A$,M)

The value M is rounded to an integer value. If the length of A$ is greater than M, then A$ is the return value; otherwise, the return value is a character string of M characters produced by padding space characters following the value of A$.

RTRM$ (A$)

This function returns a character string identical to A$ with all space characters removed from the right of the value.

SPACE$ (M)

The value M is rounded to an integer value. The function will return a character string of M space characters.

SREP$ (A$,B$,C$)

This function returns a string which is identical to A$ except all non-overlapping occurrences of B$ have been replaced by C$ in the return value.

STR$ (A$,M,N)

This function returns a string representing the part of the string A$ which starts at position M and continues for N characters. Both M and N are rounded to integer values. If N is less than one after rounding, a null string is returned. When fewer than N characters exist from position M onward, then the remainder of the string is returned.

TRANSLATE$ (A$,B$,C$)

This function returns a string formed by replacing characters in string A$ which are found in B$ by corresponding characters in C$. That is, a translation mapping of characters in B$ to characters in corresponding positions of C$ is applied to the string A$. For example, the value of TRANSLATE$('BIG CAT','ACT','ODG') is 'BIG DOG'.

UPRC$ (A$)

This function returns a character string identical to A$ except all lower case letters have been changed to the corresponding upper case letters.

VALUE (A$)

This function returns a number obtained by converting the character string A$ to the internal format of numbers. The value A$ can contain any of the formats of numeric constants.

VALUE$ (M)

This function returns a character-string representation of the number M. The representation will be identical to the one displayed by a PRINT statement, without leading or trailing space characters.

VERIFY (A$,B$)

This function returns a number which indicates whether or not all of the characters of string A$ belong to the set of characters in B$. Value zero is returned if all characters in A$ are found in B$, otherwise the value returned is the position of the first character in A$ not found in B$. For example, VERIFY('OUCH','AEIOU') returns value 3 since C is not a vowel (A,E,I,O, or U).

F-5 Time And Date Functions

These functions are used to supply the current date and time to BASIC programs. Some computer systems do not have the hardware or software components to provide this capability – when this is the case, dummy values are returned when these functions are invoked. A table of these values is given at the end of this section.

DAT$

This function returns a character string representation of the current date, e.g. '1978/09/25'.

DATE

This function returns a five-digit number in the form YYDDD where YY represents the last two digits of the year and DDD is the Julian date (the relative position of the day in the current year), e.g. 78214.

DATE$

This function returns a character string representation of the current date, e.g. '78/09/25'.

JDY

This function returns a number representing the current date as a Julian date (the relative position of the day in the current year), e.g. 214.

TIME

This function returns a number representing the number of seconds since midnight.

TIME$

    This function returns a character string representing the
current time of day using a 24-hour clock, e.g. '14:23:17'.

Dummy Values For Functions

Function	Dummy Value
DAT$	'0000/00/00'
DATE	-1
DATE$	'00/00/00'
JDY	-1
TIME	-1
TIME$	'99:99:99'

G.   Matrices

G-1   Introduction

A matrix is a collection of numbers or a collection of
character strings which can be referenced and manipulated either
individually or jointly. The statement,

    153 DIM COST(200), PRODUCT_NAME$(300)

defines two matrices named COST and PRODUCT_NAME$.   The matrix
COST has 201 numbers defined which may be referenced as COST(0),
COST(1), ..., COST(199), COST(200). The matrix PRODUCT_NAME$
is defined to consist of 301 character strings.

Matrices are named using the same rules as variable names.
A matrix of numbers is named according to the rules for numeric
variables and a matrix of character strings is named according
to the rules for character variables. It is considered good
programming practice to use a meaningful name to describe the
collection of elements.

G-2   DIM Statement

Syntax: DIM matrix(dimensions), matrix(dimensions),
                   ....,matrix(dimensions)

Examples: 103 DIM   CUSTOMER_NUMBER(300)
             107 DIM   PRODUCT$(5,100)
             108 DIM   MARK(50,30)

The DIM statement is used to define the number of elements
in a matrix. This is accomplished by specifying a list of
numbers, called dimensions, in parentheses following the matrix
name.   Up to 255 dimensions may be given, although it is rarely
useful to define more than a few dimensions. The number of
elements in the matrix is given by the product of the dimensions
all incremented by 1.

    143 DIM SIZE(20,14,33)

The matrix SIZE has 10710 = 21*15*34 elements defined.

It is an error for a particular matrix to occur more than
once in a DIM statement in a program. Although DIM statements
may be placed anywhere in a program, it is considered good
programming practice to place all DIM statements together at the
start of a program.

A matrix with one dimension is called a vector. The elements are often thought of as being in a single row or as being in a single column. A matrix with two dimensions is often considered to be a table of values arranged in rows and columns. The first dimension specifies the number of rows and the second dimension specifies the number of columns. Matrices are sometimes referred to as arrays.

Additional Rules For The DIM Statement

(1) Each dimension specification must be given as a positive integer constant.

(2) DIM statements are not executable. They are only used to specify the number of elements in a matrix.

(3) When a matrix is not specifically given a size in a DIM statement, the maximum number of elements is established by the first reference to the matrix. If the matrix is referenced in its entirety, the matrix is given one dimension with a value of 10. If the matrix is referenced with subscripts, it is given as many dimensions as there exist subscripts and each dimension has a value of 10. It is considered poor programming practice to use a matrix without explicitly defining the matrix size using a DIM statement.

G-3 Subscripts

Individual matrix elements can be referenced by using subscripts. For example, MARK(TEST,STUDENT) refers to an element in the two-dimensional matrix MARK. In this case there are two subscripts. The first subscript (TEST) is used to establish the row and the second (STUDENT) is used to establish the column.

In general, a matrix will have N dimensions. An individual element is referenced by specifying N subscripts. Each subscript is a numeric expression which is rounded to be an integer value. This value must not exceed the value of the corresponding dimension. The subscript value must not be less than 0 or 1, depending upon the BASE option specified for the program (see OPTION BASE). If no BASE option is specified, each dimension starts with a 0-th element.

A subscripted element may be used wherever a variable may be used. For example, it can be assigned values in an assignment statement or it may be used as a value in expressions.

G-4   Current Dimensions Of A Matrix

At any time during the execution of a program, a matrix has a current set of dimensions. These dimensions can vary in number and extent from those specified on a DIM statement, as long as the number of elements in the new dimension specification does not exceed the number of elements originally indicated by the DIM statement. The current dimensions of a matrix can be changed when a matrix expression is assigned to a matrix.

Two built-in functions exist to determine the extents of a matrix: LDIM and UDIM.

LDIM (A,n)

The LDIM built-in function returns a numeric value giving the lower extent (depends on the BASE option) of the n-th dimension of a matrix A.

UDIM (A,n)

The UDIM built-in function returns a numeric value giving the upper extent of the n-th dimension of a matrix A.

Using LDIM And UDIM

The LDIM and UDIM built-in functions can be used to write sequences of statements to process matrices in a manner that does not require coding dimension extents as constants.

```
00100    DIM CHARGE(100)
   ......
05200    INDEX = LDIM(CHARGE,1)
05210    TOTAL = 0
05220    LOOP
05230       TOTAL = TOTAL + CHARGE(INDEX)
05240       INDEX = INDEX + 1
05250    UNTIL INDEX > UDIM(CHARGE,1)
```

Statements 5200 to 5250 compute the sum of the numbers stored in the array CHARGE.

G-5   Matrix Assignment

    Syntax: MAT   matrix = matrix expression
                 MAT   matrix (verification specification)
                       = matrix expression

    The matrix assignment statement is used to assign values to
all elements in an array. The rules by which these elemental
values are computed are given in following sections of this
chapter.   The target matrix (i.e. the matrix to be assigned
values) can optionally be verified to have specific dimensions.
This provides a method whereby proper dimensions of arrays can
be verified as a program executes.

    When a matrix assignment occurs, the target matrix takes on
the dimensions indicated by the matrix expression. Thus, the
current dimensions of a matrix may be changed each time a matrix
assignment takes place. Whenever redimensioning occurs, the new
dimensions must not specify more elements than existed when the
matrix was originally given dimensions (see DIM statement).

        Example: MAT A = B

This matrix assignment statement causes the dimensions of A to
be set to match the dimensions of the matrix B. An error will
be detected if matrix A was not initially specified with as many
elements as are contained in matrix B.   The contents of matrix B
are then assigned to matrix A.

        Example: MAT A (20,N+4) = B

The matrix assignment in this example will be identical to the
assignment in the preceding example, except that the current
dimensions of A are verified before the assignment actually
takes place. An error will result if the matrix A does not have
two dimensions with the indicated values, before the matrix
assignment statement takes place.

G-6   Assignment Of A Matrix

    Syntax: MAT matrix = matrix
               MAT matrix (verification specification) = matrix

    Example: MAT CUST$ = NEW_CUST$
                MAT SALES (30,10) = ORDERS

    This form of matrix assignment causes the values from the
source matrix (to right of '=' character) to be assigned to the
target matrix.   There must be sufficient space in the target to
hold all elements of the source matrix.   The target matrix will

assume the dimensions of the source matrix. If a verification
specification is present, the target matrix must be dimensioned
accordingly before the matrix assignment takes place. The
source and target matrices must both be numeric matrices or both
be character matrices.

G-7   Assigning A Constant To A Matrix

    Syntax: MAT matrix = (expression)
                 MAT matrix (verification specification)
                        = (expression)

    Example: MAT NAME$ = ('')
                 MAT MARK = (-1)
                 MAT COST(PRODUCT_COUNT) = (OVERHEAD)

    This form of matrix assignment causes the expression in
parentheses to be evaluated and that value to be assigned to all
elements of the target matrix. The target matrix must have the
same type (numeric or character) as the expression. The
dimensions of the target matrix are unchanged by the assignment.
If a verification specification is present, the target matrix
must have the same dimensions as are given in the verification
specification.

G-8   Assigning The Sum Of Two Matrices

    Syntax: MAT matrix = matrix + matrix
                 MAT matrix (verification specification)
                    = matrix + matrix

    Example: MAT PRICE = COST + PROFIT

    This form of a matrix assignment statement assigns to a
target numeric matrix the sum of two numeric matrices. The two
source matrices must have the same current dimensions. These
current dimensions become the current dimensions of the target
matrix. There must be sufficient space in the target matrix to
contain the number of elements indicated by these dimensions.
An element in the target matrix is assigned a value computed as
the sum of the values in the corresponding position in the
source matrices. If a verification specification is included,
the target matrix must be dimensioned as indicated in the
verification specification before the assignment takes place.

G-9   Assigning The Sum Of An Expression and A Matrix

Syntax: MAT matrix = (expression) + matrix
             MAT matrix (verification specification)
                        = (expression) + matrix

This form of a matrix assignment statement assigns to a target numeric matrix the sum of the numeric expression added to all elements of the source numeric matrix. The current dimensions of the source matrix become the current dimension of the target matrix. There must be sufficient space in the target matrix to contain the number of elements in the source matrix. An element in the target matrix is assigned a value computed as the sum of the value of the expression and the value in the corresponding position in the source matrix. If a verification specification is included, the target matrix must be dimensioned as indicated in the verification specification before the assignment takes place.

G-10   Assigning The Difference Of Two Matrices

Syntax: MAT matrix = matrix - matrix
             MAT matrix (verification specification)
                        = matrix - matrix

Example: MAT PROFIT = PRICE - COST

This form of a matrix assignment statement assigns to a target numeric matrix the difference of two numeric matrices. The two source matrices must have the same current dimensions. These current dimensions become the current dimensions of the target matrix. There must be sufficient space in the target matrix to contain the number of elements indicated by these dimensions. An element in the target matrix is assigned a value computed as the difference between the corresponding elements in the source matrices. If a verification specification is included, the target matrix must be dimensioned as indicated in the verification specification before the assignment takes place.

G-11 <u>Assigning</u> <u>The</u> <u>Product</u> <u>Of</u> <u>An</u> <u>Expression</u> <u>and</u> <u>A</u> <u>Matrix</u>

Syntax: MAT matrix = (expression) * matrix
            MAT matrix (verification specification)
                = (expression) * matrix

Example: MAT PRICE = (1 + FACTOR) * COST

This form of a matrix assignment statement assigns to a target numeric matrix the source matrix with the expression value multiplied by each element. The current dimensions of the source matrix become the current dimensions of the target matrix. There must be sufficient space in the target matrix to contain the number of elements in the source matrix. An element in the target matrix is assigned a value computed as the product of the value of the expression and the value of the element in the corresponding position in the source matrix. If a verification specification is included, the target matrix must be dimensioned as indicated in the verification specification before the assignment takes place.

G-12 <u>Sorting</u> <u>Matrices</u>

Syntax: MAT matrix = ASORT(matrix)
         MAT matrix (verification specification) = ASORT(matrix)
         MAT matrix = DSORT(matrix)
         MAT matrix (verification specification) = DSORT(matrix)
         MAT matrix = AIDX(matrix)
         MAT matrix (verification specification) = AIDX(matrix)
         MAT matrix = DIDX(matrix)
         MAT matrix (verification specification) = DIDX(matrix)

A number of built-in matrix functions may be used to process matrix data in sorted order. For example, a matrix of customer names may be processed in alphabetical order. This data may be processed in either ascending (smallest element first) or descending order (largest element first).

There are two ways of processing data in order. One way is to assign a sorted version of a matrix to a matrix (ASORT or DSORT). Alternatively, a matrix of indices can be created (AIDX or DIDX) to indicate the position of elements in the original matrix. In the latter situation, the target matrix contains a list of the positions from which the elements may be accessed in order from the original matrix.

In many applications matrices with only a single dimension are sorted. If the source matrix has more than one dimension, it may still be sorted. In this case, the matrix is treated as if only a single dimension, equal to the number of elements in the matrix, were defined for the matrix. Thus, under OPTION

BASE 1, a matrix defined

DIM A(3,2)

would be treated as a single vector with the elements:

A(1,1), A(1,2), A(2,1), A(2,2), A(3,1), A(3,2)

Similarly, the functions AIDX and DIDX would return a vector with 6 positions in the conceptual vector.

When a verification specification is given, the target matrix is verified to have the dimensions in the verification specification.

ASORT Function

This function assigns to the target matrix a copy of the source matrix, with the elements, in ascending order. The target matrix must have sufficient space to be assigned these elements. The target matrix receives the dimensions of the source matrix. The type (numeric or character) of the source and target matrices must be identical.

DSORT Function

This function is identical to the ASORT function, except the elements are assigned to the target matrix in descending order.

AIDX Function

This function assigns to the target matrix a list of the subscripts to be used to access the source matrix in ascending order. The target matrix must be a numeric matrix and is given dimensions identical to the source matrix. The source matrix may be either a character matrix or a numeric matrix.

DIDX Function

This function is identical to the AIDX function, except that the list of positions assigned to the target matrix enable the original matrix to be accessed in descending order.

Example Of DIDX

```
00100     DIM PROD$(100), PRICE(100), ORDER(100)
  .....
10000     MAT ORDER = DIDX(PRICE)
10010     INDEX = LDIM(ORDER,1)
10020     WHILE INDEX <= UDIM(ORDER,1)
10030       PRINT PROD$(ORDER(INDEX)),PRICE(ORDER(INDEX))
10040       INDEX = INDEX + 1
10050     ENDLOOP
```

In this example, line 10000 is executed; suppose that PROD$ contains a list of products and suppose that PRICE contains a list of prices in positions corresponding to the elements in PROD$. Then, the sequence of lines 10000 - 10050 will print the products and their prices in descending order according to the price of the products.

G-13 Special Matrices: IDN, CON, ZER, NULL$

```
Syntax:   MAT matrix = special matrix definition
          MAT matrix (verification specification)
                    = special matrix definition
     where special matrix definition is one of
          ZER
          ZER (dimension list)
          CON
          CON (dimension list)
          (expression) * CON
          (expression) * CON (dimension list)
          IDN
          IDN (dimension list)
          NULL$
          NULL$ (dimension list)
```

A number of special matrices can be assigned to a matrix. In addition, the dimensions of these matrices may be specified. If the dimensions of the special matrix are not specified, a special matrix of the size of the target is assigned, when possible, to the target. When a verification specification is present, the target matrix is first verified to possess the same dimensions as are specified in the verification specification. When a dimension list is specified in conjunction with a special matrix definition, there must exist sufficient space in the target matrix to contain the indicated matrix definition. In this case, the target matrix will receive the current dimensions indicated by the dimension list.

ZER

This special matrix is a matrix of zeros. It may only be assigned to a numeric matrix.

CON

This matrix is a numeric matrix in which each element has the value one. It may only be assigned to a numeric matrix.

(Expression) * CON

This special matrix consists of elements, each of which has a value equal to the value of the numeric expression. The matrix may only be assigned to a numeric matrix.

NULL$

This matrix is a character matrix in which each element has a value of the null string. It may only be assigned to a character matrix.

IDN

This special matrix is the mathematical identity matrix. It is a square matrix (has two equal dimensions) which consists entirely of zeros, except for the elements with equal subscripts (i.e. on the diagonal) which have values of one. This matrix may only be assigned to numeric matrices. If a dimension list is specified, there must be exactly two equal dimensions in the list. If no dimension list is specified, the target matrix must have two equal dimensions.

G-14 Matrix Multiplication

Syntax: MAT matrix = matrix * matrix
            MAT matrix (verification specification)
                = matrix * matrix

Matrix multiplication is defined only for numeric source matrices with two dimensions according to the mathematical definition of matrix multiplication. In this case, the second dimension of the first source matrix must equal the first dimension of the second source matrix. The target matrix will be given two dimensions, the first being the first dimension from the first source matrix and the second being the second dimension from the second source matrix. All three matrices must be numeric matrices. The target matrix must have sufficient space to contain the number of elements for the dimensions it will receive. If a verification specification is present, the target matrix is first verified to have dimensions matching the verification specification.

An element $A(i,j)$ in the target matrix is computed as follows. The i-th row from the first source matrix and the j-th column of the second source matrix are selected. In each selection there is an equal number of elements, say n elements. The elements, one from each selection, are multiplied together in pairs to create n products. The sum of these n products is the value of the element $A(i,j)$.

```
100  !  MULTIPLY MAT A = B * C WHERE
110  !     UDIM(A,1) = UDIM(B,1)
120  !     UDIM(A,2) = UDIM(C,2)
130  !     UDIM(B,2) = UDIM(C,1)
140  !     OPTION BASE 0
150  ROW = 0
160  WHILE ROW <= UDIM(A,1)
170       COL = 0
180       WHILE COL <= UDIM(A,2)
190            TEMP = 0
200            INDEX = 0
210            WHILE INDEX <= UDIM(B,2)
220                 TEMP = TEMP + B(ROW,INDEX) * C(INDEX,COL)
230                 INDEX = INDEX + 1
240            ENDLOOP
250            A(ROW,COL) = TEMP
260            COL = COL + 1
270       ENDLOOP
280       ROW = ROW + 1
290  ENDLOOP
```

The preceding example illustrates an equivalent method of multiplying two matrices using BASIC statements.

G-15 __Matrix__ __Transposition__

Syntax: MAT matrix = TRN (matrix)
             MAT matrix (verification specification)
                       = TRN (matrix)

The mathematical transpose of a matrix may be obtained by use of the TRN function. The source matrix must be a matrix with two dimensions. The result of the assignment is a matrix with two dimensions. The rows of the target matrix are assigned the columns of the source matrix. Consequently, the columns of the target matrix will be identical to the rows of the source matrix. The target matrix must have sufficient space to hold the elements in the source matrix. If a verification specification is present, the target matrix is first verified to have dimensions identical to the verification specification.

```
100   !   COMPUTE MAT A = TRN(B)  WHERE
110   !      UDIM(A,1) = UDIM(B,2)
120   !      UDIM(A,2) = UDIM(B,1)
130   !      OPTION BASE 1
140   ROW = 1
150   WHILE ROW <= UDIM(A,1)
160        COL = 1
170        WHILE COL <= UDIM(A,2)
180             A(ROW,COL) = B(COL,ROW)
190             COL = COL + 1
200        ENDLOOP
210        ROW = ROW + 1
220   ENDLOOP
```

The preceding example illustrates an equivalent way to obtain the mathematical transpose of a matrix, using BASIC statements.

G-16 Other Functions using Matrices:

These functions return values computed from the values in a matrix or matrices.

SUM (A)

This function returns a numeric value representing the sum of the values in the matrix A.

DOT (A,B)

This function returns the mathematical "dot product" of two one-dimensional matrices A and B. The extents of the dimensions must be identical. The dot product is defined as the sum of the products created by multiplying together in pairs elements at corresponding positions in the two matrices.

DET (A)

This function returns the mathematical "determinant" of a square matrix A. The reader should refer to a text in Algebra for the definition of a determinant.

PROD (A)

This function returns the product of the elements in the matrix A.

H.   Input/Output Statements

H-1   Introduction

The primary function of input/output statements is to transmit data to and from an executing BASIC program. Data in an executing program is kept in variables or matrices and is manipulated using BASIC statements such as assignment statements.

Data outside of programs is organized into files. Each file consists of a number of records and each record contains data elements which may be transmitted to or from variables in a BASIC program. When a file is to be accessed, it must first be connected to the BASIC program by executing an OPEN statement. This OPEN statement specifies the name of the file to be processed and a file number used to reference this file in other input/output statements. When processing for a file is complete, the file is disconnected from the program using a CLOSE statement.

Data is transmitted from a program to a file using a PRINT statement. This statement specifies the values to be transmitted and the file number of the file to be used. It may also optionally specify the record where transmission is to start and the format of the data to be transmitted.

Data is transmitted from a file to BASIC variables or matrices by using the INPUT or LINPUT statements. The INPUT statement specifies a list of variables or matrices to which data is to be transmitted. The LINPUT statement specifies a single character variable to which an entire record from the file in question is transmitted.

A special type of file may be created known as a keyed or indexed file. An "index" of "keys" is maintained for this type of file. A key is a unique character-string that is associated with a particular data record of the file. A specific record of a keyed file may be accessed by naming its associated key value in a LINPUT, INPUT or PRINT statement. When such an access is requested, the index is searched for the specified key value, the position of the associated data record is identified and the record is accessed.

Keyed files are useful in many applications where it is necessary to read or update specific records of a file at random. Most data files are too large for a user to remember the actual record position of specific data. It is usually more practical to identify records by a distinguishing characteristic or key. For example, a student file, containing a record of information for each student, might be created as a keyed file using the student number as the key to identify records.

H-2 File Reference Number

    Syntax: # expression

    Examples: # 4
                 # INPUT_FILE

    The file reference number is used in many BASIC statements
to reference a file. For example, the PRINT statement may
specify a file reference number to indicate which file is to
receive the data in the print list. The OPEN statement is used
to associate a file reference number with a specific file. The
CLOSE statement is used to disassociate a file reference number
from a specific file.

    The expression in a file reference number is any valid
numeric expression. The value of this expression is rounded to
an integer value. The resulting value must be an integer from 0
to 9999.

    Two numbers, 0 and 1, are reserved to specify the terminal.
0 is used to indicate the terminal when used for input (INPUT
and LINPUT). 1 is used to indicate the terminal when used for
output (PRINT). These file reference numbers are always
associated with the terminal and cannot be used in OPEN or CLOSE
statements.

H-3 OPEN Statement

    Syntax: OPEN #file-ref, 'filename', mode

    where mode is one of INPUT, OUTPUT, OUTIN, INOUT, APPEND

                      or

    OPEN #file-ref, 'filename1', OUTPUT,
      DATAFILE = 'filename2', KEYLEN = expression

    The OPEN statement is used to associate a specific file
with a file reference number and to indicate the mode of access
to that file. When the mode is INPUT, data may only be
transmitted from the file using the INPUT or LINPUT statements.
When the mode is OUTPUT or APPEND, data may only be transmitted
to the file using a PRINT statement. When the mode is OUTIN or
INOUT, data may be transmitted to or from the file.

The file is assumed to exist when any of the modes of
INPUT, INOUT, OUTIN or APPEND are used. APPEND mode is used to
add records sequentially to the end of an existing file. APPEND
mode does not apply to keyed files since the position of a
record in such files is always associated with its corresponding
key value, and the concept of adding records to the end has no
meaning. When the mode is OUTPUT, a new file is created to
receive the data. If a file by that name already exists, it is
erased before the new file is created.

A keyed file may be viewed logically as a single file,
however, in reality two files are used to implement this method
of accessing data records. The first file contains the "index"
of key values and the positions of the associated "data" records
which are in the second file. The second form of the OPEN
statement shown above must be used when creating keyed files.
The first filename specifies the file which is to contain the
index and the second filename specifies the file which is to
contain the data records. The data filename must be simple and
unqualified for the Series/1 version. The data file is taken to
have the same qualifiers, explicit or implied, as the index
filename. File attributes such as record-size may be specified
only for the data filename. Refer to the chapter concerning
System Dependencies for a description of the attributes that may
be specified for a file. The index file is managed by the
system automatically and its attributes are defined by the
system.

The expression following 'KEYLEN =' in an OUTPUT-mode OPEN
for keyed files is any valid numeric expression. The value of
this expression is rounded to an integer value which must be
between 1 and 122 inclusive. This value specifies the maximum
length for the key values associated with the records of the
file. If a record is accessed using a key value longer than the
specified KEYLEN maximum for a file, the key value is truncated
for the purpose of searching or updating the index.

When a keyed file is to be opened in INPUT, INOUT or OUTIN
mode, the first form of the OPEN statement is used. In this
case, the filename specified is the name of the index file. The
system recognizes that the file is 'keyed' and extracts the data
file name that was stored in the index when it was created.
Users that access a previously created keyed file need not know
the data filename.

The value for the file reference number cannot be 0 or 1.
These numbers are reserved for terminal operations. A file
reference number can be associated with only one file at any
time during the execution of a program. A number of file
reference numbers may, however, reference the same file.
Normally, in this case, these files must all be OPENed with the
INPUT mode. Special facilities exist for controlling multiple
access to files using Waterloo BASIC on the Series/1 with the

CPS operating system. Refer to the chapter entitled "System Dependencies: IBM Series/1 (CPS)" for a description of these facilities.

H-4   CLOSE Statement

Syntax: CLOSE   # file-ref

The CLOSE statement is used to disassociate a file reference number from a file. Consequently, that file reference number may not be used in subsequent input/output statements until another OPEN is executed to associate that reference number with a file. It is an error to attempt to execute a CLOSE statement for a file reference number which is not currently associated with a file. File reference numbers 0 and 1 are reserved for terminal operations and cannot be used in a CLOSE statement. Refer to the chapter entitled "System Dependencies: IBM Series/1 (CPS)" for considerations regarding control of multiple simultaneous access to files.

H-5   File Positioning

Files may be processed either sequentially or randomly. When sequential processing is used, the records in the file are processed in the order that they occur in the file. This order may be modified by using the REC clause in a PRINT, INPUT, or LINPUT statement. The REC clause cannot be used to specify record position for files open in OUTPUT or APPEND mode. When the REC clause is used, any record in a file can be chosen as the next one for input or output. For example,

LINPUT #3,REC=17,REC$

will cause the record at position 17 in the file to be transmitted into the character variable REC$.

Some hardware does not have the capability to be accessed in any way except sequentially. In this case, an error diagnostic will be issued when the REC clause is executed. This situation, for example, is true with terminals being used to enter and display BASIC statements and messages.

The records which are accessed randomly using the REC clause should have been previously written on the file sequentially. This initialization can be accomplished by the following program (CPS System):

```
     OPEN #3,'MYFILE/RECSIZE:80',OUTPUT
     FOR I=0 TO 99
          PRINT #3
     NEXT I
     CLOSE #3
     STOP
```

This program creates a file name 'MYFILE' to have 100 records, each 80 characters in length. Any of the 100 records, at positions 0 through 99, can now be accessed. The equivalent program in the CMS system will have the first statement replaced by:

     OPEN #3, 'MYFILE (RECFM F LRECL 80)', OUTPUT

Waterloo BASIC with the CPS or VM/CMS system does not require sequential initialization of a file prior to random record access. The file must be created by OPENing it in OUTPUT mode and closing it. If the file is subsequently OPENed in INOUT (or OUTIN) mode, data may be transferred to specific records using the REC clause in a PRINT statement. Attempts to INPUT or LINPUT records beyond the highest record number previously written will be treated as an "end-of-file" condition. The contents of records not previously written are undefined. For example, consider a file to which record 50 has been written with the statement

     PRINT #3, REC = 50, 'RECORD FIFTY'

and no other records have been written. The statement

     LINPUT #3, REC = 51, A$

will cause an "end-of-file" error. The statement

     LINPUT #3, REC = 49, A$

will not cause an error, but the contents of A$ will be arbitrary.

File positioning for keyed files is similar to ordinary files, although record "position" relates to an associated character-string key value rather than actual location in the file. When records are read sequentially with INPUT or LINPUT statements, they are processed in order of ascending key values. Specific records may be accessed by using the KEY clause in a PRINT, INPUT or LINPUT statement. For example,

     LINPUT #3, KEY = 'HENRY', REC$

will cause the record associated with key-value HENRY to be transmitted into the character variable REC$.

The REC clause is invalid with input/output statements using keyed files. The KEY clause must be specified with PRINT statements using keyed files since each record must have an associated key value.

A new record is added to a keyed file when a key value specified with a PRINT is not found in the index. If the key value is found in the index, the associated record is updated.

An error results when a key value that is not defined in the index is specified using "KEY=" with a LINPUT or INPUT statement. Another form of the KEY clause, "KEY >=", may be used with LINPUT or INPUT statements when precise key values are not known. For example, the following program would display at the terminal all records in a keyed file with associated key values greater than or equal to 'H'.

```
OPEN #3, 'KEYFILE', INPUT
LINPUT #3, KEY >= 'H', REC$
LOOP
    PRINT REC$
    LINPUT #3, REC$
ENDLOOP
```

Since no loop control is included, the program will terminate with an 'end of file' error after the last record is displayed. Methods of handling such error conditions are described in the chapter entitled 'Error Handling'.

H-6   Image Strings

Image strings are used to describe the format of data to be transmitted to or from files. Within an image string, a number of special character sequences, called image items, can be identified. Any other characters are treated as spacing characters and may be transmitted on output or may cause data to be skipped on input (see INPUT and PRINT).

Legitimate image items are shown below:

S###	I-format (centered)
>###	I-format (right-justified)
<###	I-format (left-justified)
S###	F-format
S###.###	F-format
S.###	F-format
S###^^^^	E-format
S###.^^^^	E-format
S###.###^^^^	E-format
S.###^^^^	E-format

where:

      ###   a string of 1 or more # characters
      S   either a + character or a - character (optional)
      ^   the print positions of the exponent part of a floating
            point number

On input, only the width (the number of characters) of the image items described above is used. On output, the image item gives the exact specifications for how the data is to be transmitted. Numeric items are converted to the appropriate character image before transmission.

If a number of consecutive data items have identical image items, a "repetition factor" may be used instead of duplicating the identical image items in an image string. For example, the image string '<###<###<###' is equivalent to '<###*3' in terms of formatting results. In fact, use of repetition factors can be more efficient since fewer image items need be inspected and interpreted by the system. A "repetition factor" must follow an image item to be repeated, and consist of an asterisk and a simple integer constant value.

Another class of image items provides format directives, several alternative means of formatting numeric data on files, and features suited to formatting numbers for financial reports and documents. Image items in this class are delimited by pairs of at-symbols (@) to distinguish them from similar sequences of characters in other image items or text strings that may appear in an image string. A closing at-symbol is optional if the image item falls at the end of an image string.

Format Directives

These types of image items are useful in specifying the layout of data records, but do not correspond to data items in an INPUT or PRINT list.

Delimiter

A pair of at-symbols with no characters between them (@@) are treated as an image item delimiter. An at-symbol pair can be used to separate centered, unsigned I-format items. This provides an alternative to the following example which illustrates one means of printing centred strings adjacently on the same line.

```
PRINT USING '####', 'CAT';
PRINT USING '####', 'DOG'
```

This can be accomplished with the following single PRINT statement.

```
PRINT USING '####@@####', 'CAT', 'DOG'
```

In fact, since both image items are identical, a repetition factor may be used as follows.

```
PRINT USING '####*2', 'CAT', 'DOG'
```

Skip to New Record

Image directive, @SKIP@, indicates a record break. Processing of the current record is completed and subsequent image items are processed starting at the beginning of the next record.

Reading/Updating Portions of Records

A file record may contain more data items than are pertinent to a particular application. For example, a company's personnel file might have a record for each employee containing several types of information. If a simple report was desired consisting of employee names and telephone numbers, it would be unnecessary and superfluous to read unrelated data items from the employee records. An INPUT statement such as the following could be used in this case.

```
FORMAT$ = '###############@POS(73)@#######'
INPUT #3, USING FORMAT$, NAME$, TELEPHONE
```

In this example, data items between employee name in character positions 1 to 15 and telephone number in character positions 73 to 79 are ignored.

Similarly, individual data items of existing records may be updated without altering the contents of the rest of the record. The following example illustrates updating of a single data item in a record.

```
SALARY_POS$ = '@POS(67)@######'
PRINT #3, USING SALARY_POS$, SALARY
```

The general form of the position directive is as shown below.

```
@POS(n)@
```

where n is a positive integer constant indicating

a character position in the record.

If "n" is less than one, it is treated as one. If "n" is greater than the record-size of the file, it is treated as a @SKIP@ directive. That is, data item processing resumes in character position one of the next record.

Compact Numeric Formats

Binary Format

Binary format provides a compact means of storing numeric integer values on a file. Numbers formatted in binary are not "printable" and thus this type of image item is not appropriate for output to terminals or printers. Binary format image items may be defined to occupy from one to four character positions in a file record. The following binary format items may be used to read or write integer values in the ranges indicated next.

Image Item	Character Positions	Value Range
@B@	1	-128 to +127
@BB@	2	-32768 to +32767
@BBB@	3	-8388608 to +8388607
@BBBB@	4	-2147483648 to +2147483647

Floating-point (Internal) Format

Numeric values of a program are stored internally using floating-point representation. This type of image item allows numeric values to be transferred to and from the data records of a file without transformation. Numbers formatted in floating-point representation are not "printable" and thus this type of image item is not appropriate for input/output with terminals or printers. Two types of floating-point formats are supported:

Image Item	Precision	Character Positions
@S@	short	4
@L@	long	8

Short and long precision forms correspond to the internal representations of numbers used for program options SPREC and LPREC, respectively. Either type of floating-point image item may be used regardless of which program option is in effect.

Packed-decimal Format

Packed decimal format provides a compact way of storing numeric values with fixed decimal-point positions. The width of these items may be specified. Each character can represent 2 digits of a number except the last which contains 1 digit value and a sign indicator (positive or negative). Numeric values represented in packed-decimal format are not "printable" and thus this type of image item is not appropriate for input/output with terminals and printers. There are two forms of packed-decimal image items:

    @PD(w)@
    @PD(w.d)@

    where,
        w is the number of character positions
        d is the number of fractional digits

That is, (2*w)-1 digits may be represented in the "w" character positions, the last "d" of which are decimal (fractional) digits. If ".d" is not specified, all digit positions are integer. This type of image item occupies half the space required to store equivalent numeric values in I- or F-format.

The number of digits treated as fractional is not recorded with the digits and sign on the data record. Thus, image items must be used on input and output for consistent results.

Compact Numeric Formats used with Strings

When used to format character string data items, the special numeric image items simply define the width of the string image. String values are formatted left-justified and are padded on the right with blanks to the width of the image item on output. The following image widths apply to strings.

Image Item	Character Positions
@B@	1
@BB@	2
@BBB@	3
@BBBB@	4
@S@	4
@L@	8
@PD(w.d)@	w
@PD(w)@	w

Picture Formatting

Picture image items provide a means of formatting numeric values under edit control, allowing character insertion, leading zero suppression or substitution, different sign notations and decimal place representations. With the exception of implied decimal place notation (V), picture format is useful only for printer or terminal output, and it is not recommended for use with file input/output. However, data items transmitted to a file using picture format may be transmitted back to the program if the same format is used.

Picture image items consist of combinations of special characters which have meaning that may depend on context or the numeric value being processed. Characters other than those defined below are treated as unconditional insertion characters. The special characters, other than V, may be grouped into two categories, namely, digit specifiers and insertion characters. A picture format must contain at least one digit specifier to be used as an image item corresponding to a PRINT/INPUT list data item. If no digit specifiers are contained inside a pair of at-symbols, and the characters do not define one of the image item types previously described, the characters within at-symbols are treated as insertion or filler text between data items. Use of the special characters is illustrated by examples to follow.

Digit Specifiers

Character	Definition
#	Numeric digit.
Z	Substitute blank for leading zero.
*	Substitute asterisk for leading zero.
$	Floating dollar: substitute blanks for leading zeroes, $ for last leading zero.
+ or -	Floating sign: substitute blanks for leading zeroes, minus for last one if value negative, plus or blank if positive (+ or -).

Insertion Characters

Character	Definition
CR or DR	CR or DR (credit/debit) if amount negative, two blanks if positive.
Trailing +	+ or - according to sign if '+' is last character in image item.
Trailing -	- or blank according to negative or positive sign if '-' is last character in image item.
. or ,	Character always inserted if it follows a V (implied decimal point); otherwise inserted if following a non-blank digit position. Treated as Z or floating $+- if following such a character which suppressed a zero.

Note that if multiple V's appear in an image item, the first implies decimal position and the rest are treated as unconditional insertion characters. If multiple CR or DR sequences appear in an image item, the last is taken as the credit/debit indicator and the rest are treated as unconditional insertion text.

Use of the special characters is illustrated by example.

Implied Decimal Position

The character V implies the position of a decimal point without occupying a character position in the record. This can be useful for representing non-integer values in the records of a file. For example, the image item @####V##@ would format the number 12.5 as 001250.

Decimal and Comma Insertion

The decimal point and comma characters are treated equivalently to allow optional use of European notation. Canadians might use image item @##,###V.##@ to format the number 10,259.37. Europeans might format the same number with image item @##.###V,##@ resulting in 10.259,37.

Zero Suppression, Asterisk Fill, Floating $

The following table shows a variety of numbers printed with image items that illustrate use of zero suppression (Z), asterisk fill (*) and floating dollar ($). Asterisk fill and floating dollar formats are particularly useful when printing cheques for preventing fraudulent addition of leading digits.

Number	@ZZ,ZZZV.##@	@$$,$$$V.##@	@**,***V.##@
123.45	123.45	$123.45	**,123.45
1234.56	1,234.56	$1,234.56	*1,234.56
1.23	1.23	$1.23	**,**1.23
.12	.12	$.12	**,***.12

Floating Sign

The following examples illustrate the use of floating plus or minus.

Number	@++,+++V.##@	@--,---V.##@
123.45	+123.45	123.45
-1234.56	-1,234.56	-1,234.56
-1.23	-1.23	-1.23
.12	+.12	.12

Trailing Sign

The use of + or - as the last character in an image item is illustrated below.

Number	@###V.##+@	@###V.##-@
123.45	123.45+	123.45
-12.34	012.34-	012.34-

Credit, Debit

Credit/debit notation can be useful for financial reports. The following examples illustrate use of this format.

Number	@ZZ,ZZZV.##CR@	@ZZ,ZZZV.##DR@
123.45	123.45	123.45
-1234.56	1,234.56CR	1,234.56DR
-1.23	1.23CR	1.23DR
.12	.12	.12

Insertion Characters

Use of insertion characters can be convenient for such things as displaying date and time. For example, image item @##/##/##@ might be used to format 800215 as the date 80/02/15 (February 15, 1980). Image item @##:##:##@ might be used to format 102135 in terms of hours, minutes and seconds, resulting in 10:21:35.

Picture Formats used with Strings

When used to format character string values, the characters of a picture item which are Digit Specifiers define character positions to be used for the string value. Other characters are treated as insertion characters. String values are processed starting with the leftmost Digit Specifier. Digit Specifier positions beyond the length of the string value are filled with blanks on output. For example, the string 'HOTDOG' printed with image item @### DIGGETY ###@ would display the result HOT DIGGETY DOG.

H-7 Status of Input/Output Operations

There always exists a possibility that an input/output operation may not be successful (see Error Handling). For example, an OPEN operation may fail because there is insufficient space to create a file. Similarly, an INPUT operation may fail due to a hardware or operational malfunction.

The standard action when an input/output error is detected is to terminate the execution of the program and to display an error message indicating the error. Common error situations are diagnosed by displaying an error message describing the error condition. Less frequent situations are diagnosed by indicating a general input/output error condition and displaying a system dependent error code.

The standard action can be overridden by executing an appropriate ON-error statement. The ON-error statement provides facilities to branch to specific statements when errors occur or to ignore errors. In these circumstances the presence of errors can be detected and the type of errors diagnosed by use of the IO_STATUS, or CODE built-in functions.

H-8 PRINT statement

Syntax: PRINT #file-ref, position-clause,
                  USING image-string, output-list

             MAT PRINT #file-ref, position-clause,
                  USING image-string, matrix-list

where   position-clause   is   either   'REC=expression'   or
'KEY=expression';

the output-list is a list, separated by commas, of numeric or
character expressions or matrices preceded by the keyword MAT;

and the matrix-list is a list of matrices.

Examples: PRINT #CUST_FILE, CUST$, BALANCE
             PRINT USING FORMAT$, MAT MARK
             MAT PRINT USING FORMAT$, MARK
             PRINT #5, REC=RECRD_NUMB, X,Y,Z
             PRINT #8, KEY=PART_NAME$, QUANTITY, PRICE

The PRINT statement is used to transmit a series of values
to an output file. The file to which the transmission occurs is
determined by the file reference number, if present. If no file
reference number is specified, the transmission is to the
terminal using a default file reference number of 1.

The REC= clause is optional. If present, it is used to
position the file for output at the record indicated by the
numeric expression in the clause. If the REC= clause is not
specified, output continues in the file from the position in the
file established by the last input/output operation.

PRINT statements used with keyed files must contain the
KEY= clause. The REC= clause must not be specified in PRINT
statements with keyed files. Refer to the section entitled File
Positioning for further information concerning keyed file PRINT
statements.

The USING clause is optional. If present, the image string
is used to determine the format of the data in the output file
(formatted output).   Otherwise, the data is transmitted
according to a default format (unformatted output).

Unformatted Output

Unformatted output occurs when no USING clause is present
in the PRINT statement. Numeric items are printed as numeric
constants with insignificant 0's removed. Character items are
displayed without any conversion.

The position on a record to which an item is transmitted is controlled by a comma or semi-colon separator between items and the size of the print zones into which a record may be divided. By default, the size of a print zone is 18 characters, although this may be altered by the PRTZO option. A comma separator causes the next item to be printed at the start of the next print zone. A semi-colon separator causes the next item to be printed immediately following the previous item.

Numeric values are transmitted according to the following rules:

(1) If the absolute value of the number is greater than .0000005 and less than 99999999999.5 then the absolute value (rounded to 11 significant digits) is converted to the form shown following:

##########.##########

where # represents a digit. Zeros preceding or trailing the number are then removed. When the resulting number is an integer, the decimal point is removed. This number is then displayed preceded by either a blank character (non-negative number) or a minus sign, and followed by a trailing space character.

(2) Otherwise the number is rounded to 7 significant digits and printed in scientific notation according to the following diagram:

S#.######ES##b

where:

the # characters represent digits. If the number is negative, a - sign is inserted in front of the number. The b is one blank space.

(3) When less than a print zone remains to be filled in the current record and a numeric value is to be transmitted, the record is written to the output file and transmission continues with the subsequent record in the file. This will result in an error when using keyed files, since each record must be identified with a specific key value.

If output is directed to the user's terminal, each row of a matrix is transmitted starting with a new record and an extra blank line is transmitted following each plane. The individual elements in each row are displayed as if they were separated by commas.

When the output list contains a null item (two separators in a row) nothing is transmitted. Each comma separator, however, causes the output position to move ahead to the next print zone. This provides a mechanism for skipping print zones.

When the output list has been terminated, the current
record is transmitted to the file, unless a semi-colon is used
to terminate the list. In this case, the current record is not
transmitted but is held internally to receive data when the next
PRINT statement is executed for this file.

Examples:

                                        Output

PRINT 1.2300   1.23
PRINT 4.12 E-6   4.120000E-06
PRINT .0014   .0014
PRINT -178.69   -178.69

DIM A (2,3,3) (BASE 1)   0   0   0
PRINT MAT A or   0   0   0
MAT PRINT A   0   0   0

                          0   0   0
                          0   0   0
                          0   0   0
                          | | |
                          | | COL (37)
                          | COL (19)
                          COL (1)

Formatted OUTPUT

When the USING keyword is specified, the character
expression following that keyword is used as an image string.
This image string controls the format of data transmitted to the
output file.

Data is transmitted to the file from items in the output
list and from the image string. The process is as follows:

(1) The image string is scanned until an image item is detected
     in the string. Any characters which are scanned that are
     not part of a format item are transmitted to the output
     file.

(2) When an image item is detected, the next element from the
     output list is transmitted according to the specifications
     of the image item.

(3) When the image string is exhausted, the current record is
     written to the output file, the next record begins
     receiving transmission, and the image string is reused
     starting at the beginning. When using keyed files, an
     error will result if output spills over onto the "next"

record due to exhaustion of the image string or filling of a record. Since keyed file records are associated with a unique key value, the concept of next sequential record is not defined for output.

(4) An error is detected if at least one item is present in the output list and no image items exist in the format string.

(5) When a record is completely filled, it is transmitted to the output file and the subsequent record starts to be filled.

(6) When the REC or KEY clause is present in the PRINT statement, the indicated record is filled starting at the beginning of that record. Otherwise, the next record filled is the one following the last one accessed.

(7) When the output list is terminated with a semi-colon character, the record is not written and the next print statement commences filling that record immediately following the last position filled.

When output is directed to a file or device other than the user's terminal, matrices are printed according to the image items of the image string just as if the individual elements of the matrix appeared in the output list. This allows matrices to be read with the INPUT statement using the same image string used to PRINT them. If output is directed to the user's terminal, at the start of each matrix row a new line is used for transmission and the image string is reused, starting at its beginning. In addition, when output is directed to the user's terminal, a blank record is transmitted at the end of each plane in the matrix.

Character strings are formatted according to the following rules:

(1) If the length of the character string exceeds the width of the image item, the character string is truncated to the width of the image item and transmitted to the record.

(2) Whenever a record is filled, it is written to the output file and transmission of the character output continues on the subsequent record.

(3) When right-justified I-format is specified, the character string is padded with blanks on the left to the width of the format item and then transmitted.

(4) When left-justified I-format is specified, the character string is padded on the right with blanks to the width of the format item and then transmitted.

(5) F-format, E-format and centered I-format items cause blanks to be added to both the left and right of the character string so that the string will be centered when transmitted.

Numeric values are transmitted according to the following rules:

(1) If less space remains on the current record than the width of the image item, the current record is written to the output file and transmission will occur to the subsequent record.

(2) With I-format, the value is rounded to an integer and transmitted using centered, right-justified, or left-justified format. With centered I-format, if the image item begins with a sign, then a sign is inserted preceding the number.

(3) With F-format, the value is rounded to the indicated number of decimal places and transmitted. If a sign character is the first character in the image item, then a sign is inserted preceding the number.

(4) With E-format (scientific notation), the value is rounded to the indicated number of places and transmitted. If a sign character is the first character in the image item, then a sign is inserted preceding the number.

(5) When an image item is too small to represent the value of the number to be transmitted, it is filled with asterisks.

Examples

Format String	Item	Output
'##.##'	1.237	b1.24
'#####'	7	bb7bb
'>###'	16	b16
'<####'	191	191b
'##.###'	-.0012	-0.001
'+##.##'	.41	b+0.41

Refer to the section entitled Image Items for a description of output using image items enclosed in at-symbols (@).

H-9   INPUT Statement

Syntax: INPUT #file-ref, position-clause,
                     USING image-string, input-list

              MAT INPUT #file-ref, position-clause,
                     USING image-string, matrix-list

where position-clause is 'REC=expression', 'KEY=expression' or
'KEY>=expression';

the input-list is a list, separated by commas, of numeric or
character variables or matrices preceded by the keyword MAT;

and the matrix list is a list of matrices.

The INPUT statement is used to transmit data from a file to
a number of variables and/or matrices. The file from which the
transmission occurs is determined by the file reference number,
if present.   If no file reference number is specified, the
transmission occurs from the terminal using a default file
reference number of 0.   When input is requested from a user
terminal, a prompt (?) is normally displayed on the terminal to
indicate that the program is ready to accept input.   This
feature may be disabled by the NOPROMPT option.

The REC= clause is optional. If present, it is used to
position the file for input at the record indicated by the
numeric expression in the clause.   If the REC=clause is not
specified,   input   occurs   from   the position in the file
established by the last input/output operation on that file.

The KEY= or KEY>= clause can be used to specify file
positioning with keyed files.   The REC clause must not be
specified in INPUT statements with keyed files. The KEY clause
is optional.   Refer to the section entitled File Positioning for
further information concerning keyed file INPUT statements.

The USING clause is optional. If present, the image string
is used to determine the format of the data to be transmitted
(formatted input).   Otherwise, the data is scanned from records
in the file (unformatted input).

Unformatted Input

When no USING keyword is specified, the input is scanned
from the file.   Individual items of data are separated from one
another by commas or by the end of a record.   Numeric data is
accepted in any form allowed by the BASIC language in BASIC
statements.   Character data is whatever is entered with the
trailing spaces and leading spaces removed. A null string is
assigned when the input consists only of spaces.

Scanning data items starts at the beginning of the record specified in the REC or KEY clause if it is present. If no REC or KEY clause is specified, the scanning starts wherever it finished on the previous input/output operation. When all items in the input-list have had data assigned to them, the next scan position is set to the beginning of the next record, unless a semi-colon is added at the end of the input list. In this case, the next scan position will be immediately following the last item scanned.

An INPUT statement may process several records.

Formatted Input

The character expression, called the image string, in the USING clause indicates the location and the length of the data to be transmitted to the items in the input list. Normally, the same image string, used to PRINT the data to a file, is also used to INPUT that data.

The transmission of data is controlled by simultaneously scanning the image string (starting at the beginning) and the current record. If the REC or KEY clause is specified, the indicated record is processed starting at its beginning, otherwise, record scanning continues from where it finished on the last input/output operation. The transmission process involves locating the position and then transmitting the data. The format information is outlined below.

When an item is to be assigned a value, the following positioning process occurs:

(1) The image string is scanned until an image item is detected. An equal number of characters in the input record are skipped.

(2) When the end of the image string is encountered, the image string is reused and scanning commences at the start of the image string; this also causes the next record to be read and to be processed as noted above.

(3) When the end of a record is encountered, the next record is read and scanning continues. This does not affect scanning of the image string.

(4) It is an error if the input list contains at least one item and the image string contains no image items.

At this point, the image item in the image string determines the data to be transmitted.

(1) When a numeric item is to be assigned a value, if there is insufficient space on the current record to contain the

item, according to the image item, the next record is read. Only the width of the image item is significant. The number to be assigned is extracted from the record, in consecutive positions for the size of the format item.

(2) When a character item is to be assigned a value, the width of the image item determines the size of the character string to be transmitted.

Refer to the section entitled Image Items for a description of INPUT using image items enclosed in at-symbols (@).

When the entire input list has been assigned values, the following positioning occurs.

(1) The image string is scanned until the next image item is located or until the end of the string is encountered. An equal number of characters in the current record is skipped. When the end of that record is encountered, the next record is read and the skipping of characters continues.

(2) If the input list was not terminated by a semi-colon, the next scan position in the input file is established at the start of the next record; otherwise, the next scan position does not change.

Examples:

```
INPUT      #10,USING '##. #.##. >####',X,Y,A$
INPUT      #10,USING '##,##',X,Y,Z
INPUT      #INFILE, REC=REC_PTR,USING FMT$,MAT A
```

H-10 LINPUT Statement

      Syntax: LINPUT #file-ref, position-clause, variable

                  where position-clause is 'REC=expression', 'KEY=expression' or 'KEY>=expression'.

      Example: LINPUT RECORD$
                  LINPUT #4, CUST_REC$
                  LINPUT #XFILE, REC=CUST_NUMB, CREC$
                  LINPUT #8,KEY=NAME$, MEANING$

The LINPUT statement is used to transmit an entire record to a character variable or to an element of a character matrix. The file from which the transmission occurs is established by the file reference number, if present. Otherwise, the transmission is from the terminal using a default file reference number of 0. When input is requested from a user terminal, a

prompt (?) is normally displayed on the terminal to indicate
that the program is ready to accept input. This feature may be
disabled by the NOPROMPT option.

The REC= clause is optional. If present, it is used to
position the file for input at the record indicated by the
numeric expression in the clause. If the REC= clause is not
specified, input of the next record in the file will occur.

The KEY= or KEY>= clause can be used to specify file
positioning with keyed files. The REC clause must not be
specified in LINPUT statements with keyed files. The KEY clause
is optional. Refer to the section entitled File Positioning for
further information concerning keyed file LINPUT statements.

Trailing blank characters are removed during transmission
of the record to the specified character variable unless the
program option NOTRIM is specified. Refer to the section which
describes the OPTION statement for information concerning
NOTRIM.

H-11 SCRATCH Statement

Syntax: SCRATCH   character expression

Example: SCRATCH   'DATA'

            SCRATCH   OLD_FILE$

The SCRATCH statement is used to erase a file from the
computer system. The character expression specifies the name of
the file to be scratched. If the filename specified is that of
a keyed file, both the key (index) file and its associated data
file are erased.

H-12 Special File Names

Two special file names are defined in order to be able to
easily use the terminal as a file:

.KBIN -   terminal as input file
.KBOUT -   terminal as output file

Thus, it is possible to use the terminal as either an input or
output file. It is only possible to open .KBIN for input and to
open .KBOUT for output.

Other special file names may be used in specific systems. Refer to the chapters on System Dependencies for these names.

Additional special file names may be defined using the ASSIGN command. These may be displayed with the SHOW command. Refer to the System Command sections describing the ASSIGN and SHOW commands for further information.

H-13 REMOVE Statement

Syntax: REMOVE #file-ref, KEY=expression

where expression defines a character value

Example: REMOVE #3, KEY='HENRY'

The REMOVE statement removes a key value from a keyed file index. The associated data record is released so that it may be re-used for another record associated with a new key value. Refer to the section entitled File Positioning for more information concerning keyed files.

REMOVE statements may only be used with keyed files opened in OUTPUT, OUTIN or INOUT modes.

H-14 LOCK, UNLOCK Statements

Refer to the chapter entitled "System Dependencies: IBM Series/1 (CPS)" for information concerning record interlock facilities for controlling simultaneous multiple access to files.

H-15 RENAME Statement

Syntax: RENAME 'filename1' TO 'filename2'

where filename1 and filename2 are character-valued expressions

The RENAME statement changes the name of a file. The first filename indicates the name to be changed and the second filename specifies the new name. System-dependent restrictions apply to the class of filenames that may be changed. Refer to the chapters concerning System Dependencies for further information.

H-16 <u>Built-In</u> <u>Functions</u> <u>Used</u> <u>With</u> <u>Input/Output</u>

Several built-in functions exist to enable programs to determine the characteristics of files and records. Functions used to diagnose error conditions are described in the chapter entitled Error Handling.

<u>BLKSIZE (file-ref)</u>

This function returns a numeric value equal to the block size of the file associated with the file reference number parameter.

<u>RECSIZE (file-ref)</u>

This function returns a numeric value equal to the record size of the file associated with the file reference number parameter.

<u>RECNUM (file-ref)</u>

This function returns a numeric value equal to the relative record number of the last record accessed in the file associated with the file reference number parameter. If the parameter is not specified, the relative record number of the last record accessed in any file is returned. This function may not be used with keyed files.

<u>KEYVAL$ (file-ref)</u>

This function returns a character value containing the key value corresponding to the last record accessed in the keyed file associated with the file reference number parameter.

<u>KEYLEN (file-ref)</u>

This function returns a numeric value equal to the maximum key length permitted for the keyed file associated with the file reference number parameter.

<u>FILE$ (file-ref)</u>

This function returns a character value containing the name of the file associated with the file reference number parameter.

<u>FILE_DEFAULT$</u>

This function returns a character value containing the user's default filename subset. With the Series/1 CPS version of Waterloo BASIC, this subset is applied automatically as a prefix to simple filenames.

I. READ, DATA, RESTORE Statements

I-1 Introduction

DATA statements are used to define a list of data items which can be transferred to variables using the READ statement. This provides an alternative to files as a means to provide data values for assignment to variables. The RESTORE statement is used to make the list of variables available at the start of the list.

Items appearing in DATA statements occur on the list of items to be transferred according to the order of DATA statements in the program. When the program is placed into execution, by the RUN command, the next item to be transferred is the first item in the list. As READ statements are executed, the items in this list are transferred to items specified in the READ statements. If a READ statement exhausts the list and more transfers are requested, an error occurs. The RESTORE statement may be used to make the next available item to be transferred the first item in the list.

I-2 DATA Statement

Syntax: DATA   item, item, ..., item

where item is a numeric constant, a character string in single or double quotation characters, or a sequence of zero or more characters.

Examples: DATA   433, 'CHARLIE BROWN' , 17E1
            DATA   43.3E1, CHARLIE BROWN ,170

The DATA statement is a non-executable statement that causes an internal data list to be created. The DATA-list constants are supplied to variables and matrix elements specified in corresponding READ or MAT READ statements.

At the beginning of program execution, a list containing all the constants, in their order of appearance by statement number, is built from all the DATA statements. At the same time, a conceptual pointer is set to the first constant in the list. The pointer is advanced through the DATA-list, constant by constant, as the data is supplied to variables in READ or MAT READ statements. The pointer can be to relocated to point to the first constant again by the RESTORE statement.

The length of character constants to be assigned to character variables is limited only by line length.

Notes:

(1)   Each datum in the data sequence is delimited by a comma or by the end of the statement. Leading and trailing space characters are not significant in these data values and are removed. The resulting value must be a recognizable numeric constant if a numeric value is required. When leading or trailing spaces are required for character values, the data must be enclosed in quotation characters.

(2)   DATA statements can be placed anywhere in a program, either before or after the READ statements to which they supply data.

(3)   An error will occur if DATA statements do not contain enough constants for the READ statements issued.

(4)   The DATA statement must be the last statement in that statement line and cannot be continued.

(5)   The remark clause (!) is not permitted on a DATA statement.

(6)   If the DATA statement list is edited (i.e., DATA statements added, deleted, changed or replaced) while the program is in a paused or interrupted state, the conceptual data list pointer is set to end of list. Thus, it will be necessary to execute a RESTORE statement (in the program or in immediate-mode) before executing another READ when the program is continued.

Example:

A sample DATA statement is as shown:

        110 DATA "BILL",21.60,CHARGE,15.40

In this example, the character constants (BILL and CHARGE) and the arithmetic constants (21.60 and 15.40) are inserted into the internal data list.

I-3 __READ__ Statement

Syntax: READ item, item, ..., item
            MAT READ matrix, matrix, ..., matrix

where item is a variable, a subscripted matrix element, or a matrix preceded by the keyword MAT.

Examples: READ LINE_SIZE, PAGE_DEPTH
            READ MAT PRICE, PROFIT_FACTOR
            MAT READ PRICE

The READ statement is used to transfer data from the list of items specified in DATA statements.

At the beginning of program execution, a conceptual pointer is set to the first value in the data list. When a READ statement is encountered, successive values from the internal data list are assigned to the variables or matrix elements in a READ statement, or to entire arrays in the MAT READ statement. The values are assigned to the array by rows, beginning at the current position of the internal data file pointer. The internal DATA-list pointer can be reset by use of the RESTORE statement.

Subscripts of array variables in the READ statement are evaluated as they occur; thus, an assigned variable in a READ statement can be used subsequently as the subscript of another variable to the right of the assigned variable in the same statement.

Notes:

(1) If there are no DATA statements in the program, execution of the READ statement will cause an error.

(2) Each value read from the internal DATA-list must be of the same type (character or arithmetic) as the variable to which it is assigned. (See DATA statement).

__Examples__:

The following shows the execution of READ statements:

```
5   OPTION BASE 1
10  DATA 'JONES', 15.00, 'SMITH',20.50
20  READ A$,A1,B$,B1
30  DATA 1,2,3,4,5,6
40  READ A,B,C,X(A),X(B),X(C)
```

After execution of these statements, the character variables A$ and B$ will contain the character strings JONES and SMITH, respectively. The arithmetic variables A1 and B1 will contain the decimal values 15.00 and 20.50, respectively. The arithmetic variables A, B, and C will contain the integer values 1, 2, and 3, respectively, and the first three elements of the one-dimensional matrix X will contain the integer values 4, 5, and 6, respectively.

I-4   RESTORE

   Syntax: RESTORE

   The RESTORE statement restores the DATA-list conceptual pointer to the first item in the first DATA statement of the program.

Notes:

(1)   A RESTORE statement in a program that contains no DATA statements is ignored.

(2)   A RESTORE statement for an already RESTOREd data table pointer is ignored.

Example:

   After the following statements are executed, the variables A and C will each have a value of 1, and B and D will each have a value of 2:

```
10 DATA 1,2
20 READ A,B
30 RESTORE
40 READ C,D
```

J-1 Introduction

The statements described in this chapter are termed "unstructured control statements". Strictly speaking, there is no requirement that they be included in Waterloo BASIC since it is possible to accomplish their functions by other means. However, since an extensive collection of programs already is written using these statements, they have been included in the language. Many of the other dialects of BASIC do not have any structured control statements. Programs written in these dialects are forced to have these statements for a control purpose.

J-2 GOTO Statement

Syntax: GOTO line-number
               GO TO line-number

Examples   GOTO 4092
               GO TO 967

The execution of this statement causes control to be transferred to the statement on the line number indicated.

J-3 ON-GOTO Statement

Syntax: ON expression GOTO line-number-list
               ON expression GOTO line-number-list NONE line-number

Examples: ON TYPE+CLASS GOTO 8000,8000,9000
               ON X GOTO 5000,7000,8000 NONE 4000

The execution of this statement causes control to be transferred to one of the lines in the list of line numbers, depending on the value of the expression. The numeric expression is evaluated and rounded to be an integer value. If the resulting value is 1, control is transferred to the statement at the first line number in the list; if the result is 2, control is transferred to the statement at the second line number in the list; if the result is N, control is transferred to the statement at the N-th line number in the list.

Control is transferred to the statement at the line number specified in the NONE clause if the result of the expression evaluation is less than one or larger than the number of line numbers in the list. If the NONE clause is not specified, an error is detected when the expression result does not indicate a line number in the list.

J-4   GOSUB and RETURN Statements

  Syntax: GOSUB line-number
        RETURN

  Examples: GOSUB 10432
        RETURN

  The GOSUB and RETURN statements can be used jointly to create subroutines. A subroutine is a sequence of statements, the last one of which is a RETURN statement, that can be invoked for execution by the GOSUB statement. When the GOSUB statement is executed, control is transferred to the statement specified in the GOSUB statement. When the RETURN statement is executed, control is transferred to the statement following the GOSUB statement.

Consider the following program (lines 600-700 from a subroutine):

```
100      GOSUB   600
120      GOSUB   600
130      STOP
600      PRINT 'HI THERE'
700      RETURN
800      END
```

The output produced by this program is as follows:

```
HI THERE
HI THERE
```

In the execution of the sample program, the following statements were executed:

  100, 600, 700, 120, 600, 700, 130

Each time the GOSUB statement was executed, the statement following the GOSUB was remembered so that control could be passed to it when the RETURN statement was executed.

  At any time during the execution of a program, there exist a number of active GOSUB statements. The execution of a RETURN statement causes control to be transferred to the statement following the last active GOSUB statement. When the RETURN occurs, that GOSUB statement becomes inactive.

```
100      GOSUB      200
110      GOSUB      300
120      STOP
200      PRINT 'LINE 200'
210      GOSUB      400
220      RETURN
300      PRINT 'LINE 300'
310      GOSUB      200
320      RETURN
400      PRINT 'LINE 400'
410      RETURN
500      END
```

The output produced by executing the previous program is as follows:

```
LINE     200
LINE     400
LINE     300
LINE     200
LINE     400
```

and the order in which statements were executed is as follows:

```
100, 200, 210, 400, 410, 220, 110, 300,
310, 200, 210, 400, 410, 220, 320, 120
```

Additional Rules About GOSUB And RETURN

(1) It is an error to attempt to execute a RETURN statement when no active GOSUB statements exist.

(2) A diagnostic message is issued when a program completes execution with any active GOSUB statements.

J-5   ON-GOSUB Statement

Syntax: ON expression GOSUB line-number-list
            ON expression GOSUB line-number-list NONE line-number

Examples: ON TYPE+CLASS GOSUB 700,800,900
            ON X GOSUB 700,700,420,600 NONE 300

The execution of this statement causes control to be transferred, in same way as if a GOSUB statement were executed, to one of the lines in the list of line numbers, depending on the value of the expression. This statement is identical to the ON-GOTO statement except that transfer of control is accomplished using a GOSUB instead of a GOTO.

J-6   **IF-THEN** Statement

Syntax: IF expression THEN statement
              IF expression THEN line-number
              IF expression THEN statement ELSE statement
              IF expression THEN statement ELSE line-number
              IF expression THEN line-number ELSE statement
              IF expression THEN line-number ELSE line-number

Examples: IF X > 4 THEN Y = Z + K
              IF DEBUG$ = 'YES' THEN PRINT 'LINE 400'
              IF Z = 1 THEN 400 ELSE 500
              IF COST > 100   THEN 800

The execution of an IF-THEN statement is used to select for execution either the THEN clause or the ELSE clause. When the numeric expression evaluates as true (non-zero) the THEN clause is selected. Otherwise, the ELSE clause, if present, is selected. When the expression is false (zero) and no ELSE clause is specified, control is transferred to the next statement following the IF statement.

The THEN clause and the ELSE clause specify either a statement to be executed or a line number to which control is to be transferred. When the associated clause is selected, the statement in the clause is executed or control is transferred to the line in question.

J-7   **FOR** and **NEXT** Statements

Syntax: FOR var = expression TO expression
              ....
              NEXT var

              FOR var = expression TO   expression
                                        STEP expression
              ....
              NEXT var

Examples: FOR I=1 TO N
                 PRINT I, I**2
              NEXT I

              FOR X = 100 TO 0 STEP   -.5
                 PRINT X, X*1.07
              NEXT X

The FOR and NEXT statements may be used in pairs to create loops. The FOR statement is used to mark the start of the loop and the NEXT statement is used to mark the end of the loop. The statements between these statements form the body of the loop.

The FOR and the NEXT statement both specify a numeric variable, called the control variable for the loop. This variable is assigned the value for the expression to the immediate right of the = character in the FOR statement. This assignment occurs when the FOR statement is initially executed. At the same time the expression to the immediate right of the TO keyword is evaluated and internally saved by Waterloo BASIC. This value is called the terminal value for the loop. At the same time the expression to the immediate right of the STEP keyword is evaluated and the value is internally saved by Waterloo BASIC. This value is called the increment for the loop. If no STEP keyword is present, an incremental value of 1 is used.

The execution of a FOR/NEXT loop causes the body of the loop to be executed a number of times. At the start of each iteration the control variable is compared to the boundary value. The loop terminates when one of the following conditions is true:

(1) the increment value is non-negative and the control variable is greater than the terminal value.

(2) the increment value is negative and the control variable is less than the terminal value.

At the end of each loop, the increment is added to the control variable. A FOR-NEXT loop may be executed zero times, provided one of the two preceding conditions is true.

K. Miscellaneous Statements

K-1 Introduction

This chapter describes several statements which do not fall into any of the categories described in other chapters.

K-2 OPTION Statement

Syntax: OPTION   option option .... option

The OPTION statement is used to inform the Waterloo BASIC system of certain global information to be used to control the execution of a program. For example, the NOPROMPT/PROMPT option is used to determine whether or not '?' prompts are to be displayed on a user terminal when the program is ready to accept input from the terminal.

Some options may be entered at most once per program. These options are non-executable and may be entered anywhere in the program. These options affect the entire program and take effect as soon as the program is placed into execution. Other options are executable. They take effect when the OPTION statement is executed. These options may be entered a number of times in each program.

BASE 0 Or BASE 1

These options are used to establish the lower extent of all dimensions of matrices. When BASE 0 is in effect, each dimension starts with 0; when BASE 1 is in effect, each dimension starts with 1. This option is non-executable. It may be entered at most once per program. If no BASE option is present, each dimension starts at 0.

LPREC Or SPREC

These options are used to establish the precision maintained internally for numeric quantities. When LPREC (long precision) is specified, numbers have 16 digits of precision. When SPREC (short precision) is specified, numbers have 6 digits of precision. In certain circumstances, large programs may execute in less time when SPREC is used. At most, one of these options may be specified. If neither is specified, LPREC takes effect. The option is not executable.

NOTRIM

This option specifies that entire records are to be transmitted to the character variable specified in a LINPUT statement, without trimming of trailing blanks. If this option is not specified, trailing blanks of a record are not transmitted to the character variable of a LINPUT statement.

PROMPT Or NOPROMPT

These options are used to specify whether or not a '?' should be displayed on the terminal when a program is ready to receive data from that terminal. The NOPROMPT option can be used to disable this feature. These options, not being executable, may occur at most once per program, and may not both be specified.

PRTZO Expression

This executable option is used to set the width of print zones to be used with the PRINT statement when unformatted output is being produced. Normally, the size of a print zone is 18 characters. Execution of an OPTION statement with this option can reset the zone width to any size between 14 and the record size of a file. The numeric expression following the PRTZO keyword is evaluated and rounded to be an integer value.

K-3 STOP Statement

Syntax: STOP

The STOP statement is used to terminate execution of a program. The CONTINUE command may not be used for a program which has been terminated in this manner.

K-4   PAUSE Statement

Syntax: PAUSE

The PAUSE statement is used to suspend execution of a program. When the execution of this statement causes suspension of a program, a diagnostic message is displayed on the terminal indicating the line number of the line where the program was suspended.

This statement is often used when debugging programs. While the program is suspended, immediate-mode statements can be entered and executed. The program and/or data values can be changed. Execution of the program can be resumed by the CONTINUE command.

K-5   RANDOMIZE Statement

Syntax: RANDOMIZE

The RANDOMIZE statement causes an unpredictable starting point to be selected for the generation of random numbers using the RND built-in function. A predictable starting point can be selected by using the RND function (see RND function).

L.   Error Handling

L-1   Error Conditions

There are many potential situations in which errors can occur in a program. Some programs are written under the assumption that errors will never occur. In this case, should an error occur, an error message will be displayed at the user terminal and a standard system action (usually suspending the program) will be performed.

In other cases, it may be important that some errors be handled by a program. The ON-error statement provides a capability to select the error recovery method appropriate for various classes of errors. This statement is described in the next section. The various classes of errors are outlined in this section.

CONV

The CONV error condition occurs when a conversion error is detected. This may happen when an input field cannot be converted to a value for a variable (INPUT or READ statements or VALUE function). This condition may arise when an invalid numeric datum is attempted to be assigned or transferred to a numeric variable.

ATTN

The ATTN error condition occurs when the "attention" key is pressed on a terminal.

SOFLOW

The SOFLOW condition occurs when a string overflow occurs, i.e., when a string operation produces a string with more than 65,535 characters.

OFLOW

The OFLOW condition occurs when a numeric overflow occurs, i.e., when a numeric operation produces a result whose magnitude is larger than the capacity of the computer. The largest number the computer can store is typically greater than 10E70.

UFLOW

The UFLOW condition occurs when a numeric underflow occurs, i.e., when a numeric operation produces a non-zero result whose magnitude is smaller than the capacity of the computer. The smallest non-zero number a computer can store is typically less than 10E-70.

ZDIV

The ZDIV condition occurs when an attempt is made to divide a number by zero.

EOF

The EOF condition occurs when an attempt is made to sequentially read or write a record beyond the extent of a file.

IOERR

An IOERR condition occurs when an error occurs in an input/output statement. These errors do not include errors which are already classified by other conditions (i.e., EOF, OFLOW, CONV).

ERR

The ERR condition occurs when any error occurs that is not already classified as another condition.

L-2 ON-Error Statement

        Syntax: ON   error-condition   GOTO line-number
                     ON   error-condition   SYSTEM
                     ON   error-condition   IGNORE

The execution of an ON-error statement causes the system reaction for an error condition to be modified. When a program begins execution, there is a default system action performed for each class of error. Some errors can be ignored when they occur; this is specified by the IGNORE clause. Other errors can cause control to be transferred to a specific line-number; this is specified by the GOTO clause. Any error may be reset to be handled by the standard system action by the SYSTEM clause.

The following table specifies the actions to be performed when the various error conditions occur.

USER SPECIFIED ACTION

ON	IGNORE	{GOTO} Line Num	SYSTEM
ATTN	**not allowed**	No user Message Transfer Control	program is suspended
CONV	No User Message No Data Transferred Continue	No User Message No Data Transferred Transfer Control	User Message Fatal Error Stop
ERR	**not allowed**	No User Message No Data Transferred Transfer Control	User Message Fatal Error Stop
SOFLOW	**not allowed**	No User Message No Data Transferred Transfer Control	User Message Fatal Error Stop
OFLOW	No User Message Replace With Signed Infinity Continue	No User Message Replace With Signed Infinity Transfer Control	User Message Replace With Signed Infinity Continue
UFLOW	No User Message Replace With Zero Continue	No User Message Replace With Zero Transfer Control	User Message Replace With Zero Continue
ZDIV	No User Message Replace With Signed Infinity Continue	No User Message Replace With Signed Infinity Transfer Control	User Message Replace With Signed Infinity Continue
EOF	No User Message Continue	No User Message Transfer Control	User Message Fatal Error Stop
IOERR	No User Message Continue	No User Message Transfer Control	User Message Fatal Error Stop

ON Condition Actions

L-3 Built-In Functions Used With Errors

Several built-in functions exist to enable programs to diagnose error conditions.

LINE

This function returns a numeric value equal to the number of the line where the program was last suspended or where the last error occurred.

IO_STATUS

When used without a parameter, the IO_STATUS function returns a numeric value which indicated the status of the last input/output operation. If a parameter is specified, the numeric parameter is treated as a file reference number and the status value applies to the last input/output operation on the particular file specified. When the parameter is specified and the file in question is not open, a value of -1 is returned.

The possible return values are as follows:

```
-1  -  file not open
 0  -  last input/output operation completed successfully
 1  -  end-of-file detected on last operation
 2  -  no record was located on last input operation
 3  -  last operation specified has an invalid access mode
       (that is, writing on a file opened for input)
 4  -  a system error was detected
 5  -  file attempted to be opened a second time
 6  -  insufficient memory for allocation of file buffers
 7  -  invalid file name was specified
 8  -  conversion error during input or output
(9,10 - not applicable to interactive BASIC)
11  -  file system resources utilized
       (e.g. maximum number of open files exceeded)
12  -  not a valid keyed file; index file header format
       invalid
13  -  specified key not found
14  -  no key clause or record overflow on output to
       keyed file
15  -  invalid key length specification in keyed file
       OPEN for OUTPUT
16  -  specified file attributes conflict with
       attributes defined at file creation
       (e.g. record size, block size)
17  -  invalid or conflicting file attributes specified
18  -  keyed datafile name qualified, null or blank
       in OPEN for OUTPUT
19  -  open access mode conflicts with ASSIGNed
       access limitations
```

The IO_STATUS function should not be used without parameters in PRINT statements. The values PRINTed will be zero since they apply to the file referenced by the PRINT statement.

CODE

When used without a parameter, this function returns the system-dependent status of the last input/output operation. A numeric parameter is treated as a file reference number and the result gives the system-dependent status for the file in question. When the parameter is specified and the file in question is not open, a value of 0 is returned. This function should be used only in programs which will run on a single computer system, as the status values usually differ from system to system. The values which may arise are usually documented as part of a particular system's documentation. The CODE function should not be used without parameters in PRINT statements. The values PRINTed will be zero since they apply to the file referenced by the PRINT statement.

CONVDAT$

This function returns a character value containing the data item that caused the last conversion error during execution of a program.

ERROR

This function returns a numeric value equal to the internal error code corresponding to the last error encountered during execution of a program.

ERROR$

This function returns a character value containing the error message text corresponding to the last error encountered during execution of a program. A numeric parameter value may be specified which equals an internal error code to obtain the corresponding error message text.

L-4 RESUME Statement

        Syntax: RESUME

            or   RESUME NEXT

The RESUME statement can be used to "return" from processing an error condition. RESUME is only valid when an ON error-condition GOTO statement has been executed. The RESUME statement returns execution control to the beginning of the statement that caused the error-condition. The RESUME NEXT

statement returns execution control to the statement following
that which caused the error condition.

L-5 Error Handling Example

     The following program illustrates error handling with
files.   After each input/output operation, the status is
checked. When an error situation arises, the value of IO_STATUS
is inspected to determine the type of error message to be
displayed.

```
0100 ! PROGRAM TO ILLUSTRATE ERROR HANDLING WITH FILES
0110 !
0120 OPTION NOPROMPT
0123 ON EOF IGNORE
0124 ON IOERR IGNORE
0130 IF FN_OPEN_INPUT
0140    IF FN_OPEN_OUTPUT
0150       INVOKE= FN_COPY_FILE
0160       CLOSE #3
0170       INVOKE= FN_CHECK_CLOSE
0180    ENDIF
0190    CLOSE #2
0200    INVOKE= FN_CHECK_CLOSE
0210 ENDIF
0220 STOP
1000 !
1010 ! FUNCTION USED TO COPY FILE
1020 !
1030 DEF FN_COPY_FILE
1040    LOOP
1050       LINPUT #2,RECORD$
1060       IF FN_CHECK INPUT THEN QUIT
1070       PRINT #3,RECORD$
1080       IF FN_CHECK_OUTPUT THEN QUIT
1090    ENDLOOP
1100 FNEND
2000 !
2010 ! FUNCTION USED TO OPEN INPUT FILE
2020 !
2030 DEF FN_OPEN_INPUT
2040    PRINT 'ENTER INPUT FILE NAME'
2050    LINPUT FILE_NAME$
2060    OPEN #2, FILE_NAME$, INPUT
2070    FN_OPEN_INPUT = FN_CHECK_OPEN
2080 FNEND
```

```
3000 !
3010 ! FUNCTION USED TO OPEN OUTPUT FILE
3020 !
3030 DEF FN_OPEN_OUTPUT
3040   PRINT 'ENTER OUTPUT FILE NAME'
3050   LINPUT FILE_NAME$
3060   OPEN #3, FILE_NAME$, OUTPUT
3070   FN_OPEN_OUTPUT = FN_CHECK_OPEN
3080 FNEND
4000 !
4010 ! FUNCTION TO CHECK STATUS OF OPEN
4020 !
4030 DEF FN_CHECK_OPEN
4035   IO_STAT = IO_STATUS
4037   IO_CODE = CODE
4040   IF IO_STAT = 0
4050     FN_CHECK_OPEN = 1
4060   ELSE
4070     IF IO_STAT = 3
4080       PRINT 'INVALID ACCESS MODE'
4090     ELSEIF IO_STAT = 5
4100       PRINT 'FILE ALREADY OPEN'
4110     ELSEIF IO_STAT = 7
4120       PRINT 'INVALID FILE NAME'
4130     ELSE
4140       PRINT 'SYSTEM ERROR: IO_STATUS =';IO_STAT; &
4150 &                         'CODE =';IO_CODE
4160     ENDIF
4170     FN_CHECK_OPEN = 0
4180   ENDIF
4190 FNEND
5000 !
5010 ! FUNCTION TO CHECK STATUS OF LINPUT
5020 !
5030 DEF FN_CHECK_INPUT
5040   IF IO_STATUS(2)=0
5050     FN_CHECK_INPUT = 0
5060   ELSE
5070     IF IO_STATUS(2)<>1
5080       INVOKE= FN_CHECK_IO(2)
5090     ENDIF
5100     FN_CHECK_INPUT = 1
5110   ENDIF
5120 FNEND
```

```
6000 !
6010 ! FUNCTION TO CHECK STATUS OF PRINT
6020 !
6030 DEF FN_CHECK_OUTPUT
6040    IF IO_STATUS(3)=0
6050       FN_CHECK_OUTPUT = 0
6060    ELSE
6070       INVOKE= FN_CHECK_IO(3)
6080       FN_CHECK_OUTPUT = 1
6090    ENDIF
6100 FNEND
7000 !
7010 ! FUNCTION TO CHECK STATUS OF I/O
7020 !
7030 DEF FN_CHECK_IO(UNIT)
7040    PRINT 'SYSTEM ERROR: IO_STATUS =';IO_STATUS(UNIT); &
7045 &                      'CODE =';IO_CODE
7050 FNEND
8000 !
8010 ! FUNCTION TO CHECK STATUS OF CLOSE
8015 !
8020 DEF FN_CHECK_CLOSE
8030    IO_STAT = IO_STATUS
8040    IO_CODE = CODE
8045    IF IO_STAT<>0
8050       PRINT 'SYSTEM ERROR IN CLOSE: IO_STATUS =';STAT; &
8055 &                      'CODE =';IO_CODE
8060    ENDIF
8070 FNEND
65000 END
```

M.   CHAIN/USE

M-1 Using CHAIN And USE

     The CHAIN statement can be used to transfer control to
another program. Thus, a system may be written as a series of
programs, each one of which performs a specific function.

     The CHAIN statement can specify a list of expressions and
matrices to be passed to the program which is to receive
control. The execution of the USE statement causes the values
of these expressions and the values in the matrices to be
assigned to variables and matrices, respectively, in the program
which received control.

M-2 CHAIN Statement

     Syntax: CHAIN expression, param, param, ..., param

where expression is a character expression which is the name of
the file containing the program to receive control;

and where param is either an expression or a matrix preceded by
the keyword MAT.

     Example: CHAIN 'COSTER', MAT PRICE, PROFIT
               CHAIN 'UTSORT', 'MYFILE'
               CHAIN 'MAIN'
               CHAIN CALLER$

     The execution of a CHAIN statement causes control to be
transferred to a program in the file indicated by the character
expression immediately following the CHAIN keyword. The program
to receive control must have been placed in the file using the
STORE or STOREOBJ command. When no parameters are specified,
the action of the statement is equivalent to issuing a LOAD
command followed by a RUN command.

     Data may be passed to the program to receive control by
including parameters following the file name in the CHAIN
statement. These parameters may be numeric expressions,
character expressions, or entire matrices (in which case the MAT
keyword must be used). These values are stored internally and
may be assigned to variables in the program which receives
control (see USE statement).

     The environment of the program which executes a CHAIN
statement is replaced by the environment of the program which
receives control. Thus, all data values of the original program

are lost and all open files in the original program are closed.
When the new program begins execution, the environment in which
it executes is identical to that which is created by issuing the
RUN command.

M-3   <u>USE</u> Statement

       Syntax: USE param, param, ..., param

where param is either a variable name or a matrix name   preceded
by the keyword MAT.

       Examples: USE   MAT PRICE_MAT, PROF
                   USE   FILE_NAME$

       The execution of a USE statement causes the values of
parameters, passed by a CHAIN statement, to be assigned to
variables and matrices.   There must be the same number   of
parameters specified in the USE statement as were present in the
CHAIN statement.   The values are assigned to items according   to
the position of the items in the USE statement.   Items must have
the same type (character, numeric, character array,   or   numeric
array) as the value which occurred in the CHAIN statement.

N.   GUESS/ADMIT and QUIT Statements

N-1   Introduction

A common situation in programming occurs where two or more
alternative situations exist, but there is no data available to
use in an IF statement to select which alternative to execute.
For example, suppose three records are to be accessed with a
LINPUT statement. Two alternatives exist: no input/ output
errors will be encountered or at least one error will be
detected. An IF statement cannot be used since it is not
possible to determine if an input/output error will occur until
the actual operation is attempted.

In such situations, it is convenient to "guess" one of the
alternatives (i.e., no input/output errors will occur) is true
and to commence processing that choice. Part of the processing
of that choice must validate that the selection was correctly
made. If the validation fails, then the processing of the
alternative must be terminated and then another selection made.

```
50100   ON IOERR IGNORE
50200   GUESS
50300       LINPUT #INFILE, REC01$
50400       IF IO_STATUS (INFILE) <> 0 THEN QUIT
50500       LINPUT #INFILE, REC02$
50600       IF IO_STATUS (INFILE) <> 0 THEN QUIT
50700       LINPUT #INFILE, REC03$
50800       IF IO_STATUS (INFILE) <> 0 THEN QUIT
            .... process good records
50900   ADMIT
            .... process input/output error
51000   ENDGUESS
```

The preceding example shows how the GUESS/ADMIT, ENDGUESS, and
QUIT statements can be used to program the two alternatives.
The execution of a QUIT statement causes control to be
transferred to the next statement following the ADMIT statement.

N-2   <u>GUESS/ADMIT</u>

    Syntax: GUESS
                 .... process alternative (1)
               ADMIT
                 .... process alternative (2)
               ADMIT
                 .... process alternative (3)
                 ....
               ADMIT
                 .... process alternative (n)
               ENDGUESS

In general, a GUESS group defines a "block" of statements (see Nesting Loops and IF-groups) in the same manner as an IF-group. Within this block are a number of other blocks separated by ADMIT statements. Each of the inner blocks represents an alternative.

The execution of a GUESS group causes the first alternative to begin execution. If a QUIT statement is executed in an alternative, then control is passed to the statement following the next ADMIT statement in that GUESS group. If a QUIT statement is executed in the last alternative, then control is passed to the next statement following the ENDGUESS statement. When an alternative has been completely executed, control passes to the next statement following the ENDGUESS statement.

GUESS blocks can be nested in GUESS blocks (or IF-groups or loops) since a GUESS block is identical to a block in the same sense as loops or IF-groups. This nesting is described in the section called "Nesting loops and IF-groups".

N-3   <u>QUIT</u> <u>Statement</u>

    Syntax: QUIT
               QUIT   line-number

The execution of a QUIT statement causes control to be transferred from the current block to a statement following that block. When the QUIT is executed inside a loop, this next statement is the statement following the last statement (UNTIL, NEXT, ENDLOOP) of the loop. When the QUIT statement is executed inside an IF-group, the next statement to be executed is the one immediately following the ENDIF statement. When the QUIT statement is executed in a GUESS group, the next statement is the one following the next ADMIT statement in the group or the ENDGUESS if the QUIT is executed in the last block of the GUESS group.

Consider the following program to display a file on a terminal:

```
1000      ON EOF IGNORE
1010      OPEN #3, 'MYFILE', INPUT
1020      LOOP
1030         LINPUT #3, RECORD$
1040         IF IO_STATUS <> 0 THEN QUIT
1050         PRINT RECORD$
1060      ENDLOOP
1070      CLOSE #3
1080      STOP
1090      END
```

The execution of the QUIT statement in line 1040 will cause control to be transferred to statement 1070. This will occur when the IO_STATUS built-in function returns a non-zero value due to the attempt to read past the end of the file.

Because blocks of statements can be nested inside other blocks of statements, it is sometimes desirable to QUIT an outer block from within an inner block. This can be accomplished by specifying, in the QUIT statement, the statement number of the first statement in the outer block.

```
100     DIM NAME$(1000)
        ....
50000   DEF FN_LOOKUP(PARAM$)
50100   GUESS ! VALUE NOT IN TABLE
50200      PTR=LDIM(NAME$,1)
50300      WHILE PTR<=UDIM(NAME$,1)
50400         IF PARAM$=NAME$(PTR) THEN QUIT 50100
50500         PTR=PTR+1
50600      ENDLOOP
50700      FN_LOOKUP=0
50800   ADMIT ! VALUE IN TABLE
50900      FN_LOOKUP=1
51000      VALUE_INDEX=PTR
51100   ENDGUESS
51200   FNEND
```

This example shows a function FN_LOOKUP which returns a false indication (0) if the parameter PARAM$ is not found in the matrix of names NAME$. If the parameter value is found in the table, a true indication (1) is returned and the variable VALUE_INDEX contains the position that the parameter value was found in the table. The QUIT statement in line 50400 specifies the line number (50100) of the GUESS group. Thus, if this statement is executed, control is transferred to 50900.

O.   Sorting Files

Two statements, SORT and TAGSORT, are provided for sorting records of a file. The statements may be part of a program or be invoked directly from the terminal as immediate-mode commands. The syntax of the two statements is similar. The terms defined below are used to describe both statements.

Term	Definition
input-file	name of the file containing the records to be sorted
output-file	name of the file to receive sorted records or tag records
utility-file	name of the work file to be used for intermediate results
sort-key-list	list of sort-key-specifications separated by commas
sort-key-specification	(position, length, type, sequence)
position	starting position of the sort-key within each record
length	number of characters in sort-key
type	'C' for character 'F' for floating-point 'B' for binary 'P' for packed-decimal
sequence	'A' for ascending 'D' for descending

File names, key type and key sequence, can be specified as character constants or expressions. Similarly, key position and key length can be specified as numeric constants or expressions.

The rules that follow are common to both SORT and TAGSORT statements.

1.   If no utility-file is specified (the USING clause is omitted), a file with name SORTUTIL is created in the user's personal file area.

2.   The sum of sort-key sizes cannot exceed 244 characters. If no sort-keys are specified, the entire record is treated as

the sort-key with type character and ascending sequence, subject to the maximum of 244 characters.

3.   If multiple sort-keys are specified, they are ranked with the first being the most major and the last being most minor. A combination of ascending and descending sort-keys of various types may be used.

4.   Position and length for a sort-key must be specified. If type is omitted, it is assumed to be 'C' (character). If sequence is omitted, it is assumed to be 'A' (ascending).

5.   Type 'C' (character) is used for sort-keys consisting of numeric values not stored in binary, floating-point or packed-decimal format (refer to the section describing Image Items in the chapter entitled Input/Output Statements).

6.   For a given packed-decimal sort-key, values in each record are assumed to contain the same number of decimal (fractional) digits.

7.   The record size of the output file may be specified as part of its filename (refer to the chapters concerning system dependencies). If the record size is larger than the data to be transferred, output records are padded on the right with blanks. If the record size is smaller than the data to be transferred, the data is truncated.

O-1   <u>SORT</u> <u>Statement</u>

        Syntax: SORT 'input-file', 'output-file',
                     USING 'utility-file', sort-key-list

        The SORT statement reads the records of the specified input file and writes them to the specified output file according to the order defined by the sort-key(s).

        For example, a file of financial transaction records might contain several items of data. The following SORT statement would produce a file with the transaction records ordered by date in descending sequence within customer number in ascending sequence. Customer number starts in position 1 of the record and is 5 characters in length. Transaction date starts in position 22 of the record and is 6 characters in length.

```
SORT 'TRANS', 'SORTRANS', (1,5),(22,6,,'D')
```

```
input:      20386 ... 791021 ...
            11532 ... 800105 ...
            53782 ... 791215 ...
            11532 ... 800212 ...
            20386 ... 800201 ...
            11532 ... 791130 ...

output:     11532 ... 800212 ...
            11532 ... 800105 ...
            11532 ... 791130 ...
            20386 ... 800201 ...
            20386 ... 791021 ...
            53782 ... 791215 ...
```

O-2   TAGSORT Statement

Syntax: TAGSORT 'input-file', 'output-file',
         USING 'utility-file', sort-key-list

The TAGSORT statement reads the records of the specified input file and produces a file containing record positions and sort-key values. The resulting file may be used subsequently to access records of the original file in the order specified by the sort-key(s). Since the output file contains the sort-key values as well as the record positions, TAGSORT may be used to extract a file which contains a subset of the data items found in the records of the input file. The data items to be extracted may be specified as minor sort-keys if their order is unimportant.

If the input file is a keyed file, record position is given in terms of the key values associated with its records. Output records contain key values starting in position 1, padded on the right with blanks to the maximun key length for the file, followed immediately by the sort-key values in the order specified.

If the input file is not a keyed file, record position is given in terms of relative record number. Output records contain a 4-character relative number in binary format, followed immediately by the sort-key values in the order specified.

For example, it may be desired to extract from a company's employee file, the employees' name, age, sex and title ordered by name in ascending sequence. The file is a keyed file with a 4-digit employee number as the key. Age, sex and title are specified as minor sort-keys although their order within name is unimportant.

```
TAGSORT 'EMPLOYEE', 'TEMP', (1,15),(28,2),(20,1),(32,10)
```

input:

key-value	data
0001	BIGDOME,J.R. ... M...52...PRESIDENT
0123	SMITH,J.S. ... F...35...ADM.ASST.
0986	KIDD,W.M. ... M...17...CLERK
1252	SMART,I.M. ... F...23...PROGRAMMER

output:

```
0001BIGDOME,J.R.    52MPRESIDENT
0986KIDD,W.M.        17MCLERK
1252SMART,I.M.       23FPROGRAMMER
0123SMITH,J.C.       35FADM.ASST.
```

P-1 Overview

This chapter describes the features of Waterloo BASIC which
apply only to the version implemented on the IBM Series/1
computer with the CPS operating system. These features do not
necessarily apply to other implementations of Waterloo BASIC.
Broadly speaking, these system dependencies apply to the file
system used, to the sign-on and sign-off procedures, and to the
manner in which the program library is implemented.

P-2 Files

There are two classes of input/output devices supported by
Waterloo BASIC. The first class is file oriented whereas the
second class is record oriented, sometimes referred to as
unit-record devices. The only file-oriented type of device
supported by BASIC directly is disk. Diskettes are supported
only as a means of transferring programs or data to or from disk
files using utility programs which may be invoked by the system
manager or privileged users. The record-oriented devices
supported by BASIC are terminals and printers.

Disk files are organized into volumes, known as W-file
volumes. W-file volumes are handled by the Waterloo file system
which provides facilities beyond those supported by the CPS
operating system. Each volume may contain a number of files
which are catalogued separately into libraries for each user.
To a BASIC program, disk files are named with the following
convention:

        .WFLvol.user.dataset

    e.g. .WFL1.USER122.MARKPGM

Each of the names can be up to 8 characters in length. Volume
names must start with the three-letter prefix, WFL (W-file).

When a user signs onto the system, a default file prefix is
assigned from the password file to the user. This default
prefix is automatically concatenated before all file names used
in a program by the user. When this user prefix is of the form

        .WFLvol.user

then a user is said to be unprivileged because access is
restricted to files which are datasets found in the library
specified by the prefix. Such users need not learn CPS dataset

conventions, as all files are named with a single 8-character name.

```
LOAD 'MYPROG'
OPEN #7, 'DATAFILE', INPUT
```

This is illustrated by the preceding example.

Unprivileged users may be ASSIGNed access to the printer or program and data libraries by ASSIGN commands processed from an EXECUTE file during sign-on to the system. Each userid may have an EXECUTE filename defined in the password file entry by the system manager. Typical sign-on ASSIGNments are illustrated below.

```
ASSIGN 'LIB' TO '.WFL0.BASLIB',INPUT
ASSIGN 'PRINTER' TO '.PRNT.X',INOUT
```

In this case an unprivileged user might access files as illustrated below.

```
CHAIN '.LIB.REPORT'
OPEN #3, '.PRINTER', OUTPUT
```

Record-oriented devices are usually accessed using system device names. System device names for terminals are TERM (equivalently TERM0), TERM1, TERM2, etc. System device names for printers are PRNT (equivalently PRNT0), PRNT1, PRNT2, etc. These numbered system device names are assigned to devices of the type indicated, found at successively higher hardware device addresses.

Access to printers using these system device names is not direct. A spooling program intercepts output to printers and collects it in a disk file until the printer is CLOSEd. At this time, the output is queued to be printed when the printer is available. Print spooling has been used to eliminate problems of contention for the printer by multiple users simultaneously. A means exists to obtain exclusive, direct control of a printer. If this is necessary, the user should consult with the system manager.

Privileged users may access record-oriented devices using names of the form

```
.device.dataset
```

where device is a system device name and dataset is a dummy name which may be any valid 8-character name. Such names are illustrated.

```
.PRNT.X
.TERM2.A
```

Record Size, Block Size

Disk files contain multiple physical records. Records accessed by a BASIC program are not necessarily equivalent to physical records and are termed logical records. Logical records are typically grouped consecutively into blocks which correspond to physical records. By default, logical records are 80 characters in size and are grouped 3 records per block (i.e. blocksize is 240 characters). Record size and block size may be specified when a file is created using filename switches to be described later. Logical records are equivalent to physical records if record size is equal to block size.

The maximum block size is 256 characters. Logical records may be defined with a record size greater than 256 characters, in which case a logical record is stored in multiple physical records (256 character blocks). The maximum record size permitted is 32000 characters.

If block size is not specified, the system computes an optimal block size based on the record size. If block size is specified, it must be an even multiple of the record size except when the record size is larger than 256 characters.

Multi-user File Control

Problems can arise in many systems when multiple users are simultaneously accessing and updating the same data files. Waterloo BASIC provides three file control modes which are described below.

Control Mode	Description
SHARED	This mode permits multiple users to access common files on an input-only basis.
EXCLUSIVE	This mode gives a user exclusive control of a file, so that records may be updated without interference by other users.
INTERLOCK	This mode permits multiple users to access and update common files. Individual records may be LOCKed while they are being updated.

The following table indicates the control modes available for the different OPEN access modes.

	EXCLUSIVE	INTERLOCK	SHARED
OUTPUT)	default	invalid	invalid
APPEND)			
INOUT)	default	optional	invalid
OUTIN)			
INPUT)	optional	optional	default

Since INTERLOCK support is consumptive of limited system memory resources, it is not the default control mode for any of the access modes. Defaults may be overridden by optional control modes using filename switches to be described later.

INTERLOCK control mode may only be specified for files with logical records which are equivalent to one or more physical records. That is, record size must equal blocksize or be greater than 256 characters.

LOCK Statement

Syntax: LOCK #file-ref, REC=expression, WAIT

or   LOCK #file-ref, KEY=expression, WAIT

This statement gives the ability to LOCK a specific record so that other users may not access or update it until it is released with the UNLOCK statement. This statement is only valid for files OPENed with a control mode of INTERLOCK. Other users attempting to access or update a LOCKed record will encounter an error condition.

Record position is specified by a KEY= clause for keyed files and a REC= clause for non-keyed files. Refer to the section concerning File Positioning in the chapter entitled Input/Output Statements.

The WAIT clause is optional. If a LOCK statement is executed without the WAIT clause, and another user has the record locked, an error condition will result. If the WAIT clause is used, and another user has the record locked, program execution will be suspended until the other user UNLOCKs the record, at which time execution will resume. When a file is closed, any outstanding LOCKed records are automatically UNLOCKed.

UNLOCK Statement

      Syntax: UNLOCK #file-ref, REC=expression

         or   UNLOCK #file-ref, KEY=expression

    This statement will release a record that has been LOCKed so that other users may access it. The UNLOCK statement is only valid for files OPENed with a control mode of INTERLOCK.

    Record position is specified by a KEY= clause for keyed files and a REC= clause for non-keyed files. Refer to the section concerning File Positioning in the chapter entitled Input/Output Statements.

Extending Existing Files

    The OPEN access mode APPEND permits sequential extension of non-keyed files. Refer to the section describing the OPEN Statement in the chapter entitled Input/Output Statements.

    Files may be extended sequentially or by specifying record position if the file was OPENed with INOUT or OUTIN access mode and control mode of EXCLUSIVE. Keyed files are not extended when new records are added, until all previously REMOVEd records have been reused.

Filename Switches

    Switches may be appended to dataset names in order to supply system-dependent information about files. These switches are separated by '/' characters as illustrated below.

    OPEN #8,'CUSTOMER/INTERLOCK',INOUT
    OPEN #9,'.PRNT.X/ASA',OUTPUT

A description of the available switches follows.

ASA

    This switch is used to inform the BASIC system that ASA control characters are found in the first character of each record transmitted for output. These control characters are used to control the spacing of lines on output forms. The following control characters may be used:

    '1' - skip to the top of the next page
    '0' - leave one blank line
    ' ' - skip to next line
    '+' - overprint on previous line
    '-' - leave two blank lines

RECSIZE: integer

    This switch is used to specify the number of characters in
each record of a file. The record size of a file may only be
defined when the file is created (OPENed for OUTPUT).   If the
record size is specified when OPENing an existing file, it is
compared with the defined record size for verification.   If
unspecified, the default record size when creating disk files is
80 characters. Default record sizes for system devices PRNT and
TERM are 132 and 80, respectively.

BLKSIZE: integer

    This switch is used to specify the number of characters in
a disk file block. Refer to the earlier discussion of Record
and Block Size for further information concerning blocks.

Control mode

    Valid control mode option switches are

    SHARED, EXCLUSIVE and INTERLOCK

The following list indicates valid switch name abbreviations
with the optional portion of the name enclosed in angle
brackets.

    R<ECSIZE>
    B<LKSIZE>
    ASA
    INT<ERLOCK>
    EXC<LUSIVE>
    SH<ARED>

P-3 Public Program Library

    The public program library is a file library named
'.WFL0.BASLIB'. Individual programs are placed in the public
library by using the STORE or STOREOBJ command. Because of file
protection, this library can only be STOREd into by a privileged
user. Any user can execute a program from this library by using
the RUNLIB command.

    If a pseudo-name, such as LIB, has been ASSIGNed to this
library, users can CHAIN to library programs or access data
files created in the library.

```
CHAIN '.LIB.REPORT'
OPEN #2, '.LIB.TRANSACT',INPUT
DIR  '.LIB'
```

This is illustrated in the preceding examples.

P-4 <u>Signing</u> <u>On</u> <u>and</u> <u>Signing</u> <u>Off</u>

When the Waterloo BASIC system is first loaded into the computer, each terminal displays a logo and the prompt

USERID?

To sign on the terminal, the user enters his USERID. If applicable, the system now prompts for a password:

PASSWORD?

The user now enters his password. If the correct password is entered, a special EXECUTE file is invoked, if one is specified in the user's password file entry. This EXECUTE file may contain ASSIGN statements giving the user limited access to files outside of his personal file area. A user signs off the system by entering the command BYE.

P-5 Incremental <u>LOAD</u>

Programs loaded from disk files using the LOAD, RUN and RUNLIB commands or the CHAIN statement are affected by <u>incremental</u> <u>load</u>. When large programs were loaded from disk in previous versions, considerable delay would result which was directly related to program size. The current version of Waterloo BASIC uses a technique termed incremental load to eliminate the variable overhead previously associated with program loading. When a program is loaded, only a small portion of it is brought into the machine's memory. As the program executes or is edited, other portions of the program are brought into memory "on demand" automatically. Performance of the program is not deterred by incremental load since its overhead is equivalent to that of virtual memory paging normally performed by the system.

A side-effect of incremental load is that the program file remains open. Consequently, the program file cannot be SCRATCHed until another program is loaded or the workspace is CLEARed.

P-6   Renaming Files

The RENAME statement has the following syntax:

RENAME   'filename1' TO 'filename2'

The second filename must be a simple, unqualified dataset name.
That is, the W-file volume and library names may not be changed.
The first filename may be a fully qualified name, subject to
user privilege, or a simple dataset name to which the default
qualification prefix applies.

P-7   DIRECTORY Command

The DIRECTORY command may optionally contain a filename
specification. This filename specification may consist of a
W-file volume name and optionally a library name. It may also
consist of a pseudo-name which has been ASSIGNed to a W-file or
W-file and library. If no filename specification is present, a
list of filenames in the user's personal library is displayed.
If a W-file volume name is specified, a list of library names in
that W-file volume is displayed. If both a W-file volume name
and a library are specified, a list of filenames in the
designated library are displayed. Examples follow:

```
DIR
DIR '.WFL1'
DIR '.WFL1.BASDEMO'
DIR '.LIB'
```

Q. System Dependencies - IBM 370/303X/43XX (VM/CMS)

Q-1 Overview

This chapter describes features of Waterloo BASIC which apply only to the IBM computers which use the VM/CMS operating system. These features may not be available on other versions of Waterloo BASIC. Broadly speaking, these system dependencies apply to files and to sign-on procedures.

Q-2 Files

Waterloo BASIC uses the CMS file system for file storage and consequently uses the CMS conventions for naming datasets. In general, a file name has the form

    name   type   mode

Only 'name' is required. Default file types and modes apply according to the context in which the file name is used. These defaults may be overridden by specifying type and optionally mode in the general form of the file name. The following table illustrates default file types and the context in which they apply.

default type	commands or statements
WBASIC	EXECUTE, LIST, OLD, SAVE
WSTORE	CHAIN, LOAD, RUN, STORE, STOREOBJ
WDATA or WBASIC	TYPE
WKEY or WDATA	OPEN, SCRATCH, RENAME

A default file type of WKEY is used for the index file associated with a keyed file.

For input files, a default mode of * is used; otherwise, the default mode is A1. For example,

    HENRY
    HENRY WDATA
    HENRY WDATA *

all specify the same file.

File attributes are entered according to CMS conventions. These attributes follow the file name in parentheses. Note that the closing parenthesis is optional.

RECFM type

The RECFM option is used to specify the record format of the file. A type F is fixed format, a type V is variable format, and a type A means that ASA control characters are contained on each record. Records are stored with varying lengths in V-format files. Consequently, existing records cannot be updated and such files cannot be OPENed for INOUT or OUTIN.

LRECL integer

The LRECL attribute is used to specify the logical record length. For V-format files, this attribute defines the maximum record length.

Examples: 'FILE01   (RECFM F LRECL 128)'
             'MYFILE   (RECFM V LRECL 121)'

Q-3 Signing On And Signing Off

Once you have signed onto the VM/CMS system, Waterloo BASIC can be invoked by typing the command WBASIC. To return to the CMS level, either the BYE or FINISH command can be issued.

When WBASIC is invoked, it automatically opens and processes commands from a special EXECUTE file with the name 'PROFILE WBASIC *'. If a file with this name does not exist, normal processing continues. This facility can be used, for example, to automatically set SCREENSIZE and SLIMIT each time WBASIC is used.

When WBASIC is active, programs may be brought into the workspace, manipulated and run using commands provided for these purposes. An extended form of the WBASIC command may be issued from CMS level which allows certain of these operations to be specified in one command line and permits suppression of certain messages:

        WBASIC filename (LOAD   RUN   BYE   VERBOSE)
                         OLD   NORUN NOBYE   TERSE
                         EXEC

In the above form of the WBASIC command, groups of mutually exclusive options are listed in columns. At the top of each column, the default for each group appears. When this form of the command is used without options specified, WBASIC attempts

to LOAD and RUN a program from a WSTORE file with the specified
name, and then return control (BYE) to CMS. If no WSTORE file
is found, a program is compiled (OLD) from a WBASIC file and
RUN.   The file name may be specified as RDR if the program or
commands are to be read from a virtual reader file.   An
explanation of the various options follows.

LOAD   - load a program into the workspace from a WSTORE file

OLD   - compile a program into the workspace from a WBASIC
           file

EXEC   - process commands from a WBASIC file

RUN   - run the program loaded or compiled

NORUN   - do not run the loaded or compiled program, but leave
           it in the workspace for modification or display

BYE   - exit to CMS level after program execution

NOBYE   - remain at WBASIC level after program execution

VERBOSE- display all informational messages

TERSE   - suppress display of the logon banner,   'READY',
           'EXECUTION BEGINS' and 'EXECUTION ENDS' messages

Q-4 Special Names

     A number of special file names are supported in the VM/CMS
implementation. These names and an explanation of their meaning
appear in the following table.

name	meaning
PRINTER or PRT	virtual printer
PUNCH or PUN	virtual punch
READER or RDR	virtual reader
TERMINAL or TERM	console
CORE	a single-record pseudo file

INPUT, LINPUT and PRINT operations using the CORE file do not
perform any external input/output to a file or device. This
pseudo file is a buffer in memory with space for a single
record.   The length of this record buffer is 256 characters by
default, but may be specified using the LRECL option.   This

pseudo file can be used to transform data using the format capabilities provided for INPUT and PRINT without actual input/output to temporary files.

Q-5 Issuing CMS Commands from WBASIC

Certain CMS and CP comands may be issued without exiting from WBASIC. This capability is provided by the 'CMS subset' facility of VM/CMS. The set of commands available in the 'CMS subset' may vary from one installation to another. Users should consult with local systems personnel concerning which commands are available.

A special 'CMS subset' mode may be entered any time that WBASIC is reading a line from the terminal, whether under program control or at command level. This mode is invoked by entering the string CMS. In this mode 'CMS subset' commands may be issued at the terminal. The RETURN command terminates this special mode and the WBASIC program or command read resumes.

CMS and CP commands available in the 'CMS subset' may be executed under control of a BASIC program using the built-in function CMS. This function takes a string-valued parameter which contains the command to be executed. CP commands must be preceded in the string by the characters 'CP '. CMS EXEC files may be invoked if the string begins with 'EXEC '. Only commands available in the 'CMS subset' should be used in EXEC files that are invoked. VM/CMS will overwrite WBASIC and its workspace with command processors invoked from EXEC files if the commands are not part of the 'CMS subset'. The return value of the CMS built-in function is the return code from CMS or CP.

Q-6 Miscellaneous Features

SCREENSIZE

The default SCREENSIZE setting is zero for VM/CMS WBASIC. This default was chosen to avoid conflict with the automatic screen formatting provided by VM/CMS for the widely used 327x full-screen types of display stations. If WBASIC is not being used with a 327x display station, the user may wish to specify the number of lines per screen using the SCREENSIZE command.

Screen Clear

The screen of a 327x display station may be cleared from a BASIC program by PRINTing a line with CHR$(12) as its first character. Data following the CHR$(12) in the PRINT list appears beginning on the top line of the cleared screen.

SLIMIT

Syntax: SLIMIT number
            SLIMIT

A facility has been provided for limiting the number of statements that may be executed in each RUN of a program. This facility may be used to prevent wasteful consumption of resources by runaway programs executing from unattended terminals. This system command is illustrated below.

SLIMIT 5000

The above command limits program execution to five thousand statements. If the program exceeds this limit, it is interrupted and a diagnostic message is issued.

If the command is used with no number specified, the current statement limit is displayed.

Q-7 DIRECTORY Command

The DIRECTORY command can optionally contain a filename specification. If no filename specification is present, a list of all files with mode A is displayed. An asterisk (*) may be used in place of any of name, type or mode to designate all files matching non-asterisk qualifiers. For example,

DIR '* WSTORE A'

displays a list of all files with type WSTORE and mode A.

Q-8 Interrupting Programs

The method used to interrupt an executing program depends upon the type of terminal used. When the terminal is an ASCII terminal, the BREAK key may be depressed while the program is active. If the program is awaiting input from the terminal, the BREAK key may be depressed as the first character on the line. When an IBM 327x terminal is used, a program may be interrupted by depressing the ENTER key while the program is not awaiting terminal input or by typing the characters ATTN when the program is awaiting input.

Q-9 Unsupported Features

The following commands or statements are not supported in the VM/CMS version of Waterloo BASIC:

ASSIGN
DEASSIGN
LOCK
SHOW
UNLOCK

R.   Reserved Words

Neither keywords (i.e., DIM, USING) nor built-in functions (i.e., STR$, TIME) may be used as variable names. Strictly speaking, commands may be used as variable names although this is a dangerous practice since an assignment, without the LET keyword in immediate-mode execution, cannot be made to these variables. We have provided a list of all keywords, built-in functions, and commands in the following section for quick reference. Several names to be included in the next version of Waterloo BASIC have been included to prevent their use in current programs.

List Of Reserved Words

ABS, ACOS, ADMIT, AIDX, AND, APPEND, ASIN, ASORT, ATN, ATN2, ATTN, BASE, BLKSIZE, BYE, CALL, CEIL, CEN, CHAIN, CHR$, CLOSE, CODE, CON, CONV, CONVDAT$, COS, COSH, COT, CSC, DAT$, DATA, DATAFILE, DATE, DATE$, DEBUG, DEF, DEG, DET, DIDX, DIM, DOT, DSORT, ELSE, ELSEIF, END, ENDGUESS, ENDIF, ENDLOOP, EOF, EPS, ERR, ERROR, ERROR$, EXIT, EXP, FAH, FILE, FILE$, FILE_DEFAULT$, FNEND, FOR, FORM, FP, GALI, GO, GOSUB, GOTO, GUESS, HEX, HEX$, IDN, IDX, IF, IGNORE, IMAGE, INCM, INF, INPUT, INT, INV, IO_STATUS, IOERR, IP, JDY, KEY, KEYED, KEYFILE, KEYLEN, KEYVAL$, LBKG, LDIM, LEN, LET, LINE, LINPUT, LOCK, LOG, LOG10, LOG2, LOOP, LPAD$, LPREC, LTRM$, LWRC$, MAT, MAX, MAX$, MIN, MIN$, MOD, NEXT, NONE, NOPROMPT, NOT, NOTRIM, OCT, OCT$, OFLOW, ON, OPEN, OPTION, OR, ORD, OUTIN, OUTPUT, PAUSE, PI, PRINT, PROD, PROMPT, PRTZO, QUIT, RAD, RANDOMIZE, READ, REC, RECLEN, RECNUM, RECSIZE, REM, REMOVE, RENAME, RESTORE, RESUME, RETURN, RND, RPAD$, RPT$, RTRM$, SCRATCH, SEC, SGN, SIN, SINH, SLEEP, SOFLOW, SPACE$, SPREC, SQR, SREP$, STEP, STOP, STR$, SUB, SUM, SYSTEM, TAB, TAN, TANH, THEN, TIME, TIME$, TO, TRANSLATE$, TRN, UDIM, UFLOW, UNLOCK, UNTIL, UPRC$, USE, USING, VALUE, VALUE$, VERIFY, WHILE, ZDIV, ZER

S.   Summary of Commands And Statements

S-1   Notation

This chapter summarizes the syntax of commands and statements in Waterloo BASIC. It is included for easy reference; the details for a particular command or statement should be obtained by reference to the pertinent section of the manual.

In the next two sections various short forms are used for terms:

Short Form	Term
char-con	string constant
char-exp	string expression
file-name-ref	file name
file-num-ref	file number
line-num	line number
line-range	line range
numer-con	numeric constant
numer-exp	numeric expression
matrix-element	matrix element
matrix-name	matrix name
variable-name	variable name

The index may be used to locate the section of the manual where these terms are explained.

Some commands and statements have optional phrases or components. These are depicted by enclosing the optional section in square brackets.

        RUN   [file-name-ref]

The example indicates that the file-name-ref is optional in the RUN command.

Some components have a number of optional phrases or components of which one must be selected. This is shown in a vertical list enclosed by < and > characters.

        <   INPUT >
        <   OUTPUT >
        <   INOUT >
        <   OUTIN >

The example indicates that one of the four options must be selected.

S-2   <u>System</u> <u>Command</u> <u>Summary</u>

(1)   AS[SIGN]   name to filename-ref, <INPUT>
                                            <INOUT>
                                            <OUTIN>

(2)   A[UTOLINE]   [line-num [, increment]]

(3)   BYE

(4)   CH[ANGE]   [line-range]/literal-1/
                      literal-2/[occurrence]

(5)   CLEAR

(6)   CONT[INUE]

(7)   DEAS[SIGN]   name

(8)   DEL[ETE]   line-range

(9)   DI[RECTORY]   [file-name-ref]

(10) ENDL[OG]

(11) EX[ECUTE]   file-name-ref

(12) FINISH

(13) H[ELP]   <[ED[ITOR]]]   [command-name]   >
                      <[FU[NCTION]]]   [function-name]   >
                      <[ST[ATEMENT]]]   [statement-keyword]>

(14) LIST   [line-range]   [file-name-ref]

(15) LOAD   file-name-ref

(16) LOG[IO]   file-name-ref

(17) OLD   file-name-ref

(18) MERGE   file-name-ref

(19) RENUM[BER]   [line-num[,increment]]

(20) RESET

(21) RUN   [file-name-ref]

(22) RUNL[IB]   file-name-ref

(23) SAVE   [line-range] file-name-ref

(24) SC[REENSIZE]   [number]

(25) S[EARCH]   [line-range]/literal/[occurrence]

(26) SH[OW]

(27) STO[RE]   file-name-ref

(28) STOREO[BJ]   file-name-ref

(29) T[YPE]   file-name-ref

S-3   BASIC Statements Summary

(1)   CHAIN   file-name-ref[,param[,param]....]

                  where parameter is one of:
                  MAT array-name
                  numer-exp
                  char-exp

(2)   CLOSE   file-num-ref

(3)   DATA   [<numer-con>],<numer-con>]...]
                [<char-con >],<char-con >]...]

(4)   DEF   function-name[(variable-name[,variable-name]...)]=

                  <numer-exp>
                  <   >
                  <char-exp >

(5)   DEF   function-name[(variable-name[,variable-name]...)]
                  [statement]
                  .
                  .

          [function-name   =   <numer-exp>]
          [<   >]
          [<char-exp >]

      FNEND

(6)   DIM   array-name (n1[,n2]...)[,array-name(n1[,n2]...)]...

(7)   END

(8)   FOR   numer-var = numer-exp TO numer-exp [STEP numer-exp]
                  [statement]
                  .
                  .

      NEXT   numer-var

(9)   GO[ ]SUB line-num

(10)   RETURN

(11)   GO[ ]TO line-num

```
(12)   GUESS
              [statement]
              .
              .

       [ADMIT
              [statement]
              .
              .
              .]
       ENDGUESS
```

```
                              <line-num >  ⎡       <line-num >  ⎤
(13)   IF numer-exp THEN       <         >  ⎢ ELSE  <         >  ⎥
                              <statement>  ⎣       <statement>  ⎦
```

```
(14)   IF        numer-exp
              [statement]
              .
              .

       [ELSEIF   numer-exp
              [statement]
              .
              .
              .]

       [ELSE
              [statement]
              .
              .
              .]
       ENDIF
```

```
(15)   INPUT     [file-num-ref,][file-pos,][USING char-exp,]
                 [input-list]

                          <REC=numer-exp>
       where file-pos is: <KEY=char-exp >
                          <KEY>=char-exp>

                        <variable-name  >  ⎡  <variable-name  >  ⎤
       input-list is:   <MAT array-name  >  ⎢ ,<MAT array-name  >  ⎥ ...
                        <array-element   >  ⎣  <array-element   >  ⎦
```

```
            <variable-name>       <numer-exp>
(16)  [LET]  <             >  =  <          >
            <array-element>       <char-exp >


                                        <char-var           >
(17)  LINPUT [file-num-ref,][file-pos,]  <                   >
                                        <char-array-element>
      where file-pos is like INPUT


(18)  LOCK file-name-ref, <REC=numer-exp> [,WAIT]
                          <KEY=char-exp>


(19)  LOOP
           [statement]
           .
           .
      ENDLOOP

(20)  LOOP
           [statement]
           .
           .
      UNTIL    numer-exp

(21)  MAT INPUT [file-num-ref,][USING char-exp,][file-pos,]

                [matrix-name[,matrix-name]....]
      where file-pos is like INPUT

(22)  MAT PRINT   [file-num-ref,][USING char-exp,][file-pos,]
                  [matrix-name[,matrix-name]....]

      where file-pos is like PRINT

(23)  MAT READ    [matrix-name[,matrix-name]...]
```

```
                    <CONV    >
                    <ATTN    >
                    <ERR     >
                    <SOFLOW  >  <GOTO line-num>
(24)   ON           <OFLOW   >  <SYSTEM        >
                    <UFLOW   >  <IGNORE        >
                    <ZDIV    >
                    <EOF     >
                    <IOERR   >
```

```
(25)   ON           numer-exp GO[  ]SUB line-num[,line-num]
                    ....[NONE line-num]
```

```
(26)   ON           numer-exp GO[  ]TO line-num[,line-num]
                    ....[NONE line-num]
```

```
                                                < INPUT  >
(27)   OPEN         file-num-ref ,file-name-ref,< APPEND >
                                                < INOUT  >
                                                < OUTIN  >
```

```
(28)   OPEN file-num-ref, file-name-ref, OUTPUT
            [,DATAFILE=file-name-ref,KEYLEN=numer-exp]
```

```
                    <PRTZO   nn>    ⎡ <PRTZO   nn>  ⎤
                    <BASE   0  >    ⎢ <BASE   0  >  ⎥
(29)   OPTION       <BASE   1  >    ⎢ <BASE   1  >....⎥
                    <    SPREC>     ⎢ <    SPREC>   ⎥
                    <    LPREC>     ⎢ <    LPREC>   ⎥
                    <   PROMPT>     ⎢ <   PROMPT>   ⎥
                    < NOPROMPT>     ⎣ < NOPROMPT>   ⎦
```

```
(30)   PAUSE
```

```
(31)   PRINT   [file-num-ref,][file-pos,][USING char-exp,]
               [output-list]

                          <REC=numer-exp>
       where file-pos is: <              >
                          <KEY=char-exp >

                          <MAT array-name> <,> <MAT array-name>
       output-list is:    <numer-exp      > <;> <numer-exp        >...
                          <char-exp       >      <char-exp       >
```

(32)   QUIT   [line-num]

(33)   RANDOMIZE

(34)   READ   input-list   (see INPUT for input-list)

(35)   REM   [comment]

(36)   REMOVE   file-num-ref, KEY=char-exp

(37)   RENAME   file-name-ref   TO   file-name-ref

(38)   RESTORE

(39)   RESUME   [NEXT]

(40)   SCRATCH   file-name-ref

(41)   STOP

(42)   UNLOCK   file-num-ref, <REC=numer-exp>
                               <KEY=char-exp>

(43)   USE [var[,var].....]

        where var is:
              <MAT array-name>
              <variable-name >
              <array-element >

(44)   WHILE   numer-exp
       [statement]
         .
         .
       ENDLOOP

(45)   WHILE   numer-exp
       [statement]
         .
         .
       UNTIL   numer-exp

I N D E X